# THE FILMS OF
# AGATHA CHRISTIE

SCOTT PALMER

B.T. BATSFORD LTD • LONDON

Dedicated in Loving Memory
to My Father
Walter T. Palmer
(1926–1992)

First published 1993

Typeset by Graphicraft Typesetters Ltd., Hong Kong

and printed in Great Britain by
Butler and Tanner, Frome, Somerset

Published by
B.T. Batsford Ltd
4 Fitzhardinge Street
London W1H 0AH

A catalogue record for this book is available from the British Library

ISBN 0 7134 7205 7

Jacket illustrations: (front) David Suchet, Austin Trevor, Albert Finney, Angela Lansbury &
Edward Fox, Joan Hickson, Margaret Rutherford & Dennis Price, Peter Ustinov; (back) Ian
Holm, Tony Randall, Helen Hayes, Ralph Richardson

# ≡ CONTENTS ≡

# CONTENTS

# CONTENTS

# ═ FOREWORD ═

It gives me great pleasure to introduce Scott Palmer's new book on the films of my grandmother Agatha Christie's books.

For the last 70 years Agatha Christie's books have given enormous pleasure to millions of people all over the world. They have been published in 44 languages and with all sorts of covers, and can be found in all kinds of places – airports, high streets, super stores, newsstands, beaches, hotels, etc.

In licensing film and television rights we have always tried to find producers, directors and actors who will convey something of the mystery and atmosphere of the books. Sometimes it is necessary to reduce the cast of people (it almost always is in screenplays of books) but I hope you will find that in almost every case the *plot* remains intact.

What Scott Palmer does for you is to provide a very valuable record of all the films/TV that have been made. Some you will have seen, some you will not have seen. If you are like me, some you will like and some you will not! But in one matter I hope you will all be agreed. In the 1990s a lot of different films are made aimed at different sorts of people – I think you would find it very difficult to find a body of film, such as is described by Scott Palmer, that is such universally good entertainment for *everybody*, whether they are grandmothers or grandchildren, or wherever they live, or however much they earn. That, to me, is what Agatha Christie achieved in her books and in the films that emerged from them. When you have read Scott Palmer's book, see as many of them as you can!

MATHEW PRICHARD

# PREFACE

Just within the last decade, sales of Dame Agatha Christie's works have surpassed one billion. The phenomenon of her popularity seems to increase with the passage of time; sales of her books have *averaged* 18 million per annum, and are on the rise. To put the Christie phenomenon in perspective: William Shakespeare, acknowledged as the greatest author who ever lived, has sold some 900 million; Christie took 60 years to do what Shakespeare did in 400. Only the Bible (which had a 2,000 year head start) has outsold Agatha Christie.

Considered by many as the greatest mystery write of all time, Christie is rivalled only by Sir Arthur Conan Doyle, creator of Sherlock Holmes. Unlike Doyle however, Christie wrote about more than one detective: the dapper, eccentric Belgian sleuth Hercule Poirot; the beloved, spinsterly Jane Marple; husband and wife team Tommy & Tuppence Beresford; Ariadne Oliver; Mr Parker Pyne; Harley Quin & Mr Satterthwaite; Inspector Japp and Superintendent Battle.

Certainly the medium of film (and television) has had a great deal to do with the continuing success of Christie's work. In fact, since her death in 1976, we have seen far more film adaptations of her stories than in the nearly 50 years of her life since the first film was made in 1928 (in fact more than 80 films have been made the last 15 years!).

Christie herself, like other authors whose written works have been translated to the screen, was pleased with some aspects of the films and displeased with others. It is interesting to note that on the score or so of films made from Christie's works during her lifetime, Agatha Christie neither wrote nor collaborated on a single screenplay. One reason for this may be that Christie, a remarkably shy person, was ill-equipped to deal with the hurly-burly of film-making; she was a very private, retiring individual possessing an innate dislike of the unavoidable necessity of becoming a public figure or the focus of attention.

Nevertheless, success was inevitable, and with it media attention. Although during her lifetime relatively few films were made of her nearly 100 novels and short story collections, those that were filmed were certainly generally well done (although we can see numerous changes between the filmed and written works) and some of them rank among the great mystery films.

Agatha Christie was born Agatha Mary Clarissa Miller in Torquay, Devon, September 15, 1890. An imaginative child, by the time she was 16 she had decided on a career as an opera singer. She studied in Paris in 1906, but was told her voice lacked the needed strength, and she abandoned the idea the following year.

Shortly after the outbreak of the First World War, she married Colonel Archibald Christie, an officer in the Royal Flying Corps. After he left for France, Christie joined the Voluntary Aid Detachment and worked in a hospital dispensary. This practical experience gave her a knowledge of toxicology, the study of poisons, which she put to advantage in her first published novel, *The Mysterious Affair at Styles*, which appeared in 1920. Her only child, a daughter named Rosalind, was born in 1919.

By 1926 her marriage to Archibald Christie began to dissolve and that same year her extremely strained state of nerves brought about a temporary amnesia, which in turn culminated in her mysterious and highly publicized disappearance. Two years later, in 1928, she divorced Christie, and subsequently married 26-year-old archaeologist Max Mallowan in 1930.

By the 1930s, Christie was established as a top crime writer and many of her finest works were written during this period. *The Murder of Roger Ackroyd*, which appeared simultaneously with her enigmatic disappearance, was not only one of her finest novels, but also hugely successful due in part to the widespread notoriety that accompanied Christie's personal affairs.

During this time films and plays of her novels and short stories were being produced. She also wrote her first original play, *Black Coffee*, in 1930.

Over the years, Christie's popularity has increased tremendously, especially since her death. One of the reasons must certainly be the release of television and cinema adaptations of her work. The medium of motion pictures and, especially, television (where all the films eventually wind up) has the potential to reach millions, and serves to introduce new generations of people to the wonders of Dame Agatha Christie.

*The Films of Agatha Christie*, which has been several years in preparation, comes at a time when Christie is at the height of her popularity. The book lists, chronologically, the more than 100 films (including television films) made of Agatha Christie's works (novels, plays, short stories, original material, etc.). Cast lists, synopses, plots, character analyses, reviews and other comments will be given. Over 200 photographs, some rare and never seen before, are included; naturally more recent or popular films will be covered in greater detail, as more materials and information are available on these. Unfortunately, prints of some films are no longer extant, although rare photos were discovered by the author.

*The Films of Agatha Christie* will have a widespread appeal to Christie fans the world over (who are legion), mystery fans in general, and buffs and students of motion pictures. Christie has been translated into more than 100 languages; worldwide sales reflect her global popularity.

Finally, I would welcome and appreciate any advice, comments, corrections and criticisms, which can be addressed me to c/o the publisher, or directly to 2645 Teresita Street, San Diego, California, 92104.

Scott Palmer, 1993.

# AUTHOR'S NOTE

I have often been asked which Christie stories are the best. A number of books have been written about Christie, and the authors usually include their own favourites list. Not to be contrary, I am including my own favourite dozen Christie stories, eight of which have also been filmed.

1: *Ten Little Indians*
2: *The Murder of Roger Ackroyd*
3: *Murder On the Orient Express*
4: *Crooked House*
5: *Curtain*
6: *The ABC Murders*
7: *Witness For the Prosecution*
8: *Death On the Nile*
9: *Murder at the Vicarage*
10: *Evil Under the Sun*
11: *Hallowe'en Party*
12: *Mystery of the Blue Train*

# ACKNOWLEDGEMENTS

During the course of writing this book, several people were especially helpful to me. My sincere thanks goes to Martin Abel, Anna Barlow, Bud Barnett of Cinema Collector's Book Store, Patricia Finn, Michael Hawks of Larry Edmunds Book Store, Fiona Jackman, Sophie King, Desi Maxim, Bobbie Mitchell, Palmira Palmer, Walter T. Palmer, Victoria Ruef, Sukhmeet Sawhney Evelyn Shepherd, Roxane Sherard, John Timbers, and Malcolm Willits of Collector's Book Store.

A special note of thanks goes to Mathew Prichard, grandson of Dame Agatha Christie and head of Agatha Christie Ltd, who very kindly read the manuscript and wrote the foreword to this book.

Thanks also to the BBC, The British Film Institute, CBS Television, KPBS Television (San Diego), London Weekend Television, Rosemont Productions, Thames Television, TVS, Warner Bros Television, and WGBH-Boston, who were kind enough to supply me with and allow me to use certain photographs for the book.

I would also like to thank the following actors, all of whom appeared in Christie films, for their help in supplying film credits, photos, etc. over many years. They are: Terence Alexander, Harry Andrews, John Arnatt, Peter Arne, Dame Peggy Ashcroft, Sir Richard Attenborough, Charles Aznavour, Alan Badel, George Baker, Peter Barkworth, Colin Blakely, Lally Bowers, Peter Bowles, Peter Bull, John Castle, Geoffrey Chater, Peter Copley, Michael Craig, Michael Culver, Allan Cuthbertson, Maurice Denham, Vernon Dobtcheff, Valentine Dyall, Michael Elphick, Fabian, Robert Flemyng, Edward Fox, Leo Genn, Sir John Gielgud, Julian Glover, Michael Gough, Charles Gray, Dulcie Gray, Jeremy Hawk, Joan Hickson, Stanley Holloway, Ian Holm, Marianne Hoppe, Ronald Howard, Noel Howlett, Wilfrid Hyde-White, Frederick Jaeger, Lionel Jeffries, Freddie Jones, Peter Jones, Deborah Kerr, Roy Kinnear, Esmond Knight, Sam Kydd, Jon Laurimore, Leigh Lawson, Richard Leech, Queenie Leonard, Charles Lloyd-Pack, David Lodge, Herbert Lom, Simon MacCorkindale, Alec McCowen, Leo McKern, James Mason, Ferdy Mayne, Ralph Michael, Sir John Mills, Norman Mitchell, Robert Morley, Derek Nimmo, Ralph Nossek, Hugh O'Brian, Muriel Pavlow, Richard Pearson, Ron Pember, Donald Pleasence, Eric Porter, Denis Price, Denis Quilley, Tony Randall, Vanessa Redgrave, Oliver Reed, Ewan Roberts, Dame Flora Robson, Anton Rodgers, Peter Sallis, Tim Seely, Dinah Sheridan, Elke Sommer, David Suchet, Sylvia Syms, Dorothy Tutin, Sir Peter Ustinov, Richard Vernon, James Villiers, Thorley Walters, Jack Watson, Moray Watson, Timothy West, John Williams, Ian Wolfe, John Woodvine, and Ben Wright.

# 1928

## Die Abenteuer GMBH
## (Adventurers Inc.)

Made in Germany. Directed by Frederick Sauer.

CAST

Carlo Aldini · · · · · · · · · · · · · · · · · · · · · · · · · · · · · · · Tommy
Eve Gray · · · · · · · · · · · · · · · · · · · · · · · · · · · · · Tuppence
and: Michael Rasumny, Hilda Bayley, Shayle Gardner.

No other credits available. Based on the novel, *The Secret Adversary* (1922).

Strangely enough, the first film made from an Agatha Christie story was made in Germany rather than in Christie's native England. This was due in part to the sensational international publicity Christie had received in 1926–7 in regards to her own mysterious disappearance.

*The Secret Adversary*, written in 1922, was the first of Christie's works to introduce Tommy Beresford and Tuppence Cowley, who in subsequent works became the husband and wife team of crime solvers. For the motion picture, one of the last silents, Italian actor Carlo Aldini and British film star Eve Gray were cast as Tommy and Tuppence.

The story begins when Tommy and Tuppence meet shortly after the close of the First World War. Although they had been friends since their youth, they had not seen each other for several years; lately during the War Tuppence had been working at a hospital (note the parallel to Christie's own life during the same period) and Tommy was recouperating there from his war wounds.

Since both of them were currently unemployed, they came up with the idea of an advertisement, labelling themselves 'Adventurers Incorporated'.

Tuppence is subsequently hired by a man who wishes her to pose as an American girl travelling to Paris. He asks for her name; she tells him she

▲ Carlo Aldini and Eve Gray as Tommy and Tuppence in *Die Abenteuer GMBH*, the first film of an Agatha Christie story.

▲ Michael Rasumny (left), Hilda Bayley and Shayle Gardner in *Die Abenteuer GMBH*.

is Jane Finn (a name that had casually been mentioned to her by Tommy). She so alarms her new employer with this name that he first threatens, then bribes her to 'keep quiet'. She and Tommy shortly afterwards discover that the mysterious employer (along with his office) has disappeared. The pair also learn that a great number of people are interested in 'Jane Finn', and international intrigue and danger abound before they learn what it is all about and bring the criminal to justice.

Unfortunately, there is apparently no print of this film extant. More than 55 years later, a television remake would be made in England starring Francesca Annis and James Warwick; they would also star in the ten episode series based on the adventures of Tommy and Tuppence.

# ≡1928≡

## The Passing of Mr Quin

Made in England. Directed by Julius Hagen.

### CAST

| | |
|---|---|
| Stewart Rome | Dr Alec Portal |
| Trilby Clark | Eleanor Appleby |
| Clifford Heatherley | Professor Appleby |
| Ursula Jeans | Vera, housemaid |
| Mary Brough | Cook |
| Vivian Baron | Derek Capel/Quin |
| Kate Gurney | Landlady |

Based on the short story *The Coming of Mr Quin* (1925). 100 minutes (8,520 feet).

The character of the mysterious, magician-like Harley Quin was introduced in the 1920s in short stories, which were originally published in various magazines. The stories are gathered in a collection published in 1930 under the title *The Mysterious Mr Quin*.

Quin is a fellow who solves mysterious crimes, sometimes dealing with supernatural overtones; he appears mysteriously on the spot, solves the crime, and disappears quickly like an apparition. His friend Mr Satterthwaite is frequently also at the scene of the crime, although he arrives by more conventional and explicable means.

Stewart Rome, a popular leading man of silent films who matured into a fine character star in 150 films, played the doctor; Australian actress Trilby Clark, who had a somewhat short film career, played Eleanor Appleby (in the story the name was Appleton).

The film, which received mixed reviews, concerns a doctor, Alec Portal, who is in love with Mrs Appleby, a woman who is married to a professor (Clifford Heatherley) who is horribly cruel to her. When the professor is found murdered, suspicion naturally falls on Mrs Appleby, although we come to learn that others had a motive for his death: neighbour Derek Capel was also in love with Mrs Appleby, and Vera, the housemaid, was going to have the professor's child.

After Mrs Appleby is arrested for the crime, there follows her murder trial, which was considered one of the merits of the film; cross-examination of the witnesses are shown in double exposure with the accused woman and members of the public.

After Mrs Appleby is acquitted of the murder, she is released and returns to the village to a convent to take refuge. Portal, still in love with her, constantly visits her and eventually persuades her to marry him. On their first day at home, Portal discovers a letter his new wife had written to Capel some time previously that seems to prove her guilt.

Mr Quin, a broken down, sickly vagrant, appears in the village in need of medical attention. Portal, now convinced that his wife is a murderess, treats Quin and then leaves for a party at his home. Quin, uninvited, turns up during the party and explains to the guests the murder was committed by Capel, the neighbour who was in love with Mrs Portal. As he lies dying from self-administered poison, we learn that Quin is none other than Capel in disguise; his conscience had driven him into the wilds of Africa where, a fever-wracked wreck, he decided to return to confess and die.

Acting in the film is generally competent; Clifford Heatherley stands out among the cast as the cruel husband and received the best notices at the time. The faults of this film lie in a great unnecessary length to which many of the sequences are drawn out, an excessive use of close-ups, and the failing in part by the director to make some of the characters' actions believable at times.

Like *Die Abenteuer G.M.B.H.*, no prints are apparently available of *The Passing of Mr Quin*. All the Quin stories were written prior to 1930; this was (to date) the only film ever made with the character of Harley Quin, who only appears as a disguise of another character.

Christie remarked that she very much liked the character of Harley Quin. However, she never wrote any more Quin stories after this period (one Quin story appeared in *Three Blind Mice and Other Stories*, in 1950, but it had been written in the 1920s).

▲ Dr Alec Portal (Stewart Rome) consoles Eleanor Appleby (Trilby Clark), in *The Passing of Mr Quin*.

▲ Dr Alec Portal (Stewart Rome) ministers to Derek Capel (Vivian Baron) in *The Passing of Mr Quin*.

# ☰1931☰

## Alibi

Made in England. Directed by Leslie Hiscott.

CAST
▼

| | |
|---|---|
| Austin Trevor | Hercule Poirot |
| J.H. Roberts | Dr Sheppard |
| Franklyn Dyall | Sir Roger Ackroyd |
| Elizabeth Allan | Ursula Browne |
| John Deverell | Lord Halliford |
| Ronald Ward | Ralph Ackroyd |
| Mary Jerrold | Mrs Ackroyd |
| Mercia Swinburne | Caryll Sheppard |
| Harvey Braban | Inspector Davis |

and: Clare Greet, Diana Beaumont, Earle Grey, Agnes Brantford

Based on the novel *The Murder of Roger Ackroyd* (1926). 75 minutes.

▲ Dr Sheppard (J.H. Roberts, left) meets with Sir Roger Ackroyd (Franklyn Dyall) in *Alibi*.

Certainly *The Murder of Roger Ackroyd*, written in 1926, ranks among Agatha Christie's greatest novels. By the time Twickenham Film Studios brought the novel to the screen in 1931, it had already enjoyed a tremendous success on the London stage. It opened at the Prince of Wales Theatre on May 15, 1928, running for almost a year. The original London theatre cast was headed by Charles Laughton as Hercule Poirot, who enjoyed a great personal success (although the play ran only a month in New York when Laughton, again as Poirot, brought it to Broadway early in 1932).

When Twickenham decided to film the story, Irish-born actor Austin Trevor (who was under contract to them at the time) was chosen to play Hercule Poirot. Trevor, 34 at the time of the film, enjoyed a long and distinguished stage and film career, and was noteworthy playing Frenchmen and other continental types. The previous year, 1930, Trevor had starred in *At the Villa Rose*, also made at Twickenham Studios. That film was based on Sir Alfred Edward Woodley Mason's novel of the same title; Trevor portrayed fictional French detective Inspector Hanaud, which was really the beginning of his numerous portrayals of this genre. Trevor, who had studied in France, became expert at assuming a French accent.

The eminent J.H. Roberts repeated his stage role as Doctor Sheppard. Also in the film were

▲ The murder of Sir Roger Ackroyd in *Alibi*. L-R: Dr Sheppard (J.H. Roberts), Sir Roger Ackroyd (Franklyn Dyall), Hercule Poirot (Austin Trevor), Ursula Browne (Elizabeth Allan), Lord Halliford (John Deverell), Mrs Ackroyd (Mary Jerrold).

star character players Franklyn Dyall, Mary Jerrold and Harvey Braban.

The film begins in a quiet English village where a wealthy widow is discovered having committed suicide, apparently out of remorse for killing her alcoholic husband.

Local medico Dr Sheppard is a friend of Sir Roger Ackroyd, a man who was rumoured to have been engaged to the dead woman. Ackroyd confides to Sheppard one evening that he was in fact secretly engaged to the woman, who he believes was being blackmailed over the death of her husband. The blackmailer, Ackroyd believes, drove her to take her own life.

Ackroyd has received a letter from the dead woman, which she apparently posted just before her death. Sheppard urges Ackroyd to open it as he thinks it may contain a clue as to the blackmailer's identity (if it does not actually name the blackmailer). But Ackroyd wishes to open it later, so Sheppard leaves him and agrees to come back the next morning. Shortly after Sheppard arrives home however, he receives a telephone call to return in his professional capacity; Ackroyd has been found stabbed to death.

Meanwhile, Sheppard's sister Caryll (Mercia Swinburne – much younger and not the gossiping busybody seen in the novel) has discovered that the Sheppard's mysterious new neighbour is none other than the one and only Hercule Poirot, who is taking some time off in the country to grow vegetable marrows.

Inspector Davis (Harvey Braban) calls in the famous sleuth, and with the latter's help is able to solve this baffling and perplexing crime.

▲ L-R: Inspector Davis (Harvey Braban), Ralph Ackroyd (Ronald Ward), Lord Halliford (John Deverell) and Hercule Poirot (Austin Trevor) share a friendly drink in *Alibi*.

This was not only the first film to introduce the character of Hercule Poirot, it was also the first of three films made by Twickenham Studios, all starring Trevor as the Belgian detective. Although *Alibi* generally received favourable reviews, viewers will certainly have no difficulty in noting the startling dissimilarity between Austin Trevor and the written version of Hercule Poirot. Trevor was taller, younger, and peculiarly without the famous sleuth's moustache. His accent however, is quite fine.

▲ Poirot appears the only one amused in this scene from *Alibi*. L-R: Servant (Diana Beaumont), Inspector Davis (Harvey Braban), Hercule Poirot (Austin Trevor), Ralph Ackroyd (Ronald Ward), Lord Halliford (John Deverell), and Dr Sheppard (J.H. Roberts).

▲ Another corpse is discovered in *Alibi*; Inspector Davis takes notes while Poirot uses his little grey cells. L-R: Inspector Davis (Harvey Braban), Hercule Poirot (Austin Trevor), Ralph Ackroyd (Ronald Ward), Dr Sheppard (J.H. Roberts), and Lord Halliford (John Deverell).

The great successes of Charles Laughton in the stage version of *Alibi* and Francis L. Sullivan as Poirot in *Black Coffee* in 1930–1, not unnaturally led to comparisons. There were, at the time, certain problems in transferring a stage success to the screen, although reviewers of the film at the time liked Trevor, not commenting on the lack of consistency between the celluloid and the literary Poirot. J.H. Roberts is quite good (as he was on stage) and Franklyn Dyall does well as the doomed Ackroyd.

Christie was displeased when young, attractive Linden Travers was cast in the part of Caryll, Dr Sheppard's sister in the stage version of *Alibi*, because the character was so different from the way she had written it. Twickenham Studios followed suit, casting Mercia Swinburne in the role; she was also much younger and more attractive than the novel's spinsterish, middle-aged character.

*Variety*, reviewing the film when it opened at London's Phoenix Theatre April 28, 1931 said '. . . it deals with the good old hunt-the murderer theme in the good old way, and must be credited with likely appeal to the neighbour-hood houses as it is well knit along the familiar lines.'

# Black Coffee

Made in England. Directed by Leslie Hiscott.

## CAST

▼

| | |
|---|---|
| Austin Trevor· · · · · · · · · · · · · · · · · · · · · · | · Hercule Poirot |
| Richard Cooper · · · · · · · · · · · · · · · · · | ·Captain Hastings |
| Adrienne Allen· · · · · · · · · · · · · · · · · · | · · · Lucy Amory |
| Elizabeth Allan· · · · · · · · · · · · · · · · · | ·Barbara Amory |
| C.V. France · · · · · · · · · · · · · · · · · · | Sir Claude Amory |
| Philip Strange · · · · · · · · · · · · · · · · | ·Richard Amory |
| Dino Galvani · · · · · · · · · · · · · · · · · · | · Dr Carelli |
| Michael Shepley· · · · · · · · · · · · · · · · · | · · Raynor |
| Melville Cooper · · · · · · · · · · · · · · · · | ·Inspector Japp |
| Marie Wright· · · · · · · · · · · · · · · · · · | · Miss Amory |

and: Leila Page, Harold Meade, S.A. Cookson.

Based on the original play *Black Coffee* (1930). 78 minutes.

Just like *Alibi*, Twickenham Films' *Black Coffee* was a successful stage play in London. It opened there on December 8, 1930 at the Embassy Theatre, starring Francis L. Sullivan as Hercule Poirot and John Boxer as Captain Hastings. Although Christie admired Sullivan (they were also friends) she noted that, like Laughton before him, Sullivan was a very large man, not at all physically like the literary Poirot.

The film version of *Black Coffee* was the second of the three Poirot films made by Twickenham Studios, and once again Austin Trevor was cast as the Belgian sleuth. This film is noteworthy to Christie fans, as it marks the first screen appearance of Captain Arthur Hastings (played by Richard Cooper) as well as that of Inspector James Japp of Scotland Yard, played by the wonderful Melville Cooper, a character star who later went to Hollywood to play a gallery of pompous, supercilious characters.

The story concerns the inventor (the distinguished C.V. France) of a new formula for explosives, Sir Claude Amory. When Amory is poisoned and the formula stolen, it is not long before Poirot appears on the scene, along with Hastings, to discover the truth behind the murder and recover the missing formula.

As is true throughout the short series, Trevor is once again bereft of the famous little Belgian's moustache, although Hastings has one!

Christie later said regarding the story of *Black Coffee*: 'It was conventional spy thriller and, although it was full of cliches, it was not, I think, at all bad.'

Christie missed the play as she was in Mesopotamia with her husband doing archaeological research at the time; we do not know if she ever saw the film either.

*Variety*, reviewing the film when it opened at the Gaumont Theatre in London on August 19,

▲ Poirot questions the household in *Black Coffee*. L-R: Hercule Poirot (Austin Trevor), Richard Amory (Philip Strange), Lucy Amory (Adrienne Allen), Raynor (Michael Shepley), Barbara Amory (Elizabeth Allan), and Captain Hastings (Richard Cooper).

▲ Lucy Amory (Adrienne Allen) and Dr Carelli (Dino Galvani) discuss the situation in *Black Coffee*.

▲ Captain Hastings (Richard Cooper, left), Barbara Amory (Elizabeth Allan) and Hercule Poirot (Austin Trevor) discuss their strategy in *Black Coffee*.

▲ Raynor (Michael Shepley, left) shows Poirot (Austin Trevor) the keys to the mystery in *Black Coffee*.

1931, stated: 'Another of Twickenham's adaptations of Agatha Christie's stream of mystery thrillers, featuring the Poirot fellow, French detective (they were probably confusing Poirot with Trevor's earlier portrayal of Hanaud) played once again by Austin Trevor.

'Sort of film which is never less than interesting but never much more so. It looks as though it cost about sixty thousand pounds, and will make a good profit. It's not by any means a great film, but it's the sort of stuff which will go quite well here. This company, by the way, made the Sherlock Holmes picture which played in New York recently.' (Note: here the reviewer was obviously referring to *The Sleeping Cardinal*, made by Twickenham and starring Arthur Wontner as Sherlock Holmes; it was the first in a series of five Holmes films – also directed by Leslie Hiscott.)

C.V. France gives a good performance, as does Adrienne Allen as one of his daughters; Melville Cooper certainly puts his stamp on Inspector Japp, although he does not get as much screen time as he deserved.

# ≡1934≡

## Lord Edgware Dies

Made in England. Directed by Henry Edwards.

### CAST

| | |
|---|---|
| Austin Trevor | Hercule Poirot |
| Richard Cooper | Captain Hastings |
| Jane Carr | Lady Edgware |
| John Turnbull | Inspector Japp |
| Michael Shepley | Captain Ronald Marsh |
| Leslie Perrins | Bryan Martin |
| C.V. France | Lord Edgware |
| Esme Percy | Duke of Merton |

and: Quinton McPherson, Phyllis Morris, Ellen Pollock, Kynaston Reeves, Brenda Harvey.

Based on the novel *Lord Edgware Dies* (1933). 81 minutes.

▲ Poirot (Austin Trevor) receives an important telephone call while Hastings (Richard Cooper) looks on in *Lord Edgware Dies*.

After a two-year absence, Twickenham Film Studios produced the third and final film based on Agatha Christie's Hercule Poirot, once more starring Austin Trevor. Since *Black Coffee* in 1931, no other Christie films had been made, and the only theatre production was Charles Laughton's brief run in New York in 1932. This was the play *Alibi*, which he had so successfully performed on the London stage four years before, in 1928.

Unlike the previous films, *Lord Edgware Dies* has Poirot, along with Hastings, involved in the story a good deal before the crime is committed. Lady Edgware, a former actress (played here by Jane Carr), seeks the assistance of Poirot to obtain a divorce from her wealthy but slightly eccentric

▲ Jane Carr, a popular leading lady in the 1930s, as Lady Edgware in *Lord Edgware Dies*.

▲ Poirot (Austin Trevor, left) shows Hastings (Richard Cooper) a vital clue in *Lord Edgware Dies*.

husband, Lord Edgware. It seems she has fallen in love with the Duke of Merton (Esme Percy).

When Poirot visits Lord Edgware to discuss the situation, he is surprised to learn that Edgware has already agreed to give his wife a divorce. The next day Edgware is found murdered, Lady Edgware is arrested, and it is up to Poirot to try and unravel this mysterious case of doppelgängers and dual identities.

In this final film Trevor again made an interesting, if not ideal, Poirot; Richard Cooper was a competent Hastings, and the excellent John Turnbull gave a good performance as Inspector Japp; at least the producers gave him a bit more to do than Melville Cooper playing the same part in *Black Coffee*.

This film would mark the last appearance in motion pictures of the Hercule Poirot character for 32 years; he would not again return until 1966 when Tony Randall essayed him in MGM's British production *The Alphabet Murders*. Curiously enough, *The Alphabet Murders* would also mark the last screen appearance of Austin Trevor's long and distinguished motion picture career.

Fans of the Poirot character would have to be very patient. Two unsuccessful attempts were made to bring him to the small screen: Jose Ferrer in 1960 and Martin Gabel in 1962 both filmed pilots for possible television series; neither, however, was picked up by the networks.

# ≡ 1937 ≡

## Love From a Stranger

Made in England. Directed by Rowland V. Lee.

### CAST

Basil Rathbone· · · · · · · · · · · · · · · · · · · Gerald Lovell
Ann Harding· · · · · · · · · · · · · · · · · · · Carol Howard
Binnie Hale · · · · · · · · · · · · · · · · · ·Kate Meadows
Bruce Seton · · · · · · · · · · · · · · · · · · ·Ronald Bruce
Jean Cadell· · · · · · · · · · · · · · · · · · · · · Aunt Lou
Bryan Powley · · · · · · · · · · · · · · · · · Doctor Gribble
Joan Hickson · · · · · · · · · · · · · · · · · · · · · Emmy
Donald Calthrop · · · · · · · · · · · · · · · · · ·Hobson
Eugene Leahy· · · · · · · · · · · · · · · · · · · · Mr Tuttle
and: Ben Williams.

Based on the short story *Philomel Cottage* (1934). 87 minutes.

*Philomel Cottage* appears in the 1934 publication *The Listerdale Mystery*, a Christie short story collection. *Love From a Stranger*, based on this story, opened as a play at London's New Theatre on March 31, 1936, starring Frank Vosper. Praised by the London *Times*, the play ran a respectable five months (although it ran only one month when Vosper presented the play on Broadway. Since he was the only actor from the well-casted original London production, this may have had something to do with the short-lived American run).

When Trafalgar Studios produced the film in 1937, Basil Rathbone (an excellent choice) was cast in the role of Gerald Lovell. Rathbone was still two years away from the character that would give him screen immortality: Sherlock Holmes. American actress Ann Harding was chosen to play Carol Howard, and there was a fine supporting cast.

Gorgeously photographed and splendidly cut, *Love From a Stranger* is a macabre story of a neurotic, unbalanced scoundrel masquerading as a suave gentleman, who marries women for their money, then murders them.

Ann Harding plays Carol Howard, a girl who wins a lottery, meets, falls in love with, and marries handsome suave Gerald Lovell (Rathbone). Lovell appears to be thoughtful without being obsequious, and nothing is suspected of his past, either by the audience or his new wife.

The first inkling we have that he is dishonest, not even then suspecting anything worse, is the look on his face after he has persuaded his bride to sign away her fortune, on the pretext that she is merely affixing her signature to a mortgage transfer.

We soon begin to realize that Gerald has other, more sinister plans for Carol, and the steps bringing him to the point where the murder of his wife is planned are deliberate and testing; by the time we reach the denouement we are at a

▲ Ronald Bruce (Bruce Seton, left) shakes hands with Gerald Lovell (Basil Rathbone) while Carol Howard (Ann Harding) looks on in *Love From a Stranger*.

▲ Basil Rathbone as Gerald Lovell and Carol
Howard as Ann Harding in *Love From a Stranger*.

nerve-breaking tension. The powerful sequence
when Carol finally realizes what Gerald has
planned, is gripping. She parries his actions, tries
to save herself, succeeding when his weak heart
gives out after she makes him believe she has
poisoned his coffee. This is the only weak point
in the film; it seems hard to believe, given the
character and temperament of Gerald Lovell, that
he would simply die of fright.

Rathbone's character study of the suave, men-
tally deranged man who has married and killed
three women begins slowly and builds up to a
tense finish. He skillfully avoids the pitfalls of
overacting, which might normally come to an
actor not possessing Rathbone's talents. Ann
Harding gives a carefully thought out performance; she is especially good throughout the final
tense moments with Rathbone.

In the supporting cast, Bruce (later Sir Bruce)
Seton gives a solid performance in the relatively
small part of Ronald Bruce, and Binnie Hale, a
stage actress mainly associated with musical
comedy and revue, offers a good performance
in a comparatively small but telling role. Donald
Calthrop in the role of Hobson, the elderly gardener, is excellent.

It is of special interest to Christie fans that
Joan Hickson plays Emmy; 50 years later, after
a distinguished career on stage and in over 100
films, she would receive her highest popular and
critical success when she starred as Miss Marple
in several television films for the BBC.

*Variety*, which reviewed *Love From a Stranger*
at the London Pavilion on January 7, 1937, stated:
'Provincially, these films enjoy heavy patronage
here, and this one has the additional advantage
of having been produced in classy drawing room
environment which has the effect of creating an
even more sinister atmosphere.'

## And Then There Were None

Made in Hollywood. Directed by Rene Clair.

CAST
▼

| | |
|---|---|
| Barry Fitzgerald | Judge Francis J. Quincannon |
| Walter Huston | Dr Edward G. Armstrong |
| Louis Hayward | Philip Lombard |
| Roland Young | William Henry Blore |
| June Duprez | Vera Claythorne |
| Sir C. Aubrey Smith | General Sir John Mandrake |
| Judith Anderson | Emily Brent |
| Mischa Auer | Prince Nikita Starloff |
| Richard Haydn | Thomas Rogers |
| Queenie Leonard | Ethel Rogers |
| Harry Thurston | Boatman |

Based on the novel *Ten Little Niggers* (1939). 97 minutes.

When Septimus Winner wrote the poem *Ten Little Indians* in Philadelphia in 1868, Victorian minstrel writer Frank Green substituted the word niggers for indians when he adapted it as a minsteral song in London the following year. Certainly England at that time, and even well into the twentieth century, had a very tiny black population, and the word nigger did not have the contemptuous connotation it does today, especially in America. Agatha Christie grew up with the rhyme, which has been a favourite for generations in Great Britain.

Christie wrote the novel under the title *Ten Little Niggers* in 1939, and the story is frequently regarded as her masterpiece. She once said: 'It was so difficult to do that the idea fascinated me. It was well received and reviewed, but the person who was really pleased with it was myself, for I knew better than any critic how difficult it had been.'

American publishers, however, regarded the title as a racial offence, so the book's title was changed to *And Then There Were None* for American distribution.

The novel was adapted to the stage by Christie herself, the major change being that, unlike the novel, two of the play's (and all the subsequent film versions') characters survive. It must be remembered that it was Christie and no one else who was responsible for the altered ending; fans

▲ The distinguished cast of the 1945 version of *And Then There Were None*. L-R, front: Dame Judith Anderson as Emily Brent, Barry Fitzgerald (Judge Quincannon), Sir C. Aubrey Smith (General Mandrake), Louis Hayward (Philip Lombard), and June Duprez (Vera Claythorne). L-R, back: Roland Young (William Henry Blore), Walter Huston (Dr Armstrong), Mischa Auer (Prince Starloff), Richard Haydn (Thomas Rogers), and Queenie Leonard (Ethel Rogers).

▲ Thomas Rogers (Richard Haydn, standing) looks on while (L-R) Philip Lombard (Louis Hayward), Vera Claythorne (June Duprez), General Mandrake (Sir C. Aubrey Smith) and Emily Brent (Dame Judith Anderson) play cards in *And Then There Were None*.

who have read the book and then seen the play or one of the five film versions of the story would do well to keep this in mind. A popular ending for the rhyme in Christie's time was 'He got married and then there were none', instead of 'He went and hanged himself and then there were none'.

The original play, which opened at the St James Theatre in London November 17, 1943, played to capacity crowds every night for nearly a year in spite of the War; only Hitler's Luftwaffe put an end to it when a bomb destroyed part of the theatre (fortunately no one was inside at the time). The London production starred Allan Jeayes and Terence De Marney; it also enjoyed a great success in New York (unlike most of Christie's previous plays) with a fine cast including Halliwell Hobbes, Estelle Winwood, and J. Pat O'Malley. There are those who believe that had German bombs not cancelled the play, '*Ten Little Indians*' would have been the national institution '*The Mousetrap*' was destined to become.

The motion picture of the story, entitled *And Then There Were None*, marked the first time Hollywood attempted the filming of a Christie

work. Twentieth Century-Fox had the talented French director Rene Clair to helm the project, and assembled a prestigious cast that included some of the finest star character actors in Hollywood.

Barry Fitzgerald, fresh from his Oscar-wining performance as the gruff Father Fitzgibbon in *Going My Way*, played the judge; Walter Huston, a truly great actor of many films (he would win his own Oscar three years later for *The Treasure of the Sierra Made*) played Doctor Armstrong; swashbuckling Louis Hayward played Lombard. Roland Young, the wonderful Cosmo Topper of the Topper series was cast as Blore; June Duprez, an Alexander Korda discovery, was Vera Claythorne. Sir C. Aubrey Smith, knighted the previous year by King George VI, played General Mandrake; Judith Anderson (herself later to be made Dame Judith) appeared as Emily Brent.

Talented Russian actor Mischa Auer, usually seen in comedy parts, was cast as Prince Nikita Starloff, a character not in the novel (replacing young Anthony Marston) and obviously tailored to suit Auer's persona. Richard Haydn and Queenie Leonard (Elsa Lanchester turned down the latter's role because she thought it was too small), both of whom had been revue stars in England, were cast as Mr and Mrs Rogers; Fox Studios deserves high marks for this casting, as Haydn and Leonard were the living personifications of the book's characters (Smith's General is very close to the mark too).

▲ General Mandrake questions the butler, Thomas Rogers, in *And Then There Were None*. L-R: General Mandrake (Sir C. Aubrey Smith), Philip Lombard (Louis Hayward), Ethel Rogers (Queenie Leonard), Thomas Rogers (Richard Haydn), Dr Armstrong (Walter Huston), and William Henry Blore (Roland Young).

▲ Judge Quincannon (Barry Fitzgerald, left) reads a message to the guests from their absent host, U.N. Owen, in *And Then There Were None*. L-R: Prince Starloff (Mischa Auer), Emily Brent (Dame Judith Anderson), General Mandrake (Sir C. Aubrey Smith), Philip Lombard (Louis Hayward), William Henry Blore (Roland Young), and Vera Claythorne (June Duprez) give him their full attention.

The film remains generally faithful to the novel (and taking into consideration its ending, Christie's play). It opens as eight persons, strangers to one another, are ferried by boat (a wonderful cameo by Harry Thurston as the boatman – apparently his only screen role) to Indian Island, a small island off the English coast of Devon. (It is believed that Burgh Island, between Salcombe and Plymouth near Bigbury Bay, was Christie's model for Indian Island.)

The passengers have come there to spend the weekend as guests of Mr and Mrs U.N. Owen.

Upon arrival at the island's large, lonely house, introductions are made and the guests are shown to their rooms by butler Rogers. Mrs Rogers assists the female guests.

Meeting later at dinner, they discover the absence of their host as well as the 'indian' motif. Rogers explains the island is so named 'because it's shaped like the head of an indian'. A china centrepiece, as well as the nursery rhyme (which Auer has fun singing at the piano) are preambles of things to come.

After dinner, the guests retire to the drawing room where drinks are served. After the Prince finishes his song, they are startled by a voice on a gramophone record which accuses each person of having committed a crime for which he or she has gone unpunished. Thinking it a bad practical joke, they are shocked when the Prince suddenly collapses while choking on a drink and is pronounced dead by Dr Armstrong.

▲ General Mandrake responds to the news of another murder in *And Then There Were None*. L-R: Dr Armstrong (Walter Huston), Judge Quincannon (Barry Fitzgerald), William Henry Blore (Roland Young), Vera Claythorne (June Duprez), Philip Lombard (Louis Hayward), General Mandrake (Sir C. Aubrey Smith), and Emily Brent (Dame Judith Anderson).

Upon rising the following morning, they are doubly distressed to learn that Mrs Rogers has died in her sleep. Similarities between the two deaths and the lines of the nursery rhyme do not go unnoticed. Although the deaths can be attributed to suicide (the Prince) or accidental overdose (Mrs Rogers), it is also remarked that a china indian has been broken from the dining room centerpiece after each death.

▲ L-R: William Henry Blore (Roland Young), Vera Claythorne (June Duprez), Judge Quincannon (Barry Fitzgerald), Philip Lombard (Louis Hayward), and Dr Armstrong (Walter Huston) wonder how the killer managed to get in and break the china Indian when the door was locked. Dr Armstrong holds the weapon used to dispatch the last victim in *And Then There Were None*.

▲ Confrontation or conspiracy? Judge Quincannon (Barry Fitzgerald, left) and Dr Armstrong (Walter Huston) play a lethal game of pool in *And Then There Were None*.

Lombard, Blore, Judge Quincannon and Dr Armstrong conclude that their still missing host may be playing a macabre game and possibly hiding somewhere; a search proves fruitless. When General Mandrake is found stabbed to death, they realize that they have been marked for annihilation, and the missing Mr Owen is in fact one of them.

A secret vote is taken in order to air their suspicions; Rogers is chosen by a margin of one vote. The following morning he is discovered with an axe buried in the back of his head. After Miss Brent is murdered, the remaining guests hold a conference by candlelight (the generator has run down) to discuss the crimes of which the gramophone record had accused them.

Miss Claythorne returns to her room to get a coat. 'Stay here Mr Lombard,' remarks the judge. 'Nothing can happen to her if we all remain in this room,' adds Armstrong.

But something does; she screams and the rest rush to her aid. In the confusion in the dark a shot rings out and the judge is found with a bullet hole in the forehead. Lombard's revolver, stolen earlier, is found on the staircase.

After everyone has turned in, Lombard remains outside Miss Claythorne's window, ostensibly to protect her from the murderer. When footsteps are heard in the hallway, Lombard rushes out, wakes Blore, and discovers that Dr Armstrong is missing.

The next morning, Armstrong still cannot be found. Blore, already outside, calls up to Vera and Lombard, telling them to get dressed and come down. The next we see, as Blore is looking through binoculars, is a hand protruding from a window directly above him. The hand loosens a stone pyramid from the roof which falls and crushes Blore. Lombard and Vera discover Blore's body, look through the binoculars, and race down to the beach where they find the drowned body of Armstrong, who has been dead for hours.

Vera, who has just begun to trust Lombard, realizes that there are only the two of them left alive. She pulls out the revolver to shoot him, but he convinces her to fire wild, falling to the sand. When she returns to the house she (along with the audience) gets quite a surprise – a noose hanging from the ceiling awaits.

*And Then There Were None* received critical praise at the time of its release, and has become regarded as one of the great classic mystery films. A great period atmosphere, stylish sets and sublime orchestral touches (even the murderer's eerie whistling of the title song) are all flavourful ingredients to a great film.

The cast is uniformly excellent; marvellous performances are turned in by Barry Fitzgerald as the judge, Walter Huston as Dr Armstrong, and Sir C. Aubrey Smith as the deafish, quixotic General (in real life Smith was practically stone deaf). Richard Haydn and Queenie Leonard are perfect as the servants.

*And Then There Were None* also blends just a touch of comedy with the mystery, and is cleverly scripted by Dudley Nichols. This film would be remade in 1949, 1965, 1975, and 1989.

# ≡ 1947 ≡

## Love From a Stranger

Made in Hollywood. Directed by Richard Whorf.

CAST

| | |
|---|---|
| John Hodiak · · · · · · · · · · · · · · · · · · · | Manuel Cortez |
| Sylvia Sidney · · · · · · · · · · · · · · · · | Cecily Harrington |
| John Howard · · · · · · · · · · · · · · · · | Nigel Lawrence |
| Ann Richards · · · · · · · · · · · · · · · · · | Mavis Wilson |
| Isobel Elsom · · · · · · · · · · · · · · · · | Auntie Loo-Loo |
| Frederic Worlock · · · · · · · · · · · · · · | Inspector Hobday |
| Ernest Cossart · · · · · · · · · · · · · · · · · | Billings |
| Anita Sharp-Bolster · · · · · · · · · · · · · · | Ethel |
| Philip Tonge · · · · · · · · · · · · · · · · · | Dr Gribble |
| Billy Bevan · · · · · · · · · · · · · · · · · | Cab Driver |
| John Goldsworthy · · · · · · · · · · · · · · · · | Clerk |
| David Cavendish · · · · · · · · · · · · · · · | Policeman |
| Keith Hitchcock · · · · · · · · · · · · · · · | Policeman |
| Phyllis Barry · · · · · · · · · · · · · · · · | Waitress |
| Gerald Rogers · · · · · · · · · · · · · · · · | Postman |
| Colin Campbell · · · · · · · · · · · · · · · | Bank Teller |
| Bob Corey · · · · · · · · · · · · · · · · · | Cab Driver |
| Clark Saunders · · · · · · · · · · · · · · · | Sergeant White |
| Eugene Eberle · · · · · · · · · · · · · · · · | Bellboy |
| Charles Coleman · · · · · · · · · · · · · · · | Hotel Doorman |
| Nolan Leary · · · · · · · · · · · · · · · · | Man in Bar |
| Keith Kenneth, Donald Kerr, Abe Dinovitch · · · · · · · · · | Men |

Based on the short story *Philomel Cottage* (1934). 80 minutes.

It had been 13 years since Christie's short story *Philomel Cottage*, on which this film was based, had been written; 11 years since it had first been a play and ten years since the 1937 film with Basil Rathbone.

Eagle-Lion Films, an American independent film studio, has the distinction of being the first to remake a Christie film. The result, however, is far from superior and does not compare favourably to the earlier film.

No vital plot changes were made for this film. However, for some reason, every character's name was changed (with the sole exception of Dr Gribble). Unlike Rathbone in the previous film, John Hodiak plays the homicidal psychotic with a glowering sort of intensity that would make even the most credulous wary. Instead of having a paralytic stroke in this film, the murderer is

▲ John Hodiak as the evil Manuel Cortez in the 1947 remake of *Love From a Stranger*.

▲ Inspector Hobday (Frederic Worlock) questions Mavis Wilson (Ann Richards, left), Auntie Loo-Loo (Isobel Elsom) and Nigel Lawrence (John Howard) in *Love From a Stranger*.

▲ Manuel Cortez (John Hodiak) menaces Cecily Harrington (Sylvia Sidney) in *Love From a Stranger*.

trampled to death by a team of rampaging horses after a climactic fisticuffs with the detective and the heroine's devoted suitor amidst a violent downpour.

The compelling atmosphere and mounting terror of the story are never really captured in this film; most of the characters never seem plausible, although Hodiak is adequate. Sylvia Sidney fares somewhat better, giving a direct and spirited performance, while John Howard is believable as the dedicated and ardent suitor.

Isobel Elsom is fine as the dotty aunt, and in smaller parts Frederic Worlock and Philip Tonge lend their usual dignity. Ernest Cossart and Anita Sharp-Bolster as the domestics are also good – in fact, in this version of *Love From a Stranger* the best work is turned in by the supporting players.

*Variety*, reviewing the film in New York on October 30, 1947, said: 'The old bluebeard story, staple of literature and drama for generations, is given standard treatment in *Love From a Stranger*. The result is a fair thriller, without novelty or any viewpoint, with little suspense, surprise or excitement, and only moderate box office prospects.'

The *New York Times*, in its review of the film on November 28, 1947, stated: 'The thrill is gone from *Love From a Stranger*. When first filmed ten years ago it was a pretty good piece of antimacassar melodrama. The audience knows only too well how the honeymoon will end; no suspense or surprise is left to stimulate the spectator. The average movie goer is a pretty hep customer, and the chances are he will be so far ahead of the story that its climactic scene will explode with all the thunder of a cap pistol.'

This film's screenplay was written by the renowned mystery writer Philip MacDonald, author of the Anthony Gethryn stories.

# ≡ 1949 ≡

## Ten Little Niggers (TV)

Made in England. Directed by Kevin Sheldon.

### CAST

| | |
|---|---|
| Bruce Belfrage | Sir Lawrence Wargrave |
| John Stuart | Dr Edward Armstrong |
| John Bentley | Philip Lombard |
| Arthur Wontner | General Mackenzie |
| Campbell Singer | William H. Blore |
| Sally Rogers | Vera Claythorne |
| Margery Bryce | Emily Brent |
| Douglas Hurn | Antony Marston |
| Stanley Lemin | Rogers |
| Elizabeth Maude | Mrs Rogers |
| Barry Steele | Fred Narracot |

Based on the novel *Ten Little Niggers* (1939). 90 minutes.

After having been impressed by the brilliant stage version of Agatha Christie's classic, theatre director Kevin Sheldon decided to produce and direct a television version of *Ten Little Niggers* when he was hired by the BBC in 1949.

This was the first time Agatha Christie's work was to appear in the relatively new medium of television. Christie herself was happy to hear of this, as Sheldon had decided to use her own script from the play and remain generally faithful to Christie's original work.

Sheldon also hand-picked a cast, which included veterans such as Arthur Wontner (best remembered as Sherlock Holmes in several 1930s films for Twickenham), John Stuart, a leading man and later character star of some 180 films, Bruce Belfrage, a character star of stage, screen, and radio, and John Bentley, the hero of many crime and adventure films. Campbell Singer, who made a career of portraying policemen in films and on television, was cast as Detective William H. Blore.

The programme, aired as a live drama, appeared on Saturday, August 20, 1949 at 8:30 p.m. and was seen by an estimated audience of several hundred thousand. Although there there were several faux pas, such as a piece of scenery falling down and cameras occasionally in the wrong position, the adaptation went smoothly for the most part, in some spots even faultlessly played by a professional cast, especially considering that television as a medium was still in its infancy.

*Ten Little Niggers* had a bigger budget than most of the other programmes of the time, which was reflected in the cast, who executed their respective parts admirably. It was certainly no fault of the talented Arthur Wontner (who also played the part of Mr Lawrence Wargrave in the theatre) when, after having been stabbed to death, the camera remained focused on him for so long that he got up and strolled away with his hands in his pockets, quite unaware that he was still in view!

All in all, an auspicious debut. Certainly, selecting arguably the best and most famous of her tales was not a hindrance, and the professional, highly competent cast was an asset to the production. Also noteworthy were Richard Greenough's set design, and Kevin Sheldon's script. The flaws of this adaptation were more on the technical than the acting side.

The story itself stuck faithfully to the original written work in plot, dialogue, and manner of deaths, the exception being that producer/director Sheldon used the ending that Christie had written when she adapted her novel to the stage. This ending has also been used in all four film versions – in 1945, 1965, 1975 and 1989.

Christie herself, who was living in the West Country at the time of the telecast and could not

▲ The first television film of a Christie story was *Ten Little Niggers*. Made by the BBC in 1949 it starred (L-R) John Bentley as Philip Lombard, Sally Rogers (Vera Claythorne), Bruce Belfrage (Sir Lawrence Wargrave), Campbell Singer (William H. Blore) and John Stuart (Dr Armstrong).

receive the transmission from Alexandra Palace, nevertheless was informed about the production. It was unfortunate that the technical faults were emphasized to Christie, which may have had something to do with the fact that only one further television film was made of her works during her lifetime (which she also never saw).

Happily for Christie fans, beginning in the 1980s, numerous adaptations of her stories have been produced for the small screen. The majority have remained faithful to the original works, and the technical advances in the medium have been a tremendous asset as well.

▲ 'And then there were four': Sir Lawrence Wargrave (Bruce Belfrage) has just been murdered. L-R: Philip Lombard (John Bentley), Vera Claythorne (Sally Rogers), William Blore (Campbell Singer) and Dr Armstrong (John Stuart) remain.

# A Murder is Announced (TV)

Made in USA. Directed by Paul Stanley.

## CAST
▼

| | |
|---|---|
| Gracie Fields | Miss Jane Marple |
| Jessica Tandy | Letitia Blacklock |
| Roger Moore | Patrick Simmons |
| Betty Sinclair | Dora Bunner |
| Josephine Brown | Miss Murgatroyd |
| Pat Nye | Miss Hinchcliffe |
| Malcolm Kuin | Inspector Dermot Craddock |

Based on the novel *A Murder is Announced* (1950). 55 minutes.

Advertised by her publishers as Agatha Christie's fiftieth novel, *A Murder is Announced* appeared for the first time in print in 1950. This television adaption was the debut of the character Miss Jane Marple. Previous to this television film, she had not appeared on stage, television, or in motion pictures.

*A Murder is Announced* was broadcast on December 30, 1956. It was presented on NBC television as an episode of the Goodyear Television Playhouse series. Gracie Fields, the extremely popular British stage and music hall singer, actress and comedienne (who was also at one time the world's highest paid film actress) was selected to play Miss Marple.

The fine stage actress Jessica Tandy was also in the production as Miss Letitia Blacklock. And Roger Moore, who was starring in the television series 'Ivanhoe', long before his fame as Simon Templar and James Bond, appeared as Patrick Simmons.

The story line is fairly faithful to the Christie novel, although due to the short length of the film it does lose a bit of its detail and characterization.

A murder is announced in the newspaper in the village of Chipping Cleghorn at the home of Miss Letitia Blacklock. Locals believe this is a rather quaint way to announce an upcoming party, so several of them arrive at the house at the sheduled time.

However, Miss Blacklock, her relatives and servants are just as puzzled as the guests; nobody admits knowledge of the announcement. As the

▲ Dame Gracie Fields (1898–1979), who played Miss Marple in *A Murder is Announced*, was at one time the world's highest paid film star.

lights go out, an intruder bursts in yelling, 'Stick 'em up!', followed by three shots. When the lights come on again it is the intruder whose corpse lies on the floor, and it is up to Miss Marple to solve the riddle.

The *New York Times*' review was not enthusiastic about the television film, and it was a good many years before television would produce another Christie work (although two abortive attempts were made in the early 1960s to bring off a Hercule Poirot television series). Thirty years later in 1986, a very fine television adaptation of *A Murder is Announced* was produced in England by the BBC starring Joan Hickson as Miss Marple.

◀ Roger Moore, who played Patrick Simmons in *A Murder is Announced*. He subsequently rocketed to stardom as Simon Templar in *The Saint* and became even more popular playing James Bond.

# ≡ 1957 ≡

## Witness For the Prosecution

Made in Hollywood. Directed by Billy Wilder.

### CAST
▼

| | |
|---|---|
| Charles Laughton | Sir Wilfred Robarts |
| Tyrone Power | Leonard Vole |
| Marlene Dietrich | Christine Vole |
| Elsa Lanchester | Miss Plimsoll |
| John Williams | Mr Brogan-Moore |
| Henry Daniell | Mayhew |
| Ian Wolfe | Carter |
| Una O'Connor | Janet MacKenzie |
| Torin Thatcher | Mr Myers, Prosecutor |
| Philip Tonge | Inspector Hearne |
| Norma Varden | Mrs Emily French |
| Francis Compton | Judge |
| Jack Raine | Doctor |
| Ruta Lee | Diana |
| Molly Roden | Miss McHugh |
| Ottola Nesmith | Miss Johnson |
| J. Pat O'Malley | Bermuda Shorts Salesman |
| Ben Wright | Court Reporter |

Based on the short story *Witness For the Prosecution* (1933). 114 minutes.

▲ Christine Vole (Marlene Dietrich) responds to Sir Wilfred's monocle test while solicitor Brogan-Moore (John Williams) takes notes in *Witness for the Prosecution.*

*Witness For the Prosecution* was originally published in 1933 as part of a short story collection entitled *The Hound of Death and Other Stories.* In 1948, it was released with short stories again, although this time the book's title was *Witness For the Prosecution and Other Stories.*

It was 20 years after the story's original release, in 1953, that *Witness For the Prosecution* first appeared in play form, with a new, dramatic, and violent ending concocted by Christie.

David Horne, Derek Blomfield and Patricia Jessel had the leading roles when the play opened at the Winter Garden Theatre in London on October 28, 1953. Its New York Broadway debut, on December 16, 1954, had Patricia Jessel repeating her role as Romaine. Horne was replaced by Francis L. Sullivan as Sir Wilfred Robarts (we will remember that Sullivan had already played Christies' famous Belgian detective Hercule Poirot 20 years before on stage).

*Witness For the Prosecution* was extremely successful both in London, where it ran for over a year, and on Broadway, where the play won the coveted New York Drama Critics Circle Award in 1955.

Christie had put quite a great deal of effort

into researching this play to get as much authenticity as possible; she read numerous trial transcripts as well as attending several trials, and consulted with barristers regarding details and points of law.

As with *Ten Little Indians* ten years before, Christie wrote a new ending especially for the stage presentation of *Witness For the Prosecution.* Therefore when seeing the film after having read the book, you will naturally notice a drastic change. But again, as with *Ten Little Indians*, it was Christie, not the theatre producers nor the film producers, who wrote the new ending for stage and screen. In fact, Christie insisted on the new ending to the point of refusing to allow the play to be put on if the producers insisted on the same ending as in the original story.

Apparently this persistence, along with the hours of tireless effort into research paid off, as *Witness For the Prosecution* opened to rave reviews in both London and New York, and enjoyed very long runs.

Christie was most pleased. In her autobiography she stated: 'One night in the theatre stands out in my mind specially – the opening night of *Witness For the Prosecution.* I can safely say that that was the only first night I have enjoyed.'

Arthur Hornblow Jr, who had been impressed with the play, very much wanted to make *Witness For the Prosecution* as a film in 1957. After the rights to this film were secured from Christie (at the very high price of £116,000) United Artists

▲ Leonard Vole (Tyrone Power, second left) is about to be arrested in *Witness for the Prosecution* by Inspector Hearne (Philip Tonge, left) while his legal advisors (L-R) Brogan-Moore (John Williams), Mayhew (Henry Daniell) and Sir Wilfred Robarts (Charles Laughton) show concern.

set Billy Wilder to direct, and chose a marvellous cast including Charles Laughton, Tyrone Power, Marlene Dietrich, and Elsa Lanchester.

Set designer Alexander Trauner spent the enormous sum (in 1957, that is) of $75,000 building a meticulous reproduction of London's Old Bailey Courthouse, providing accuracy and authenticity down to the smallest detail. A table-sized model was first built from sketches Trauner had made; he was not permitted to take photographs.

The story concerns likeable Leonard Vole, who has formed an innocent-appearing relationship with wealthy widow Emily French, who he first encountered looking through a store window when she was selecting hats. Mrs French takes quite a shine to Leonard – and why not? He is cheerful, friendly and helpful, and the middle-aged widow naturally finds his attentions flattering, even if her dour housekeeper Janet MacKenzie does not.

When Mrs French is found murdered, Vole is arrested and tried for the crime, mainly on circumstantial evidence; we discover even before he is arrested that Mrs French has changed her will, leaving him, £80,000.

Vole's solicitor Mayhew takes him to see barrister Sir Wilfred Robarts, a famous trial lawyer who has recently had a heart attack. This was a plot development thrown in for the film by Wilder to add another bit of suspense. Robarts is very interested in the case, and despite the warnings of his finicky private nurse, Miss Plimsoll, decides to appear for the defence.

Vole's German wife Christine serves to complicate matters when interviewed by Mr Brogan-Moore, who is serving as Sir Wilfred's junior in the case. Christine shows a detached, and almost antagonistic, attitude towards her husband.

After investigation into Christine's background discloses that she had a previous husband that she never divorced, her marriage to Leonard is declared bigamous and she is called to testify as a witness for the prosecution.

As the circumstantial evidence mounts against Vole, a cockney tart comes to the aid of the defence; it seems she has certain letters in her possession written by Christine, vital to the defence, which she is willing to turn over for a price. These letters, written to a man named Max, throw a completely new light on the evidence in the case and show Christine to have been guilty of perjury in her testimony.

At the conclusion of the trial (Vole is acquitted) we learn that Christine has perpetrated a fantastic deception; she has faked the letters in order to deliberately discredit her own testimony, which in turn destroys the case against Leonard by making him appear the dupe of a clever couple.

'You see,' says Christine to Robarts, 'you thought Leonard was innocent.' 'I see,' he replies, 'and you KNEW he was.' 'No Sir Wilfred,' she replies, 'I knew he was guilty.'

The true ending of the tale is yet to come however. This was the main change from the original story and one that certainly works better (as Christie knew it would) for the medium of films (as well as in the theatre).

The story line is cleverly handled where the audience, along with the defence attorney, is

▲ Prisoner in the dock: Leonard Vole (Tyrone Power) looks grave as Sir Wilfred (Charles Laughton) addresses the court. The faithful Carter (Ian Wolfe, back left), Brogan-Moore (John Williams, seated with wig) and Mayhew (Henry Daniell, right front) are pensive about Vole's prospects in *Witness for the Prosecution*.

wholly convinced that the likeable Vole could not possibly be a murderer.

The only character change is the addition of the private nurse, Miss Plimsoll, played to the hilt by Laughton's eccentric wife, Elsa Lanchester. She constantly and persistently pursues her charge with hypodermic syringes and pills, continually berating him with quips and insults regarding his cigar-smoking and brandy-drinking.

Laughton plays the part of Sir Wilfred with a robust vigour that refrains from the credulous; Tyrone Power is winning as the seemingly-innocent Vole, and Marlene Dietrich turns in a fine performance as well. The flawless supporting cast, including John Williams as Brogan-Moore, austere Henry Daniell as Mayhew, Ian Wolfe as the loyal Carter, Una O'Connor as the no-nonsense, hard-of-hearing Janet MacKenzie, Torin Thatcher as the earnest Mr Myers (note his salute to Laughton in the courtroom), Norma Varden as Mrs French and Francis Compton as the judge, are all uniformly excellent.

Witty, crisp dialogue by Harry Kurnitz ('Sir Wilfred, you've forgotten your brandy') is also employed, along with first-rate technical credits, photography, music, and editing.

*Witness For the Prosecution* received six Academy Award nominations including Best Motion Picture, Best Actor (Charles Laughton), Best Supporting Actress (Elsa Lanchester), Best Director (Billy Wilder), Best Film Editing, and Best Sound. Unfortunately, it failed to win a single award.

The critics were unanimous in their praise of the film version of *Witness For the Prosecution*, which was equally successful (more so financially when you consider it earned $4 million at the box office in 1957–8) as the stage versions. *The New York Times'* review of November 22, 1957 stated: '*Witness For the Prosecution* comes off extraordinarily well. This results mainly from Billy Wilder's splendid staging of some splintering courtroom scenes and a first-rate theatrical performance by Charles Laughton. There is never a dull or worthless moment; the air in the courtroom fairly crackles with emotional electricity until that staggering surprise in the last reel. Then the whole drama explodes. But it is Mr Laughton who runs away with the show . . . Mr Laughton adds a wealth of comical by-play to his bag of courtroom tricks . . . the added dimensions of Mr Laughton bulge this black-and-white drama into a hit.'

Twenty-five years later, in 1982, *Witness For the Prosecution* would be remade in England as film for television starring Sir Ralph Richardson as Sir Wilfred and Deborah Kerr as nurse Plimsoll.

# ≡1960≡

## Spider's Web

Made in England. Directed by Godfrey Grayson.

CAST

▼

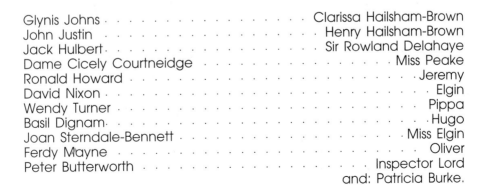

| | |
|---|---|
| Glynis Johns | Clarissa Hailsham-Brown |
| John Justin | Henry Hailsham-Brown |
| Jack Hulbert | Sir Rowland Delahaye |
| Dame Cicely Courtneidge | Miss Peake |
| Ronald Howard | Jeremy |
| David Nixon | Elgin |
| Wendy Turner | Pippa |
| Basil Dignam | Hugo |
| Joan Sterndale-Bennett | Miss Elgin |
| Ferdy Mayne | Oliver |
| Peter Butterworth | Inspector Lord |
| | and: Patricia Burke. |

Based on the original play *Spider's Web* (1954). 89 minutes.

▲ John Justin and Glynis Johns as the Hailsham-Browns in *Spider's Web*.

Like so many previous films based on Agatha Christie's works, *Spider's Web* was first a stage play (and a very successful one too). Margaret Lockwood, a great fan of Christie's and one of the biggest film stars in England, approached stage producer Peter Saunders (who had produced *The Mousetrap* and *Witness For the Prosecution*) in order to ask Christie to write an original part especially for her. The result was the character Clarissa Hailsham-Brown.

The play, which opened at the Savoy Theatre on December 13, 1954 (*The Mousetrap* was into its second year and *Witness For the Prosecution* was still going strong) received critical and public acclaim; it ran for two years.

Christie, who admired Margaret Lockwood, was pleased with her in the role of Clarissa. 'She was enchanting; she has a tremendous flair for comedy as well as drama,' Christie remarked.

Danziger Studios acquired the rights to the film, and selected Glynis Johns for the role of Clarissa, along with John Justin for her husband Henry. Husband and wife team Jack Hulbert and Dame Cicely Courtneidge, long favourites as entertainers in Britain, were also cast.

The plot concerns Clarissa Hailsham-Brown, wife of a diplomat, who have recently rented the house of a deceased antique dealer. Along with Pippa, Henry's daughter from a previous marriage, the couple move in.

When Oliver (Ferdy Mayne), the first Mrs Hailsham-Brown's new husband, arrives one night, he explains to Clarissa that Pippa's mother (who still retains legal custody of her) now wants her daughter to live with her. When he offers to back off for a price, he is shown the door by Miss Peake. Unfortunately Pippa has heard the conversation, and declares that she will kill Oliver.

When Henry leaves to pick up some diplomats he will be entertaining, Clarissa starts to get the house in order but trips over Oliver's dead body!

We are then treated to some comedy antics involving Sir Rowland, Jeremy, and Hugo, and the disappearing, reappearing and disappearing corpse. When the police arrive unexpectedly, Clarissa is accused of the murder, but the real culprit is soon caught and the mystery solved.

*Spider's Web* is a moderately interesting comedy-drama, something that MGM would do quite successfully during the next few years with Margaret Rutherford (although in *Spider's Web* the comedy was emphasized more by circumstance than by character).

The cast is competent, Glynis Johns lends her quirky charm to the part of Clarissa, and John Justin is fine as Henry. The best notices were received by Jack Hulbert and Dame Cicely Courtneidge, who were up to their usual high standards of acting.

The film, although not without interest, was not as successful as the play, perhaps in part because Clarissa was a role written especially for Margaret Lockwood, and the action, which for the most part takes place during the course of an evening, is material better suited to the theatre.

*Spider's Web* was not released in the United States (although it very occasionally turns up on television), a somewhat strange circumstance considering that *Witness For the Prosecution* enjoyed such a success. More than 20 years later, *Spider's Web* would be made as a television play starring Penelope Keith as Clarissa.

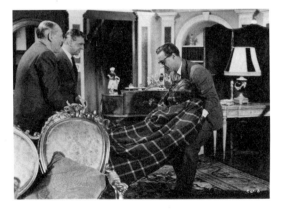

▲ L-R: Family friends, Sir Roland Delahaye (Jack Hulbert), Hugo (Basil Dignam) and Jeremy (Ronald Howard), attempt to hide the body in *Spider's Web*.

# ≡ 1962 ≡

## Murder She Said

Made in England. Directed by George Pollock.

CAST
▼

Margaret Rutherford · · · · · · · · · · · · · · Miss Jane Marple
Arthur Kennedy · · · · · · · · · · · · · · · · Dr Quimper
Muriel Pavlow · · · · · · · · · · · · · · Emma Ackenthorpe
James Robertson Justice · · · · · · · · · · Mr Ackenthorpe
Thorley Walters · · · · · · · · · · · · · Cedric Ackenthorpe
Charles Tingwell · · · · · · · · · · · Inspector Craddock
Conrad Phillips · · · · · · · · · · · · Harold Ackenthorpe
Ronald Howard · · · · · · · · · · · · · · · Brian Eastley
Joan Hickson · · · · · · · · · · · · · · · · Mrs Kidder
Stringer Davis · · · · · · · · · · · · · · · Mr Stringer
Ronnie Raymond · · · · · · · · · · Alexander Ackenthorpe
Peter Butterworth · · · · · · · · · · · · Train Conductor
Richard Briers · · · · · · · · · · · · · · · 'Mrs Binster'
Gerald Cross · · · · · · · · · · · · · · · · · · · Albert
Michael Golden · · · · · · · · · · · · · · · · · · Hillman
and: Barbara Hicks, Sidney Vivian, Vincent Harding.

Based on the novel *4.50 From Paddington* (1957). 86 minutes.

MGM's *Murder She Said*, based on the 1957 novel *4.50 From Paddington*, was the first film in the 1960s series chronicling the adventures of Miss Jane Marple starring Dame Margaret Rutherford. Although admired by Agatha Christie as an actress, Christie felt Rutherford was physically all wrong to play Miss Marple.

MGM had a different point of view, and cast Rutherford as the acidulated spinster. Rutherford had an aversion to appear in a film whose main subject matter was murder; the producers convinced her that the subject would be treated light-heartedly and she agreed.

The main change in the motion picture version from the original novel is the removal of the character Elspeth MacGillicuddy (in America the book was released under the title *What Mrs MacGillicuddy Saw*), with Miss Marple taking on her character as well.

When returning from London by train (from Paddington Station), Miss Marple witnesses a woman being strangled on another train going in the same direction on adjacent tracks. She can only see the back and hands of the murderer, a man, and the killing is over in a flash. Reporting the incident to the railway authorities, who in turn inform the police, she is nevertheless unable to convince them of the crime since a body cannot be found; they put it down to a hallucination or over-active imagination.

▲ Margaret Rutherford as Miss Marple and her real-life husband Stringer Davis as Jim Stringer in *Murder She Said*.

▲ Family conference in *Murder She Said*.
L-R: Cedric Ackenthorpe (Thorley Walters), Emma Ackenthorpe (Muriel Pavlow), Brian Eastley (Ronald Howard), Dr Quimper (Arthur Kennedy), Hillman (Michael Golden) and Mr Ackenthorpe (James Robertson Justice, sitting).

Despite the scepticism of Inspector Craddock (Charles Tingwell, who is well cast and appears in this role throughout the series), Miss Marple determines to get to the bottom of the mystery, enlisting the aid of librarian Jim Stringer (Stringer Davis, Rutherford's husband: he appeared with Rutherford in generally smallish roles in almost all her films).

Clues lead Miss Marple to the Ackenthorpe family, and she secures a position in the household in the guise of a maid to further her investigations.

After considerable personal jeopardy, and two more murders, Miss Marple is able to solve the crime and bring the perpetrator to justice, turning down a marriage proposal in the bargain.

Although not the true literary counterpart of Miss Jane Marple, Dame Margaret Rutherford nonetheless endeared herself to millions with the portrayal, putting her own inimitable stamp on it.

In this film, she is ably assisted by the performances of James Robertson Justice as the domineering invalid Ackenthorpe, Arthur Kennedy as Doctor Quimper, Thorley Walters, Conrad Phillips and Gerald Cross as the Ackenthorpe offspring, and the touching and effective portrayal of Stringer Davis.

Joan Hickson, who played Mrs Kidder, had appeared in a similar part 25 years previously in the Christie film *Love From a Stranger*. She would essay an extremely well-received characterization 25 years later as Miss Marple.

*Murder She Said* is skillfully directed by George Pollock, who is most ably assisted by cameraman Geoffrey Faithfull; composer Ron Goodwin, and art director Harry White also turn in first-rate work.

*Variety*'s review of January 10, 1962 called Murder She Said 'an engaging murder mystery' and went on to say about Rutherford that she was: 'One of filmdom's foremost character comediennes. The thread of humour weaving through the whodunit is in good histrionic hands.'

In 1988, Joan Hickson starred in the British-made television remake of this film, which returned to the novel's original title, *4.50 From Paddington.*

# ≡ 1963 ≡

## Murder at the Gallop

### Made in England. Directed by George Pollock.

### CAST

| | |
|---|---|
| Margaret Rutherford | Miss Jane Marple |
| Robert Morley | Hector Enderby |
| Dame Flora Robson | Miss Gilchrist |
| Charles Tingwell | Inspector Craddock |
| Stringer Davis | Mr Stringer |
| James Villiers | Michael Shane |
| Robert Urquhart | George Crossfield |
| Katya Douglas | Rosamund Shane |
| Duncan Lamont | Hillman |
| Finlay Currie | Old Enderby |
| Gordon Harris | Sergeant Bacon |
| Noel Howlett | Mr Trundell |
| Kevin Stoney | Dr Markwell |
| | and: Fred Griffiths. |

### Based on the novel *After the Funeral* (1953). 81 minutes.

The main difference between the film and the novel it was based on is that the detective in the novel is none other than the Belgian sleuth, Hercule Poirot, but since MGM had bought the rights to the novel and were producing a series of Miss Marple films, naturally the character was altered for the motion picture.

When Miss Marple, accompanied by her friend Mr Stringer, visit the home of Old Mr Enderby (Finlay Currie) while collecting for a charity fund, they find an open door and Mr Enderby near death (he shortly dies of an apparent heart attack). Miss Marple notices a cat in the house, which is odd since Mr Enderby is known to have hated cats – Miss Marple believes the cat was put there in order to frighten him to death.

Four of Mr Enderby's relatives are under suspicion, as they all stand to gain financially by his death (Miss Marple has overheard the reading of the old gentleman's will), so she determines to investigate the matter.

She appears at the Gallop, a hotel and riding academy run by Hector Enderby. She seems to be getting on the right track, discovering that a pair of riding boots match marks made in the soft earth at Old Enderby's house on the day of the crime.

The owner of the boots, George Crossfield (one of the heirs), appears to be the most likely suspect, but before Miss Marple is able to question him he is locked in a barn and trampled to death by a deliberately startled horse.

With Mr Stringer's help, Miss Marple discovers the true value of an old painting, and the motive behind the murders.

With the assistance of Inspector Craddock (Charles Tingwell), Miss Marple fakes a heart attack at a dance in order to entrap the mur-

derer, who she believes will attempt to employ the same method used on old Mr Enderby, i.e. frightening her to death.

Rutherford is her delightful self once again in this film, as *Variety* stated: 'giving a joyous, energetic performance.'

Robert Morley (who three years later would appear as Captain Hastings in *The Alphabet Murders*) gives one of his patented wonderfully comic acting jobs. Like James Robertson Justice in the previous film, he proposes to Miss Marple (she turns him down too) and he is a joy to watch.

Dame Flora Robson, Charles Tingwell, Stringer Davis, Duncan Lamont, Robert Urquhart and James Villiers turn in fine acting performances; George Pollock's direction is smooth and Arthur Ibbetson's camera work is first class.

▲ Hector Enderby (Robert Morley, right) is pleased to have Miss Marple (Margaret Rutherford) introduce him to Mr Stringer (Stringer Davis) whom he believes to be an art expert in *Murder at the Gallop*.

▶ Miss Marple (Margaret Rutherford) is assisted after her 'heart attack' by Hector Enderby (Robert Morley, left), Miss Gilchrist (Dame Flora Robson) and Inspector Craddock (Charles Tingwell).

# ≡1964≡

## Murder Ahoy

Made in England. Directed by George Pollock.

CAST

Margaret Rutherford · · · · · · · · · · · · · · · · · · Miss Jane Marple
Lionel Jeffries · · · · · · · · · Captain DeCourcy Rhumstone
Charles Tingwell · · · · · · · · · · · · · · Inspector Craddock
William Mervyn · · · · · · · · · Commander Breeze-Connigton
Stringer Davis · · · · · · · · · · · · · · · · · · · · · Mr Stringer
Francis Matthews · · · · · · · · · · · · · Lieutenant Compton
Joan Benham · · · · · · · · · · · · · · Matron Alice Fanbraid
Nicholas Parsons · · · · · · · · · · · · · · · · Doctor Crump
Derek Nimmo · · · · · · · · · · · Sub-Lieutenant Humbert
Gerald Cross · · · · · · · · Lieutenant Commander Dimchurch
Miles Malleson · · · · · · · · · · · · · · · · · · · · · · Bishop
Henry Oscar · · · · · · · · · · · · · · · · · · · Lord Rudkin
Henry Longhurst · · · · · · · · · Cecil ffolly-Hardwicke
Norma Foster · · · · · · · · · · · · · · · · · · · · · Shirley
Terence Edmund · · · · · · · · · · · · Sergeant Bacon
Lucy Griffiths · · · · · · · · · · · · · · · · · · · · Millie
Bernard Adams · · · · · · · · · · · · · · · · Dusty Miller
Tony Quinn · · · · · · · · · · · · · · · · · Kelly/Tramp
Edna Petrie · · · · · · · · · · · · · · · · · Miss Pringle
Roy Holder · · · · · · · · · · · · · Petty Officer Lamb.
and: Ivor Salter, Denys Peek.

Based on characters created by Agatha Christie (original film screenplay).
93 minutes.

▲ Poisoned snuff kills Cecil ffolly-Hardwicke (Henry Longhurst) to the suprise of Miss Marple (Margaret Rutherford, left) in *Murder Ahoy*. The Bishop (Miles Malleson) and Lord Rudkin (Henry Oscar) look suitably shocked.

The third film in the series of Margaret Rutherford's Miss Marple films for MGM, *Murder Ahoy* was not based on an original Christie novel, short story or play. David Pursall and Jack Seddon, who had scripted the previous films, created an original story, with a nautical background, based on characters created by Christie.

Set aboard a cadet naval training vessel, the film opens as Miss Marple is attending a meeting of trustees of the Cape of Good Hope Reclamation Trust (she is a Member of the Board). Before he can disclose important news concerning the cadet ship, Cecil ffolly-Hardwicke suffers a seizure and dies. Miss Marple discovers he has been murdered (poison in his snuff) and sets about to solve the crime.

In order to do this, she inveigles herself aboard the cadet ship, ostensibly for a visit in her trustee capacity but eventually worming her way for a

▲ Captain DeCourcy Rhumstone (Lionel Jeffries) allows Miss Marple (Margaret Rutherford) to inspect the ship's company, which includes Lieutenant Compton (Francis Matthews, saluting), Sub-Lieutenant Humbert (Derek Nimmo), Shirley (Norma Foster) and Matron Alice Fanbraid (Joan Benham), in *Murder Ahoy*.

stay of several days. There is an amusing bit as she takes over Captain DeCourcy Rhumstone's cabin; he takes over the cabin of his second-in-command, who in turn takes over the next officer's cabin, culminating in a chain of cabin-switches until the unfortunate officer last in line is forced to move into a cupboard.

Miss Marple discovers a motley group of officers aboard the vessel, all with something to hide. While Mr Stringer gathers information on land (he and Miss Marple have worked out a morse light-signal code), Miss Marple uncovers the innocent secrets most of the suspects are hiding.

Eventually Miss Marple is able to solve the mystery, but not before Lieutenant Compton has been run through with a sword and hung from the ship's yardarm, and another victim is killed with a poisoned mousetrap. The film's climax is centred around an amusing if somewhat improbable sword duel between Miss Marple and the villain.

By this time, the Rutherford name coupled with that of Agatha Christie's Miss Marple had developed quite a following for the series, and *Murder Ahoy*, along with the other films, is quite an entertaining comedy-mystery.

Notable amongst the cast are Lionel Jeffries as the bearded, eccentric captain, Gerald Cross as the officer who has been effectively hiding sea-sickness for years, and Nicholas Parsons as the brisk doctor, who has a quip for every corpse.

*Variety*'s review of September 11, 1964 was enthusiastic: 'This latest escapade of England's best-known female hawkshaw is up to slick, workmanlike standards of the others in producer Lawrence P. Bachmann's series. Director Pollock and editor Ernest Walter, along with scripters David Pursall and Jack Seddon, share credit for the smooth and well-organized story, sans loose ends too often found in whodunits. Photography by Desmond Dickinson, while not over obtrusive, catches the spirit of the production, and Ron Goodwin's musical score is bouncy and listenable.'

# Murder Most Foul

### Made in England. Directed by George Pollock.

## CAST

Margaret Rutherford· · · · · · · · · · · · · · · Miss Jane Marple
Ron Moody · · · · · · · · · · · · · · · · · · H. Driffold Cosgood
Dennis Price · · · · · · · · · · · · · · · · · · · · Harris Tumbrill
Terry Scott · · · · · · · · · · · · · · · · · Police Constable Wells
Charles Tingwell · · · · · · · · · · · · · · · Inspector Craddock
Andrew Cruickshank· · · · · · · · · · · · · · · Mr Justice Crosby
Ralph Michael· · · · · · · · · · · · · · · · · · · Ralph Summers
Megs Jenkins · · · · · · · · · · · · · · · · · · · · Mrs Thomas
James Bolam · · · · · · · · · · · · · · · · · · · · Bill Hanson
Stringer Davis · · · · · · · · · · · · · · · · · · · Mr Stringer
Francesca Annis· · · · · · · · · · · · · · · · · Sheila Howard
Allison Seebohm· · · · · · · · · · · · · · · · · Eva McGinigall
and: Pauline Jameson, Windsor Davies, Annette Kerr, Neil Stacy,
Maurice Good, Stella Tanner, Garard Green, Eric Francis, Ross Parker.

### Based on the novel *Mrs McGinty's Dead* (1952). 90 minutes.

Margaret Rutherford's popularity was at a high point at this time; the previous year she had won the Academy Award for best supporting actress in the all-star 1963 film *The VIPs*, and it is a pity that this was to be the last of the Miss Marple films.

MGM was unable to purchase any more film rights as Christie, although benefiting financially

▲ Theatrical agent Harris Tumbrill (Dennis Price) points out an important clue to Miss Marple (Margaret Rutherford) in *Murder Most Foul.*

from the success of the series, nonetheless was tired of seeing the comedy elements of action and characterization exploited in these films. Aside from a cameo in *The Alphabet Murders* the following year, this would be Rutherford's last screen role as Miss Marple.

The story opens as Miss Marple, to the annoyance of everyone, is the lone holdout on a murder jury (we see the corpse hanging before the opening credits roll). Discovering that the murdered woman had once been an actress, further investigations lead her to an amateur theatrical company with whom the dead woman had once been associated.

Miss Marple decides to join the company and there's a hilarious bit when she auditions for a part in the company, reading *The Legend of Dan McGrew*, amidst a cacophony of noises.

There is a mixture of daredevil melodrama along with satiric comedy; the theatrical company is comprised of an amusing group of unusual characters, all of whom come under suspicion.

Miss Marple learns a vital clue from theatrical agent Harris Tumbrill (Dennis Price, who would later that year appear in the remake of *Ten Little Indians*); it seems that the murdered woman had a child named Evelyn.

This narrows down the file of suspects, but the name Evelyn can either be masculine or feminine, and there are a few of both gender fitting the right age involved with the company.

Miss Marple is confronted by the murderer during the performance of a play while waiting offstage to make her entrance; the killer has a nifty alibi (he is supposed to be on stage at the time) prearranged, but, with the help of the police, Miss Marple once again triumphs.

This film has the usual comedy delight and charm of the others in the series, and Margaret Rutherford is in fine form with her lip-puckering, facial grimacing, and general bulldog-type tenacity.

Ron Moody also shines as affected theatre director/producer H. Driffold Cosgood, as do Andrew Cruickshank as the cantankerous judge, Terry Scott as the dense police constable, and Ralph Michael as actor Ralph Summers.

Francesca Annis, 20 years later to star as Tuppence Beresford in the *Partners in Crime* series, has a good part as a young actress.

*Variety* stated: 'Production values are highlighted by Ron Goodwin's music with its tingling clavichord sound. Desmond Dickinson's photography, with acute angles and interesting lighting, gives it a sensitive, mysterious look.'

▲ Miss Marple (Margaret Rutherford) shares her theory of the crime in *Murder Most Foul* with Inspector Craddock (Charles Tingwell, centre) while Mr Stringer (Stringer Davis) looks on.

# ≡ 1965 ≡

## Ten Little Indians

### Made in England. Directed by George Pollock.

CAST

| | |
|---|---|
| Wilfrid Hyde-White | Judge Arthur Cannon |
| Dennis Price | Dr Edward Armstrong |
| Stanley Holloway | William Henry Blore |
| Hugh O'Brian | Hugh Lombard |
| Leo Genn | General Sir John Mandrake |
| Shirley Eaton | Ann Clyde |
| Mario Adorf | Josef Grohmann |
| Daliah Lavi | Ilona Bergen |
| Marianne Hoppe | Elsa Grohmann |
| Fabian | Michael Raven |

### Based on the novel *Ten Little Niggers* (1939). 91 minutes.

*Ten Little Indians*, the third of five film versions of Agatha Christie's classic tale, was directed by George Pollock (who directed all of the Margaret Rutherford Miss Marple films) for Seven Arts Pictures.

This film had a number of changes from the previous version. The first and most noticeable is the location – while in the novel, stage and first film versions of the story action takes place on a remote island, in this film the guests are stranded in a remote castle atop an Austrian alp in the dead of winter.

▲ The cast of the 1965 version of *Ten Little Indians*. L-R: Hugh O'Brian as Hugh Lombard, Shirley Eaton (Ann Clyde), Fabian (Michael Raven), Leo Genn (General Mandrake), Mario Adorf (Josef Grohmann), Wilfrid Hyde-White (Judge Cannon), Dennis Price (Dr Armstrong), Daliah Lavi (Ilona Bergen) and Stanley Holloway (William Henry Blore).

The film itself was shot entirely on location (the first Agatha Christie film not shot at a studio) at an unoccupied mansion at Rush, near Dublin, Ireland.

The story involves eight guests (and two servants) who have been invited to the remote schloss, which can only be reached by cable car. None of them knows the others; they are all there at the request of a Mr U.N. Owen.

Comprising the house party are retired Judge Arthur Cannon (Wilfrid Hyde-White), Harley Street's Doctor Armstrong (Dennis Price), Mr William H. Blore, a private detective (Stanley Holloway), American engineer Hugh Lombard (Hugh O'Brian), Second World War veteran General Sir John Mandrake (Leo Genn, updated from Sir C. Aubrey Smith's General of World War One), German-born screen actress Ilona Bergen (Daliah Lavi) and pop singer Michael Raven (Fabian – 'Haven't you ever heard of Mike Raven and the black-birds?'). Ann Clyde (Shirley Eaton) was hired by a London agency as the Owen's secretary; the servants, Austrian couple the Grohmanns (Mario Adorf and Marianne Hoppe) were likewise hired through a Vienna agency; they have never met the Owens.

After introductions, the guests are shown to their rooms. General Mandrake, annoyed at the absence of their host, considers leaving but remains when he is told that Mr Owen will arrive for dinner.

During dinner, at which Mr Owen is still absent, the guests remark on the ten little indian boys centerpiece, as well as the fact that the nursery rhyme 'Ten Little Indians' is hanging framed in each guest's room.

After Mike Raven sings an updated version of 'Ten Little Indians' at the piano, a voice on a tape recorder bursts into the silence and accuses each member of the house party of a crime.

Passing it off as a practical joke in the poorest of taste, they are startled when Raven (immediately after confessing to his crime) chokes to death on his drink. Later that night the doctor tells Blore and Judge Cannon that Raven's whisky glass contained a solution of cyanide. Suicide? Or something else?

Sleep seems to be eluding most of the guests;

Grohmann discovers Lombard and Miss Clyde having milk in the kitchen. It seems that Frau Grohmann (Hoppe) is missing. After a brief search, they discover that she has taken the cable car. But she will not get far; the cable-rope has been cut and before they can bring her back it breaks, sending her crashing to her death hundreds of feet below.

After the other guests are awakened in order to discuss the situation, Dr Armstrong voices his opinion that Mr Owen, who may be responsible for these deaths and hiding somewhere, is 'out of his mind'.

General Mandrake takes charge and organizes a search of the house. Splitting in pairs to search the massive underground cellar, the General selects Miss Bergen – it seems he knows the truth about what happened to her late husband. When everyone becomes separated in the dark the General becomes victim number three.

It is obvious at this point that Mr Owen is one of the remaining guests and equally clear that he intends to punish everyone for his or her past crime. The murders are also recognized to be following the pattern of the 'Ten Little Indians' nursery rhyme, not to mention the missing indians from the centerpiece.

▲ Butler Grohmann (Mario Adorf, left) responds emphatically to the questions of William Henry Blore (Stanley Holloway) in *Ten Little Indians*.

▲ Although General Mandrake (Leo Genn, below) is anxious to leave immediately, Lombard (Hugh O'Brian) discovers their means of transportation has been cut off in *Ten Little Indians*.

After a fistfight between Lombard and Grohmann, the latter takes off in an attempt to climb down the mountain. Unfortunately the killer has seen him go out, chops the rope, and sends him to the same snowy grave where his wife rests.

When Miss Bergen is murdered in her room, the five remaining discuss their past crime; only Miss Clyde denies her guilt. While playing snooker, the Judge and Dr Armstrong form an alliance to catch the murderer – it seems he has made a mistake (putting the lights out of commission) which apparently clears these two, but that is no consolation for the judge as he is found in his room with a bullet hole in his head.

Since Miss Clyde is the only person to deny guilt of a past crime, Dr Armstrong reasons that she must be 'Mr Owen', and she's locked in her room. When Lombard opens her bedroom door (he kept the key), he gives her his revolver for protection and some mutual trust is reached. Hearing noises in the corridor, Lombard investigates; he rouses Blore and a following search reveals Dr Armstrong to be missing.

Next morning outside, Mr Blore is crushed to death when a statue shaped like a bear ('Three little Indians walking in the zoo; a big bear hugged one and then there were two') is dropped from the roof. After Lombard and Ann find this latest corpse, they look through Blore's binoculars and discover what he saw – the body of Dr Armstrong, who has been dead for hours (no footprints in the snow). At this point the audience is presented with a 'whodunit break', a 60-second flashback in order to solve the mystery.

▲ Judge Cannon (Wilfrid Hyde-White, left) and Dr Armstrong (Dennis Price) may have slept well in *Ten Little Indians*, but Ilona Bergen (Daliah Lavi) had a restless night.

▲ The guests note the macabre fact that another little Indian has been removed from the centrepiece in *Ten Little Indians*. L-R: Judge Cannon (Wilfrid Hyde-White), Dr Armstrong (Dennis Price), William Henry Blore (Stanley Holloway), Ilona Bergen (Daliah Lavi), Hugh Lombard (Hugh O'Brian), and Ann Clyde (Shirley Eaton).

The change of locale brought about other changes too. The servants have been changed from the English retainers to a Viennese couple. Other character changes (for a complete list see the 1989 version of *Ten Little Indians*) include Fabian as a rock-n-roll singer. Obviously this character was not in the 1939 novel, although Fabian was closer in age to the character than Mischa Auer's Russian Prince in the previous film.

Miss Brent, the 65-year-old spinster in the novel, was changed to 25-year-old Daliah Lavi's German actress character, for no other apparent reason than to have another young female in the film. Although all of the novel's characters are definitely English, only five of this film's characters are played by Britons; this film as well as the next two remakes used international players and altered roles accordingly.

Hugh O'Brian is quite good as Lombard and is in many respects very close to the novel's character. Shirley Eaton works well, especially in scenes with O'Brian. Swiss-born Mario Adorf, who had been likened to a European Marlon Brando, does well as does Marianne Hoppe, one of the biggest pre- and post-war film stars in Germany, although she has relatively little to do.

Outstanding performances are given by Wilfrid Hyde-White, perfectly cast as the judge; Dennis Price (by far the closest to the novel's character than any of the other actors in the other film versions) as the alcoholic doctor, and Stanley Holloway, who always looked years younger than his actual age, as a vigourous Blore. Leo Genn, who was 60 at the time of this film (Sir C. Aubrey Smith at 82 in 1945 was closer to the character's age) offers an excellent performance, typically intelligent, level-headed and quietly authoritative.

*Variety* agreed, saying in their review of October 12, 1965: 'It's a bad situation for the tyro talent, as Hyde-White, Holloway, Price and Genn, all first-rank character actors, effortlessly dominate all the scenes they're in.'

They also praised the film as 'technically excellent', adding: 'Ernie Steward's chilly and foreboding black-and-white camera-work is an important asset to the suspense building and Peter Boita's editing is crisp without being choppy. What will create the most comment is a two-minute "whodunit break" near the end when the action is suspended although the film continues, while the audience is encouraged to guess the murderer's identity. By inserting the "break" within the film, there's no problem of timing for projectionists to mishandle and no lapse of continuity for the viewer. While rapid, brief, still flashbacks to murders up to that point are shown, an animated clock ticks off the break.'

The manner of deaths in this film was more spectacular (two of the victims fall to their deaths) than in the first version, but tastefully handled. Malcolm Lockyer's music also adds to the film.

*Ten Little Indians*, itself a remake, would be made again in 1975 with Sir Richard Attenborough, Oliver Reed, Elke Sommer and Herbert Lom, and again in 1989 with Donald Pleasence, Frank Stallone and (in a different part) Herbert Lom.

# 1966

## The Alphabet Murders

Made in England. Directed by Frank Tashlin.

CAST

| | |
|---|---|
| Tony Randall | Hercule Poirot |
| Robert Morley | Captain Arthur Hastings |
| Anita Ekberg | Amanda Beatrice Cross |
| Maurice Denham | Inspector Japp |
| Guy Rolfe | Duncan Doncaster |
| Sheila Allen | Lady Diane |
| James Villiers | Franklin |
| Julian Glover | Don Fortune |
| Clive Morton | 'X' |
| Cyril Luckham | Sir Carmichael Clarke |
| Austin Trevor | Judson |
| Richard Wattis | Wolf |
| Grazina Frame | Betty Barnard |
| Patrick Newell | Cracknell |
| Alison Seebohm | Miss Sparks |
| Windsor Davies | Dragbot |
| Sheila Reed | Miss Fortune |
| Dame Margaret Rutherford | Miss Marple |
| Stringer Davis | Mr Stringer |

and: Norman Mitchell, Vincent Harding, Drewe Henley, Sally Douglas.

Based on the novel *The ABC Murders* (1936). 90 minutes.

Thirty years after Christie's original novel, *The ABC Murders* was written, MGM Studios brought it to the screen under the title *The Alphabet Murders*.

The film was directed by Frank Tashlin, perhaps best known for directing comedy films starring Jerry Lewis and also associated with the Bugs Bunny cartoon character. A good many of the same people who worked on the Margaret Rutherford Miss Marple films were on hand here as well – music by Ron Goodwin; camera, Desmond Dickinson; and of course the familiar team of screen-writers, David Pursall and Jack Seddon.

Hercule Poirot had been curiously neglected as a celluloid detective. An abortive attempt had been made in the early 1960s to bring him to television in series form; pilots filmed with Jose Ferrer and Martin Gabel did not, however, sell to the networks.

▲ Captain Hastings (Robert Morley, left) keeps a watchful eye on visiting Belgian detective Hercule Poirot (Tony Randall) in *The Alphabet Murders*.

▲ Hercule Poirot (Tony Randall, left) looking for a clue with Judson (Austin Trevor, who was the screen's first Poirot) in *The Alphabet Murders*. This was Trevor's last film appearance.

The last appearance on screen made by Poirot was in the 1934 Twickenham Film Studios production of *Lord Edgware Dies*, starring Austin Trevor, the last of his three films in the role. Coincidentally, 32 years later in this film, Trevor would make his last motion picture appearance.

Zero Mostel was originally cast as Poirot for this film, but the producers changed their minds (and Christie's objection probably had something to do with it), and American light comedy star Tony Randall, who would become a household name in the 1970s as finnicky Felix Unger in *The Odd Couple* on television, was selected.

The film opens and Randall introduces himself, pointing to the credits, then in make-up as Poirot goes about his business. The story starts with the murder of an aquatic clown, and Poirot begins his investigation, aided by the gout-ridden British Intelligence Agent, Captain Arthur Hastings (Robert Morley). After subsequent murders and the discovery of clues lead Poirot to the realization of an AA BB CC pattern, action culminates on a train as Poirot solves the crime and unmasks the killer.

There are some genuinely funny moments in this film, such as Poirot's continuously trying to ditch Hastings (including a very funny scene in a bowling alley), Poirot's arrest and time in jail, and a cameo appearance by Margaret Rutherford and Stringer Davis.

Tony Randall seems an odd choice for Poirot, but he delivers a very precise comic characterization, which in his capable hands is well-played. Robert Morley, who offered a fine portrayal in

*Murder at the Gallop*, once again shows us his flair for comedy through his inimitable style and timing as Captain Hastings.

The fine supporting cast includes Maurice Denham as Inspector Japp, Guy Rolfe as psychiatrist Duncan Doncaster, James Villiers as Franklin, Clive Morton as X, Cyril Luckham as Sir Carmichael Clarke, Richard Wattis as Wolf, and Austin Trevor as Judson, the butler.

The film is a very interesting comedy–mystery; one may have expected a series of Poirot films along the same lines as the Rutherford–Marple films, but apparently no further plans were made.

*Variety*, reviewing the film March 9, 1966, complimented the film's excellent production values, noting: 'It makes handsome use at times of London street backgrounds, Frank Tashlin's direction is attuned to the type of comedy intended and he has at his disposal an accomplished cast, as well as expert technical backing. On the technical end, Desmond Dickinson's black-and-white photography interestingly limns movement and Ron Goodwin's music score catches the action appropriately. Editing by John Victor Smith is as sharp as script allows, and Bill Andrews' art direction is fresh.'

► Former model Anita Ekberg as Amanda Beatrice Cross in *The Alphabet Murders*.

## Endless Night

Made in England. Directed by Sidney Gilliat.

CAST

▼

| | |
|---|---|
| Hayley Mills | Ellie |
| Hywel Bennett | Michael Rogers |
| Britt Ekland | Greta |
| George Sanders | Andrew Lippincott |
| Leo Genn | Psychiatrist |
| Per Oscarsson | Santonix |
| Peter Bowles | Reuben |
| Lois Maxwell | Cora |
| Aubrey Richards | Dr Philpott |
| Ann Way | Mrs Philpott |
| Patience Collier | Miss Townsend |
| Madge Ryan | Mother |
| Walter Gotell | Constantine |
| Helen Horton | Aunt Beth |
| David Bauer | Uncle Frank |
| Geoffrey Chater | Coroner |
| David Healey | Jason |
| Robert Keegan | Innkeeper |
| Mischa De La Motte | Maynard |
| Windsor Davies | Sergeant Keene |
| Robert O'Neil | Broker |
| and: Ewan Roberts. | |

Based on the novel *Endless Night* (1967). 98 minutes.

Five years after *Endless Night* was written, EMI–MGM Elstree Films acquired the rights and made it into a film starring Hayley Mills and Hywel Bennett.

The film opens where Michael Rogers is recounting events to an unidentified person. Rogers is a young Walter Mittyish, daydreaming chauffeur; his mother warns him that his fantasies (such as bidding on a Renoir at an auction at Christie's) will one day land him in trouble.

When he is hired to drive a Greek tycoon (Walter Gotell), he tells the man's architect, Santonix, of one of his fantasies: to own a piece of land he has seen called Gipsy's Acre, near the village of Market Chadwell, and build a fine house. The architect tells him: 'If the wish can be willed, perhaps the means will follow.'

A few days later, he takes a camera to Gipsy's Acre, and through the lens spies a girl dancing on the grass. After they introduce themselves, he lets her in on his secret of owning the property; before they get very far they encounter a mysterious woman who warns them to leave and that no good will come to them there.

Dismissing her as 'a nut case', they go to a local pub to get better acquainted, and after driving to London (he by scooter, she by car) they agree to meet again at Gipsy's Acre in the near future.

When the day arrives, Michael is there but Ellie stands him up; she does call, however (from Rome) and they make a date to meet in London the following Saturday.

At this rendezvous, Michael confronts Ellie with her picture in the newspaper; he is quite upset as it seems she is one of the world's richest young women, and he is only an unemployed chauffer. However Ellie tells him she loves him

▲ Hayley Mills and Hywel Bennett as the young couple at the centre of *Endless Night*.

(she has also bought Gipsy's Acre) and before you can blink they are secretly married.

After a brief honeymoon on the Continent where they meet Santonix and commission him to build their house, they return to England to meet the bride's family, who are openly hostile. Lawyer Lippincott even tries to buy Michael off.

The oft-mentioned Greta, a sort of companion to Ellie, is finally seen the next day down at Gipsy's Acre. While they are waiting for completion of the house, Michael and Ellie take over the local antique shop.

Santonix announces the house is finished, and the couple is shown the fabulous new house, complete with indoor fountains and swimming pools and other accoutrements, all remote-controlled. Right after they move in, Greta comes, ostensibly to spend the weekend but ends up staying much longer.

Shortly afterwards, a series of accidents occur, the first when Ellie is thrown off her horse. Is it the curse foretold to them by the mysterious woman, or something more sinister? Later, Ellie sprains her ankle badly; Greta now has an excuse to stay on.

Michael resents Greta's presence; she is rather overstaying her welcome. After a row at a party, Greta decides to leave but is forestalled by Michael, who apologizes for his manners, despite the warnings of Santonix that Greta is evil.

When Michael goes to an auction, Ellie goes for a last ride – this time she turns up dead. Michael blames himself as he made her stay behind; he wanted to buy her a surprise birthday gift.

Lawyer Lippincott informs Michael that Ellie's will specified her burial in New York, so he leaves for the USA. While in New York he visits Santonix, who dies mysteriously in a local hospital. It seems everyone connected with Gipsy's Acre is cursed.

Returning home, he finds Greta has dismissed the servants and it is then that we find these two have been having an affair. After a letter from Lippincott arrives with a picture of Greta and Michael, taken before they supposedly met, Michael (who has been acting a bit peculiar throughout the film) realizes the game is up and

▲ Miss Townsend (Patience Collier, left) warns Michael (Hywel Bennett) and Ellie (Hayley Mills) to stay away from Gipsy's Acre in *Endless Night*.

▲ Architect Santonix (Per Oscarsson, centre) shows Michael (Hywel Bennett) and Ellie (Hayley Mills) the model for their new home, which he has been commissioned to build in *Endless Night*.

▲ Family lawyer Andrew Lippincott (George Sanders) proposes a toast to the newlyweds in *Endless Night*. L-R: Uncle Frank (David Bauer), Michael Rogers (Hywel Bennett), Ellie (Hayley Mills), Andrew Lippincott (George Sanders), Aunt Beth (Helen Horton), Reuben (Peter Bowles), and Cora (Lois Maxwell).

snaps completely, drowning Greta in the pool.

When the police arrive, Michael also admits to the murder of Ellie, telling how he put cyanide in an antihistimine capsule.

The action concludes when we see that Michael, narrating the story, is in a sanitarium talking to a psychiatrist; he is now completely insane.

*Endless Night* is an interesting, if odd film. It was not released in American theatres, and only shows up occasionally on television. The London *Times* said that the film was 'rotten with the stink of red herrings', although perhaps the reviewer did not read the novel, as the film version was fairly faithful to it.

The acting is competent, if not spectacular;

Hywel Bennett, has a difficult role, and Hayley Mills, is well cast as an American Heiress. Per Oscarsson, as Santonix, often mumbles his lines and is hard to follow.

This was one of the last films of George Sanders, who committed suicide the same year. Leo Genn, who was cast as General Mandrake in the 1965 film of Christie's *Ten Little Indians*, has a small part at the end of the film as the psychiatrist.

*Endless Night* was directed and scripted by Sidney Gilliat; his brother, Leslie Gilliat, produced it. Some location scenes were shot in France and Italy.

# ≡1974≡

## Murder on the Orient Express
### Made in England. Directed by Sidney Lumet.

CAST

| | |
|---|---|
| Albert Finney | Hercule Poirot |
| Lauren Bacall | Mrs Hubbard |
| Martin Balsam | Bianchi |
| Ingrid Bergman | Greta Ohlsson |
| Jacqueline Bisset | Countess Andrenyi |
| Jean Pierre Cassel | Pierre Paul Michael |
| Sean Connery | Colonel Arbuthnot |
| Sir John Gielgud | Beddoes |
| Dame Wendy Hiller | Princess Dragomiroff |
| Anthony Perkins | Hector McQueen |
| Vanessa Redgrave | Mary Debenham |
| Rachel Roberts | Hildegard Schmidt |
| Richard Widmark | Ratchett |
| Michael York | Count Andrenyi |
| Colin Blakely | Cyrus Hardman |
| George Coulouris | Dr Constantine |
| Denis Quilley | Antonio Foscarelli |
| Vernon Dobtcheff | Concierge |
| Jeremy Lloyd | Aide-de-camp |
| John Moffatt | Chief Attendant |
| | and: George Silver. |

Based on the novel *Murder on the Orient Express* (1934). 127 minutes.

Producer Lord John Brabourne, in association with EMI Films, was chiefly responsible for getting the rights for the 1974 film *Murder on the Orient Express*. Brabourne's father-in-law, Lord Louis Mountbatten, was also instrumental in persuading Christie to sell the film rights.

An all-star international cast was assembled, and special attention was paid to period detail (the real Orient Express was used) with first-class sets and costumes.

The film begins with newsreel-like footage of the Armstrong kidnapping case (Christie was doubtless influenced here by the real-life Lindbergh case) in which little Daisy Armstrong is kidnapped, then murdered.

We are then transported several years later where Mr Hercule Poirot, after having successfully concluded a difficult case, is on his way home to London.

Trying to make a reservation on the Orient

▲ The Orient Express chugs along between Belgrade and Zagreb.

Express, he is told there are no berths left, which is unusual for that time of year. Coming to his rescue is his old friend Mr Bianchi, a director of the company, who also happens to be travelling aboard the train; he secures accommodation for Poirot.

The passengers include a wide variety of people: Colonel Arbuthnot, a stiff-upper-lip British army officer; the Count and Countess Andrenyi, an ardent and titled young married couple; imperious Russian Princess Dragomiroff and her German maid; irritating widow Mrs Hubbard; Swedish missionary Greta Ohlsson; businessman Mr Ratchett and his valet and nervous secretary, among others.

Shortly after the train gets underway, Ratchett approaches Poirot for protection, as he has received some threatening letters. He keeps a loaded gun under his pillow as a precaution (he tells Poirot he has retired from the baby food business), but Poirot refuses to take the case. 'I have enough money to satisfy both my needs and my caprices', he tells Ratchett as the latter increases the money offered.

The following morning Ratchett is found murdered in his bed, stabbed a dozen times or so, and Bianchi enlists the help of Poirot to solve the crime aboard the snowbound train.

With the help of Greek Doctor Constantine (George Coulouris), Poirot sets about his investigation. He is able to discover a vital clue by

◀ Albert Finney as the indomitable Belgian sleuth Hercule Poirot in *Murder on the Orient Express*.

means of the aid of a hatbox and some moustache wax. An apparently burnt scrap of paper has the message 'aisy Arms', which calls Poirot's (and the audience's) attention to the events at the opening of the film.

Setting up headquarters in the dining car, Poirot interviews the suspects one by one, separating bogus clues ('There are too many clues in this room,' says Poirot to the doctor, referring to Ratchett's bedchamber) from the genuine.

After interviewing the passengers, he is able to put together a picture of the victim, discovering that Ratchett was in fact a notorious gangster responsible for the kidnapping and subsequent murder of little Daisy Armstrong several years before.

Assembling everyone in the dining car, he informs them that he has come up with two possible solutions to the crime, both of which will be discussed.

The first solution presumes that an unidentified person or persons boarded the train, posing as a Wagon Lit Conductor (the clue of the button and tunic) and killed Ratchett. There is other physical evidence to support what Poirot refers to as 'the simple solution'.

The second, more complicated solution supposes the murderer is one or more of the travellers on the train, and Poirot expounds further on this theory, which signifies a vendetta murder.

After a detailed outline of the solution, Poirot leaves it up to Mr Bianchi as director of the

▲ Hercule Poirot (Albert Finney) tries to establish the ownership of a handkerchief found in the murder room in *Murder on the Orient Express*. L-R: Hercule Poirot (Albert Finney), Dr Constantine (George Coulouris), Beddoes (Sir John Gielgud), Cyrus Hardman (Colin Blakely), Hildegard Schmidt (Rachel Roberts), and Princess Dragomiroff (Dame Wendy Hiller).

company to choose which of the solutions he will offer to the police, as workmen dig the train out of the snow.

*Murder on the Orient Express* was one of Agatha Christie's best novels, and it gets a brilliant cinematic treatment in this 1974 film. Every aspect of the film is wonderfully conceived and realized; Tony Walton's production design and costumes are excellent, as is the cinematography of the renowned Geoffrey Unsworth; Sidney Lumet's direction is both sharp and clear.

Albert Finney makes an outstanding Hercule Poirot; by far the finest ever in the cinema. He really captures the essence of the Belgian detective with the little grey cells.

The entire cast is well-chosen and execute their roles with distinction. There is Sean Connery as the typically British army officer on his way home from India, romancing strong-willed Mary Debenham (Vanessa Redgrave) along the way. Dame Wendy Hiller's aged Princess is a joy, as

▲ Poirot (Albert Finney) offers two solutions to the crime in *Murder on the Orient Express*. L-R: Pierre Paul Michael (Jean Pierre Cassel), Hector McQueen (Anthony Perkins), Mary Debenham (Vanessa Redgrave), Colonel Arbuthnot (Sean Connery), Greta Ohlsson (Ingrid Bergman), Dr Constantine (George Coulouris), Hercule Poirot (Albert Finney), Hildegard Schmidt (Rachel Roberts), Princess Dragomiroff (Dame Wendy Hiller), Antonio Foscarelli (Denis Quilley), Count Andrenyi (Michael York), Countess Andrenyi (Jacqueline Bisset), Mrs Hubbard (Lauren Bacall), and Bianchi (Martin Balsam).

is Sir John Gielgud's snobbish manservant.

Jean-Pierre Cassel as the composed conductor, Lauren Bacall as the abrasive Mrs Hubbard, and Ingrid Bergman as the humble Swedish missionary ('I come here to teach little brown babies who are even more backwards than myself') also give good performances.

Richard Widmark exudes the proper amount of disagreeability as Ratchett, a sternly unsympathetic (and guilty) victim; Anthony Perkins' nervousness is quite in keeping, as is Rachel Roberts' loyalty, reading Goethe poetry to her mistress.

Denis Quilley as Italian used car salesman Antonio Foscarelli, and Colin Blakely as the detective are also quite good. Martin Balsam provides an amusing performance as Bianchi, suspecting in turn each of the passengers, while the always excellent George Coulouris as the Greek doctor emits competent authority.

Christie fans will certainly be grateful for the care put into the production as well as the faithfulness to Christie's original novel.

*Murder on the Orient Express* became the biggest money-making British film up to that time, and was also a huge critical success. It received six Academy Award nominations including Best Actor (Albert Finney), Best Supporting Actress (Ingrid Bergman, the only winner), Best Screenplay, Best Cinematography, Best Music and Best Costumes.

The British Film Academy selected *Murder on the Orient Express* as 1974's best film, and cited Albert Finney best actor, as well as awards in the supporting catagory to Sir John Gielgud and Dame Wendy Hiller.

*Variety* (November 11, 1974) stated: 'This is one of those strange goings-on plots, where the missing crucial pieces do not come up until the ace sleuth gathers all the suspects in the drawing room, or bedroom, or in this case, a sleeper car, and in a tour de force sequence such as Finney carries off to triumph here, painstakingly lays out the problems, clues, and guilty parties.'

They went on in their praise: 'The ensemble artistic accomplishment here is brilliant; a few decades from now only a copyright date and the subtle technicolor printing will give the film away as not being some famed British film of its own story time.'

# ≡1975≡

## Ten Little Indians

Made in England. Directed by Peter Collinson.

CAST

| | |
|---|---|
| Sir Richard Attenborough | Judge Arthur Cannon |
| Oliver Reed | Hugh Lombard |
| Elke Sommer | Vera Clyde |
| Herbert Lom | Dr Edward Armstrong |
| Gert Frobe | Wilhelm Blore |
| Adolfo Celi | General Andre Salve |
| Stephane Audran | Ilona Morgan |
| Charles Aznavour | Michel Raven |
| Maria Rohm | Elsa Martino |
| Alberto De Mendoza | Otto Martino |
| Orson Welles | Voice of Mr Owen |

Based on the novel *Ten Little Niggers* (1939). 98 minutes.

Following the tremendous success of *Murder on the Orient Express* the previous year, producer Harry Alan Towers came out with a new version of *Ten Little Indians*, with an international cast, for Avco-Embassy Films. This was ten years after the marvellous 1965 film.

▲ L-R: Vera Clyde (Elke Sommer), Michel Raven (Charles Aznavour), Dr Armstrong (Herbert Lom), Hugh Lombard (Oliver Reed), Judge Cannon (Sir Richard Attenborough), Ilona Morgan (Stephane Audran), Wilhelm Blore (Gert Frobe) and General Salve (Adolfo Celi) in the 1975 version of *Ten Little Indians*.

Once again, the main difference is the location – whereas in 1945 and 1949 the setting was a remote island and an Austrian alp in 1965, the 1975 version takes place at a luxurious, isolated hotel in the Iranian desert. The film was shot on location – something that would be improbable and highly dangerous today.

The film opens as the guests are flown by helicopter to the remote hotel. None of them knows the other; they are there at the invitation of Mr U.N. Owen to spend a weekend.

After performing introductions, the guests are shown to their rooms. Assembling for dinner, they comment on the continued absence of their host as well as the fact that a copy of the *Ten Little Indians* nursery rhyme hangs on the wall of each of their rooms.

French singer Michel Raven (Charles Aznavour) sings the title song, followed by *Dance in the Old-Fashioned Way* (one of Aznavour's own songs) before the voice of Mr Owen (spoken by Orson Welles) accuses them of their crimes.

Raven is the first to die, by poison, followed by Mrs Martino, who is strangled by a rope. By this time it is clear that they have been marked for murder and a search of the massive hotel is underway for their missing host; the only result is another murder (General Salve).

There is no telephone, radio or car at the hotel so Martino tries to walk out on foot but does not get very far. Mademoiselle Morgan is the next victim; she is bitten by a poisonous snake.

After Judge Cannon is found shot through the head, the four remaining guests discuss the crimes of which Mr Owen accused them, as this may be the key to the whole business.

During the middle of the night Dr Armstrong disappears and the others believe he may be in hiding ('Four little Indians going out to sea; a red herring swallowed one and then there were three'). Blore thinks he knows where the doctor is, but before he is able to tell the others he is pushed off the roof of the hotel.

Vera and Hugh discover his body and, minutes later, that of the doctor. Miss Clyde, realizing that there are now only two left, decides to shoot Lombard as he must be the killer. Returning to the hotel, she discovers two things – a hangman's noose and the explanation to the mystery.

*Ten Little Indians*, the fourth filming of the Christie classic, did not receive overwhelming critical praise. Comparisons to its three marvellous predecessors were unavoidable, and it was difficult to live up to them.

Also, Peter Collinson's direction of the film was not up to the standards of either Rene Clair in 1945 or George Pollock in 1965. Suspense is lacking throughout most of the film and is really only generated in the last half hour or so.

A very good cast is assembled for this film, and best among the performances are Sir Richard Attenborough as the no-nonsense Judge and versatile Herbert Lom stolidly and steadily reliable as Dr Armstrong.

▲ Elsa Martino (Maria Rohm) is found strangled against a pillar. Hugh Lombard (Oliver Reed, left) and Vera Clyde (Elke Sommer) try to console her husband Otto (Alberto De Mendoza).

▲ And then there were five: Dr Armstrong (Herbert Lom) discovers the latest victim, Miss Morgan (Stephane Andran).

A few of the performers in this film spoke native languages other than English and at times are difficult to understand. Gert Frobe, as Blore, (probably best remembered as James Bond villain Goldfinger) turns in a notable performance; Italian actor Adolfo Celi, who played Bond villian Emilio Largo in *Thunderball*, plays his part without much flair or distinction.

The rest of the cast is adequate without being electrifying; Oliver Reed and Elke Sommer lack the spark Hugh O'Brian and Shirley Eaton had in the previous version.

*Variety's* review of the film February 1, 1975 said: 'This is at least the third remake of Agatha Christie's whodunit classic, and though it's far less distinguished than its forerunners it should do modest-to-okay biz in multiple release patterns around the world for those new audiences who aren't familiar with the story.'

Fourteen years later, in 1989, *Ten Little Indians* would be filmed yet again with Donald Pleasence, Herbert Lom (in a different part this time) and Frank Stallone, and an even more bizarre change of setting.

▲ Judge Cannon (Sir Richard Attenborough) sits in the not-quite-empty Shah Abah Hotel in Isfahan, Persia, in *Ten Little Indians.*

# ≡ 1978 ≡

## Death on the Nile

Made in England. Directed by John Guillerman.

### CAST

| | |
|---|---|
| Peter Ustinov | Hercule Poirot |
| David Niven | Colonel Race |
| Bette Davis | Mrs Van Schuyler |
| Maggie Smith | Miss Bowers |
| Mia Farrow | Jacqueline De Bellefort |
| Simon MacCorkindale | Simon Doyle |
| Angela Lansbury | Salome Otterbourne |
| Lois Chiles | Linnet Ridgeway |
| Jon Finch | Mr Ferguson |
| Olivia Hussey | Rosalie Otterbourne |
| George Kennedy | Andrew Pennington |
| Jane Birkin | Louise Bourget |
| Jack Warden | Dr Bessner |
| Harry Andrews | Barnstaple |
| I.S. Johar | Manager of the *Karnak* |
| Sam Wanamaker | Rockford |

and: Alfie Bass, Victor Maddern, Reg Lye, Ann Way, Brigid Bates,
Celia Imrie.

Based on the novel *Death on the Nile* (1937). 140 minutes.

▲ Colonel Race (David Niven, left) cracks his knuckles while Hercule Poirot (Peter Ustinov) discusses a case in *Death on the Nile*.

More than 30 years before the 1978 film version of *Death on the Nile*, which was one of Christie's own favourite stories, a theatre adaptation of the tale was presented.

Under the title *Murder on the Nile* the play opened in London at the Ambassador's Theatre March 19, 1946. David Horne, who would later play Sir Wilfred Robarts in *Witness For the Prosecution*, was cast as Father Borrondale, a replace-ment of the Hercule Poirot character. This play was not a critical success, and did not have a very long run.

Six months to the day later, the play opened on Broadway in New York under the curiously altered title of *Hidden Horizon*. Archdeacon Pennyfeather (Halliwell Hobbes, who had played Mr Justice Wargrave three years before on Broadway in *Ten Little Indians*) was the story's hero this time, but the play fared even worse than it did in London, running only two weeks.

When Lord Brabourne and Richard Goodwin announced plans for another Hercule Poirot film following the tremendous success of the 1974 film *Murder on the Orient Express*, naturally Albert Finney was the first choice to play Poirot. Unfortunately, Finney's asking price was somewhere in the neighbourhood of one million dollars,

▲ The manager of the *Karnak* (I.S. Johar, extreme right) explains the ship's delay to his passengers, including (L-R): Colonel Race (David Niven), Andrew Pennington (George Kennedy), Hercule Poirot (Peter Ustinov), Linnet Ridgeway (Lois Chiles), Simon Doyle (Simon Mac-Corkindale), Mrs Van Schuyler (Bette Davis), Dr Bessner (Jack Warden), Miss Bowers (Maggie Smith), Mr Ferguson (Jon Finch), and Salome Otterbourne (Angela Lansbury), in *Death on the Nile*.

which the producers considered too high, so Peter Ustinov got the part instead.

Filmed on location in Egypt, the story begins in England, where young American millionairess Linnet Ridgeway purchases a large estate and begins plans for redesign.

Her oldest friend, Jacqueline De Bellefort, recently left penniless by the stock market crash, arrives on the scene and tells Linnet of her forthcoming marriage to the charming Simon Doyle, who Jacqueline hopes will be hired by Linnet to manage her estate.

Linnet does more than this; she marries the young man. This throws the emotionally wrought Jackie into a daze; she takes it on herself to turn up where-ever the couple may be. On their honeymoon in Egypt, Linnet and Simon think they have eluded Jacqueline, only to be annoyed at her appearance at their hotel.

Hercule Poirot is also at the hotel, and the couple engage him to act as their ambassador to Jackie to persuade her to go away and leave them alone.

Poirot is unable to do this however, and a subsequent trip down the Nile on the *Karnak* introduces a number of colourful characters who will all become involved, either directly or peripherally, in the upcoming tragedy.

When Linnet is murdered and Simon is shot, Poirot, along with his friend Colonel Race, who happens to be on board, investigate the case.

Linnet's pearls have been stolen, and before too long her maid Louise is murdered, along with the alcoholic author Salome Otterbourne, just as the latter is about to impart some important information to Poirot. Before anyone else is killed, Poirot is able to explain all the nuances of the case as he arrives at the correct, fantastic solution.

'Death on the Nile is a clever, witty, well-plotted, beautifully produced and splendidly acted screen version of Agatha Christie's mystery,' said *Variety* in its review of September 18, 1978. 'It's an old-fashioned stylized entertainment with a big cast and lush locations. The Paramount release of the EMI presentation, produced by John Brabourne and Richard Goodwin, can look forward to a long and steady run across the country. Outlook world-wide is equally optimistic.'

The choice of using Ustinov as Poirot turned

▲ Members of the cast of *Death on the Nile*. L-R, back: Simone McCorkindale as Simon Doyle, I.S. Johar (Manager of the *Karnak*), David Niven (Colonel Race), Peter Ustinov (Hercule Poirot), Jane Birkin (Louise Bourget), Jack Warden (Dr Bessner), Maggie Smith (Miss Bowers), Jon Finch (Mr Ferguson), and George Kennedy (Andrew Pennington). L-R, front: Lois Chiles (Linnet Ridgeway), Mia Farrow (Jacqueline De Bellefort), Angela Lansbury (Salome Otterbourne), Bette Davis (Mrs Van Schuyler), and Olivia Hussey (Rosalie Otterbourne).

out to be a good one: although physically he was set in the same mold as Francis L. Sullivan and Charles Laughton, two actors who previously essayed the character in the theatre and were all very large, Ustinov nonetheless etches a memorable characterization. He portrays the Belgian sleuth as witty, thoughful and introspective, and pretty much tones down the comedic aspects of the character that he would too often use in future films when he played Poirot.

Ustinov's performance is nicely complimented by the able performances of the big-name cast. David Niven is properly urbane as Colonel Race, Bette Davis supplies the right amount of hauteur as Washington socialite Mrs Van Schuyler (she would later make another appearance in a Christie film, 1985's *Murder With Mirrors*), and Maggie Smith earns our sympathy as her long-suffering companion, Miss Bowers.

Jon Finch is fine as the young man with the communist set of mind, and Mia Farrow is quite good as the jilted lover. Simon MacCorkindale, who had previously played mostly small roles in films, does an excellent job in the role of Simon Doyle.

The versatile Angela Lansbury is downright funny in the role of alcoholic romantic novelist Salome Otterbourne.

In smaller parts Indian actor I.S. Johar is noteworthy as the concerned manager of the *Karnak*, and Harry Andrews offers his usual sobering performance as the estate butler.

George Kennedy does a good job of displaying bogus honesty as the lawyer. Jack Warden, a fine character actor, is terribly miscast in the role of the German Doctor, Bessner. A cross between Gert Frobe and Oscar Homolka comes more to mind when reading the novel.

The story remains faithful to the novel, and the film is highlighted by the location filming, period atmosphere, and Anthony Powell's costumes.

Anthony Shaffer's screenplay is first-rate, as is John Guillerman's direction, which uses clever visual devices in the denouement scene that are augmented by Ustinov's narration.

*Death on the Nile* was the first, and probably the best, of Ustinov's six performances on film and television as the Belgian sleuth.

# ≡ 1979 ≡

## Agatha

Made in England. Directed by Michael Apted.

CAST

| | |
|---|---|
| Vanessa Redgrave | Agatha Christie |
| Dustin Hoffman | Wally Stanton |
| Timothy Dalton | Archie Christie |
| Helen Morse | Evelyn Crawley |
| Celia Gregory | Nancy Neele |
| Paul Brooke | John Foster |
| Timothy West | Kenward |
| Tony Britton | William Collins |
| Alan Badel | Lord Brackenbury |
| Carolyn Pickles | Charlotte Fisher |
| Robert Longden | Pettelson |
| Donald Nithsdale | Uncle Jones |
| Yvonne Gillian | Mrs Braithwaite |
| Barry Hart | Superintendant MacDonald |
| David Hargreaves | Sergeant Jarvis |
| Tim Seely | Captain Rankin |
| Peter Arne | Manager |
| Jill Summers | Aunt |
| Sandra Voe | Therapist |
| Chris Fairbank | Luland |
| Liz Smith | Flora |
| D. Geoff Tomlinson | Hotel Receptionist |
| John Joyce | Hotel Waiter |
| Irene Sutcliffe | Dress Shop Manageress |
| Ann Francis | Jane |
| Hope Johnstone | Royal Bath Clerk |
| John Ludlow | Royal Bath Clerk |
| Ray Gatenby | Official, Literary Luncheon |
| Hubert Rees | Official, Literary Luncheon |
| Tommy Hunter | Pierrot |
| Pamela Austin | Pierrot |
| Bert Ward | Pierrot |
| Harry Segal | Pierrot |
| Howard Blake, Jim Archer, Reginald Kilbey | Hotel Trio |

Based on Agatha Christie's disappearance of 1926. 98 minutes.

Several important things happened to Agatha Christie in 1926. Firstly, *The Murder of Roger Ackroyd* was published, and secondly, her marriage to Archibald Christie was disintegrating.

The failing of her marriage brought about a horribly strained nervous condition in Agatha Christie, leading to a form of temporary amnesia, culminating in her mysterious 11-day disappearance in December of 1926.

The film is the only one dealing with Christie herself (aside from a 1990 TV documentary). It begins with Agatha (Vanessa Redgrave) present-

# AGATHA

▲ Vanessa Redgrave and Dustin Hoffman (inserts) star as Agatha Christie and newspaperman Wally Stanton in the mystery-romance *Agatha*, about what might have happened during Christie's actual 1926 disappearance. Below, police drag a pond near Christie's abandoned car.

ing her husband with an inscribed loving cup, then they head off to a literary luncheon.

American newspaperman Wally Stanton is there, and notices Christie is very shy, giving a speech that only consists of one sentence.

Next morning at breakfast Colonel Christie tells his wife that he is in love with another woman and desires a divorce, stating it should be handled 'with a minimum of fuss'. Mrs Christie refuses, begging him to stay, but he remains adamant and tells her he will make plans to move out.

Stanton meanwhile is rebuffed at his attempts to interview Mrs Christie, who has just learned that her husband's mistress is about to take a holiday at the Valencia Hotel in Harrogate in order to attend the Royal Spa.

While driving Mrs Christie has an accident; the police are called in when her abandoned car is discovered. John Foster, an English journalist, informs Stanton of Christie's disappearance. Stanton goes to the scene of the accident where the police are dragging a nearby lake, as Mrs Christie has left a 'rather disturbing letter'.

Meanwhile Agatha arrives at Harrogate, registering at the hotel under the name 'Mrs Neele'. Miss Nancy Neele happens to be the name of the Colonel's mistress. While there she makes the acquaintance of Evelyn Crawley, a young woman who is in Harrogate to attend the Royal Spa for her back problems.

The hue and cry is on to find Christie; Stanton is informed by newspaper owner Lord Brackenbury to 'not waste any more time' on the Christie story. But he proceeds on anyway, tracking her to Harrogate by way of a newspaper ad.

Colonel Christie has a belligerent attitude regarding the affair, and tells the police that the incident is being grossly exaggerated, which only arouses their suspicions.

Agatha is familiarizing herself with the procedures and apparatus of the Royal Bath Spa, taking copious notes. Stanton meets Christie in order to get the scoop, but is also attracted to her and a mild romance develops. He is unable to discern whether Christie is genuinely amnesiac or merely perpetrating a deception.

When it becomes evident that Agatha is planning something, Stanton intervenes just in time to avoid a tragedy at the Royal Spa involving Mrs Christie and her husband's mistress.

*Agatha* is a stylish, engaging mystery, perfectly capturing the mood and atmosphere of post-World War One England. Kathleen Tynan and Arthur Hopcroft's screenplay has the right element of plausibility and mystery, and Michael Apted's direction is crisp and unobtrusive.

Vanessa Redgrave and Dustin Hoffman offer fine performances, although the romantic aspects of the characterizations are never fully explained.

▲ Timothy Dalton starred as Colonel Archibald Christie in *Agatha*. Here, the couple has just come from a literary luncheon.

The superb supporting cast has Timothy Dalton as Colonel Christie, Helen Morse as the amorous Evelyn Crawley, Paul Brooke as fellow-journalist John Foster, and Timothy West as Superintendant Kenward.

*Variety*, in its July 2, 1979 review said: 'The Warner Brothers release of the First Artists pre-sentation should score at the wickets, thanks to the ingenious plot and stellar performances of Dustin Hoffman and Vanessa Redgrave. *Agatha* is one of the smartest-looking films of this year, and packs a surprise twist that the real Agatha Christie might have envied.'

# ≡ 1980 ≡

## The Mirror Crack'd

Made in England. Directed by Guy Hamilton.

### CAST
▼

| | |
|---|---|
| Angela Lansbury | Miss Jane Marple |
| Edward Fox | Inspector Dermot Craddock |
| Elizabeth Taylor | Marina Gregg |
| Rock Hudson | Jason Rudd |
| Kim Novak | Lola Brewster |
| Tony Curtis | Marty N. Fenn |
| Geraldine Chaplin | Ella Zielinsky |
| Charles Gray | Bates |
| Richard Pearson | Dr Haydock |
| Wendy Morgan | Cherry |
| Margaret Courtenay | Mrs Bantry |
| Anthony Steel | Sir Derek Ridgeley |
| Dinah Sheridan | Lady Amanda Ridgeley |
| Allan Cuthbertson | Peter Montrose |
| Nigel Stock | Inspector Gates |
| Charles Lloyd-Pack | Vicar |
| Hildegard Neil | Lady Foxcroft |
| Kenneth Fortescue | Charles Foxwell |
| Peter Woodthorpe | Scoutmaster |
| Maureen Bennett | Heather Babcock |
| Carolyn Pickles | Miss Giles |
| Oriane Grieve | Kate Ridgeley |
| Eric Dodson | The Major |
| John Bennett | Barnsby |
| Richard Leech | Assistant Director |
| Sam Kydd | Property Master |
| George Silver | DaSilva |
| Marella Oppenheim | Margot Bence |
| Pat Nye | Mayoress |
| Thick Wilson | Mayor |

and: Richard Todd, Norman Wooland, Peter Bull, Robert Raglan, Charles Lamb.

Based on the novel *The Mirror Crack'd* (1962). 105 minutes.

▶ Some big-name stars appeared in *The Mirror Crack'd*, including (above) Tony Curtis as Marty N. Fenn, Elizabeth Taylor (Marina Gregg), (centre) Rock Hudson (Jason Rudd), Kim Novak (Lola Brewster), (below) Edward Fox (Inspector Craddock), and Geraldine Chaplin (Ella Zielinsky).

Set in 1953, the motion picture *The Mirror Crack'd* remains faithful to the 1962 novel. The film features some of Hollywood's biggest film stars from precisely the same period as the story takes place.

It is set in the village of St Mary Mead, where an American film crew is preparing to film *Mary Queen of Scots* at Gossington Hall, home of the widowed Mrs Bantry.

At a village party held at the hall, American actress Marina Gregg, making a return to motion pictures after an absence of several years, is a big hit with the locals. Also on hand is Marina's husband Jason Rudd, who is to direct the film.

After the film's co-star Lola Brewster arrives with her husband Marty N. Fenn, who is also the producer of the film, sparks (and insults) begin to fly between the two women.

When local woman Heather Babcock dies after taking a drink, the news reaches Miss Marple, arousing her suspicions; she is always interested in unexplained deaths. The inquest revealed that the victim had ingested poison in her cocktail, and returns a verdict of wilful murder against person or persons unknown.

Chief Inspector Dermot Craddock of Scotland Yard (who also happenes to be Miss Marple's nephew) is soon on the scene, and exchanges theories and information with Miss Marple. Miss Marple calls the victim 'quite a bore', but tells Craddock that it is hardly a motive for murder.

When investigations uncover the fact that the victim spilled her drink and took Marina's in its place, it appears that the intended victim was the actress.

Inspector Craddock does most of the investigating in the case, Miss Marple has hurt her leg and is spending a great deal of time lying down, although her brain does not remain inactive.

It takes several accidents, as well as another murder before Miss Marple, with the invaluable aid of Craddock, is able to come up with the solution.

Angela Lansbury, who had previously portrayed a tipsy novelist in 1978's *Death on the Nile*, does well as Miss Marple, offering a crisp, efficient performance, although her part is small in its size as compared to its importance.

The excellent Edward Fox gives another fine performance as Inspector Craddock, quietly effective and intelligent while actually doing most of the detective work in the picture. *Variety*, in its review of December 10, 1980 complimented him: 'Fox is a delight as a film buff who uses his knowledge of the company's past careers to help crack the case.'

They also went on to admire Elizabeth Taylor's portrayal of Marina Gregg: 'Taylor comes away with her most genuinely affecting dramatic performance in years as a film star attempting a comeback following an extended nervous breakdown.'

Kim Novak is also quite good, especially when exchanging taunts and bitchy insults with Taylor, and Rock Hudson and Tony Curtis give creditable acting jobs in their somewhat smaller roles.

The producers should also be highly commended for the obvious care that went into selec-

▶ Miss Marple (Angela Lansbury) points out a clue to Inspector Craddock (Edward Fox) in *The Mirror Crack'd*.

tion of the rest of the cast; an example of this can be seen in the film within the film, shown for several minutes at the outset – some of the finest British character players and former stars appeared in this small scene. Even the smallest parts are played by highly qualified and experienced actors, much to the audience's benefit.

The lighting by Christopher Challis suitably recaptures the mood of the period, and another plus is without question composer/conductor John Cameron's wonderful score. Jonathan Hales and Barry Sanders have done well adapting the screenplay from the original material. John Brabourne and Richard Goodwin, who did several other Christie film adaptations, produced the film for EMI.

# ≡1981≡

## The Seven Dials Mystery (TV)

### Made in England. Directed by Tony Wharmby.

CAST

| Sir John Gielgud | Marquis of Caterham |
| --- | --- |
| Harry Andrews | Superintendant Battle |
| Terence Alexander | George Lomax |
| Cheryl Campbell | Lady Eileen Brent |
| James Warwick | Jimmy Thesiger |
| Lucy Gutteridge | Loraine Wade |
| Rula Lenska | Countess Radzsky |
| Leslie Sands | Sir Oswald Coote |
| Christopher Scoular | Bill Eversleigh |
| Brian Wilde | Treadwell |
| Joyce Redman | Lady Coote |
| James Griffiths | Rupert Bateman |
| Henrietta Baynes | Vera |
| John Vine | Ronny Devereaux |
| Robert Longden | Gerry Wade |
| Sandor Eles | Count Andras |
| Jacob Witkin | Mr Mosgorovsky |
| Norwich Duff | Howard Phelps |
| Noel Johnson | Sir Stanley Digby |
| Charles Morgan | Dr Cartwright |
| Thom Delaney | Terence O'Rourke |
| Lynne Ross | Nancy |
| Roger Sloman | Stevens |
| John Price | Alfred |
| Sarah Crowden | Helen |
| Douglas W. Iles | John Bauer |

Based on the novel *The Seven Dials Mystery* (1929). 131 minutes.

*The Seven Dials Mystery* is the first of numerous television adaptations in the 1980s of Christie's works. Jack Williams produced this film, and Tony Wharmby directed. These two would team up for other TV films, notably the Hercule Poirot series.

Christie had written the story as a sequel to *The Secret of Chimneys* (1925), and indeed the

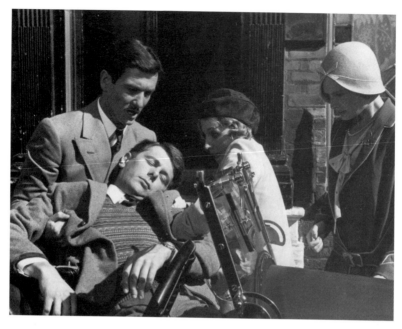

▲ Bill Eversleigh (Christopher Scoular) is attended by Jimmy Thesiger (James Warwick), Lady Eileen Brent (Cheryl Campbell) and Loraine Wade (Lucy Gutteridge, right) in *The Seven Dials Mystery*.

setting and many of the characters are the same in both stories.

The story concerns Chimneys, the house belonging to the Marquis of Caterham. His daughter, Lady Eileen Brent, is shocked to learn that a guest of the Cootes, a couple the Marquis had rented the house to, has died in her bedroom.

The guest in question is Gerry Wade, a fellow whose late-sleeping habits prompt a trick from some of his friends – they put a number of alarm clocks in his room and set them to go off earlier than Wade normally wakes. But when the clocks go off, Wade still does not rise; he has been poisoned by chloral hydrate.

Lady Eileen gets more involved in the mystery when Ronny Devereaux meets the same end, but not before he tells her of the clue of the Seven Dials.

With the aid of Jimmy Thesiger, a friend of both the victims, we are led to the Seven Dials Club, where a secret, hooded society meets to discuss political intrigue and the theft of an important document.

With the help of Superintendant Battle (Harry Andrews) the whole case comes to a head at Wyvern Abbey, home of Sir Oswald Coote, where the mystery is ultimately solved.

Agatha Christie's home, Greenway House in Devon, was used for this television film. Classy period costumes and atmosphere were created, and performances were good by the entire cast.

Cheryl Campbell makes a good Lady Eileen, and she is ably assisted by the distinguished Sir John Gielgud as her father, and Harry Andrews (who had appeared in another Christie film, 1978's *Death on the Nile*) made an excellent Battle. James Warwick, later to star as Tommy Beresford in the *Partners in Crime* series, is also winning in the role of Jimmy Thesiger.

The same group was largely responsible for *Why Didn't They Ask Evans?* later in the same year.

▲ Sir Oswald Coote (Leslie Sands), Countess Radzsky (Rula Lenska), Bill Eversleigh (Christopher Scoular) and Rupert Bateman (James Griffiths) in *The Seven Dials Mystery*, which was filmed in Agatha Christie's home, Greenway House, in Devon.

# Why Didn't They Ask Evans? (TV)

Made in England. Directed by John Davies and Tony Wharmby.

CAST

| | |
|---|---|
| Sir John Gielgud | Reverend Jones |
| Lord Bernard Miles | Dr Thomas |
| Francesca Annis | Lady Frances Derwent |
| James Warwick | Bobby Jones |
| Leigh Lawson | Roger Bassington-ffrench |
| Eric Porter | Dr Nicholson |
| James Cossins | Henry Bassington-ffrench |
| Robert Longden | Badger Beadon |
| Madeleine Smith | Moira Nicholson |
| Connie Booth | Sylvia Bassington-ffrench |
| Joan Hickson | Mrs Rivington |
| John Horsley | Mr Spragge |
| Doris Hare | Rose Pratt |
| Rowland Davies | Dr George Arbuthnot |
| Mitzi Rogers | Mrs Amelia Cayman |
| John Pennington | Mr Cayman |
| Lynda Marchal | Mrs Roberts |
| Deddie Davies | Postmistress |
| Frank Tregear | Mr Roberts |
| Charles Morgan | Coroner |
| Leon Sinden | Mr Owen |
| Elaine Wells | Nurse Fletcher |
| Annette Robertson | Julie |
| Eirik Barclay | Tommy Bassington-ffrench |
| Raymond Francis | Earl of Marchington |
| Sally Grace | Nurse Willard |
| Chris Cregan | Reeves |
| Michael Stainton | Mr Askew |
| Hugh Morton | Barker |
| Debbie Armstrong | Mary |
| Arnold Peters | Innkeeper |
| Norman Mitchell | Constable Browning |
| Artro Morris | Ticket Inspector |
| Terence Soall | Doctor |
| Kate David | Hotel Waitress |
| Penny Ryder | Cafe Waitress |
| Roy Boyd | Alan Carstairs |
| Mischa De La Motte | Ross |
| Colin Cunningham | Fred Pratt |
| Derek Hollis | Police Constable Bunner |

Based on the novel *Why Didn't They Ask Evans?* (1934). 169 minutes.

While playing golf on a course situated near a cliff on the Welsh coast, young Bobby Jones and his friend Dr Thomas look down a chasm and see the crumpled body of a man.

The man is not quite dead: his back has been broken in the fall and Dr Thomas goes to fetch help.

Regaining consciousness briefly, the injured man asks Bobby, 'Why Didn't They Ask Evans?' and then dies. When Bobby reaches into the man's pocket for a handkerchief to cover the victim's face, an intruging photo of a girl falls out.

Later in London, he meets old friend Lady Frances Derwent, who suggests it would be 'more fun' if the man had actually been pushed over the cliff, but the inquest verdict is death by accident.

When Bobby mentions the dying man's words in front of the wrong people, an attempt is made to poison him with a large dose of morphia.

When a newspaper photograph of the picture Bobby took from the dead man's pocket turns out to be a fake, Bobby and Lady Frances investigate.

Pretending to have a concussion from an auto accident she has staged, Frances works her way into the home of Roger Bassington-ffrench, one of the suspects in the case.

This ruse leads to Dr Nicholson, a sinister man running a sanitorium where virtually helpless people are kept against their will.

After Bassington-ffrench's brother Henry dies (an apparent suicide), Frances and Bobby discover not only the true identity of the murdered man on the cliffside, but also the reason for his death and the answer to the mysterious question.

The London *Times* said that this TV film was 'nicely acted' and the *New York Times* found it 'a diverting way to pass an evening'.

Producer Jack Williams and directors John Davies and Tony Wharmby have come up with a very good film of *Why Didn't They Ask Evans?* Joseph Horowitz's hauntingly beautiful theme music is certainly an asset, as is the stellar cast including such renowned performers as Sir John Gielgud, Lord Bernard Miles, and Eric Porter. In smaller roles, a number of performers can be seen who would later appear in other Christie dramatizations by London Weekend Television.

Joan Hickson, who had already appeared in the first version of *Love From a Stranger* as well as *Murder She Said*, is again on hand as Mrs Rivington. Hickson, who certainly had a connec-

tion with Christie's work (she also played Miss Price in the theatre in *Appointment With Death* in 1945) was still four years away from her wonderful Miss Marple series.

Francesca Annis is lovely as usual, and works well here with James Warwick; three years later they would star in the Tommy and Tuppence series *Partners in Crime* also produced by Jack Williams for London Weekend Television.

▲ Members of the cast of *Why Didn't They Ask Evans?*. L-R, back: Eric Porter as Dr Nicholson, Madeline Smith (Moira Nicholson), and Leigh Lawson (Roger Bassington-ffrench). L-R, front: James Warwick (Bobby Jones), Francesca Annis (Lady Frances Derwent), and Connie Booth (Sylvia Bassington-ffrench).

## Evil Under the Sun

Made in England. Directed by Guy Hamilton.

### CAST

| | |
|---|---|
| Peter Ustinov | Hercule Poirot |
| James Mason | Odell Gardener |
| Maggie Smith | Daphne Castle |
| Roddy McDowall | Rex Brewster |
| Diana Rigg | Arlena Marshall |
| Denis Quilley | Kenneth Marshall |
| Colin Blakely | Sir Horace Blatt |
| Nicholas Clay | Patrick Redfern |
| Jane Birkin | Christine Redfern |
| Sylvia Miles | Myra Gardener |
| Emily Hone | Linda Marshall |
| Richard Vernon | Flewitt |
| Cyril Conway | Police Surgeon |
| Robert Dorning | Concierge |
| Barbara Hicks | Flewitt's Secretary |
| John Alderson | Police Sergeant |
| Paul Antrim | Police Inspector |
| Dimitri Andreas | Gino |

Based on the novel *Evil Under the Sun* (1941). 116 minutes.

▲ Hercule Poirot (Peter Ustinov) and Daphne Castle (Maggie Smith) in *Evil Under the Sun.*

The fourth EMI film by Lord Brabourne and Richard Goodwin, *Evil Under the Sun*, boasts an excellent all-star cast, beautiful location photography in Majorca, and some of Cole Porter's greatest music.

The outset of the film has detective Hercule Poirot visiting millionaire Sir Horace Blatt on behalf of an insurance company, as it seems Sir Horace is attempting to insure a paste imitation of a valuable gem. But someone has switched the gems, and it is up to Poirot to find out whom.

Poirot arrives on an island in the Adriatic where Daphne Castle runs the lush hotel. With the arrival of actress Arlena Marshall, her husband and stepdaughter, things begin to happen.

Arlena is not dearly beloved, and there are a number of guests on the island who have had problems with her in the past. These include theatre producers Odell and Myra Gardener, whose play Arlena walked out on; Rex Brewster, whose book Arlena is squashing, and stepdaughter Emily, who just hates her.

Everyone, it seems, dislikes Arlena. When she carries on an indiscreet and undisguised affair with Patrick Redfern, who is on the island for a holiday with his mousy wife Christine, things come to a head.

When Arlena is found strangled on the beach,

it is up to Poirot to get his little grey cells going, breaking down alibis and checking on the clues; needless to say he clears up the murder, which in turn solves the mystery of the jewels, which brought him to the island to begin with.

Ustinov is in good form as Poirot, his second outing in the role. The comedy aspects of the character are suitably subtle and toned down, such as when Poirot takes his morning swim, which consists of wading in shallow water while making swimming movements with his arms.

The rest of the cast is first class, including Diana Rigg as the acid-tongued stage star and murder victim; Maggie Smith (who had appeared

▲ Hercule Poirot (Peter Ustinov, for left) stays at a resort hotel with some very suspicious guests in *Evil Under the Sun.* L-R, back: Sir Horace Blatt (Colin Blakely), Christine Redfern (Jane Birkin), Patrick Redfern (Nicholas Clay), Daphne Castle (Maggie Smith), Arlena Marshal (Diana Rigg), and Kenneth Marshall (Denis Quilley). L-R, centre: Myra Gardener (Sylvia Miles), Odell Gardener (James Mason), and Linda Marshall (Emily Hone). Front: Rex Brewster (Roddy McDowall).

▲ Daphne Castle (Maggie Smith, left) and Linda Marshall (Emily Hone) look on while Kenneth Marshall (Dennis Quilley) reads an important letter in *Evil Under the Sun.*

▲ Peter Ustinov in his second outing as Hercule Poirot in *Evil Under the Sun.*

with Ustinov in *Death on the Nile*) as the hotel proprietress, Sylvia Miles and James Mason as the garrulous Mrs Gardener and her long-suffering husband Odell, and Roddy McDowall as Rex Brewster.

Two veterans of *Murder on the Orient Express*, Colin Blakely and Denis Quilley, give excellent performances, the first as the self-made millionaire Sir Horace Blatt and the latter as Kenneth Marshall, husband of the victim.

Nicholas Clay is fine as the handsome young Patrick Redfern, and Jane Birkin, also from the 1978 *Death on the Nile*, does well here, effecting the chameleon-like change from the mousy wife to anything but.

Christopher Challis' splendid photography, along with Anthony Powell's costumes, are both definite pluses to *Evil Under the Sun*. Also an asset is the use of wonderful Cole Porter music throughout. The watercolours seen near the opening credits were done by Hugh Casson.

# ≡ 1982 ≡

## Murder is Easy (TV)

Made in England. Directed by Claude Whatham.

### CAST

| | |
|---|---|
| Lesley Ann Down | Bridget Conway |
| Bill Bixby | Luke Williams |
| Olivia DeHavilland | Honoria Waynflete |
| Timothy West | Lord Gordon Easterfield |
| Helen Hayes | Lavinia Fullerton |
| Freddie Jones | Constable Reed |
| Patrick Allen | Major Horton |
| Leigh Lawson | Jimmy Lorrimer |
| Shane Briant | Dr Thomas |
| Anthony Valentine | Mr Abbott |
| Jonathan Pryce | Mr Ellsworthy |
| Ivor Roberts | Vicar |
| Trevor T. Smith | Rivers |
| Carol MacReady | Mrs Pierce |
| Diana Goodman | Rose Humbleby |
| Frederick Wolfe | Avery |
| Patrick Wright | Attendant |

and: Melinda Clancy.

Based on the novel *Murder is Easy* (1939). 97 minutes.

*Murder is Easy* opens as elderly Lavinia Fullerton makes the acquaintance of research professor Luke Williams (the character's name in the novel, Luke Fitzwilliam, has been Americanized to suit actor Bill Bixby) on board a train. She tells him she is on her way to Scotland Yard to report three murders that have taken place in her small town, Wychwood.

After Miss Fullerton is run down by a car outside the station in London, Luke becomes suspicious – perhaps she was telling the truth.

With the aid of his friend Jimmy Lorrimer, who has connections with some of the villagers, Luke returns to Wychwood for Miss Fullerton's funeral. There he learns that Dr Humbleby, who Miss Fullerton said would be the next victim, has in fact died of blood poisoning.

Lord Easterfield invites Luke to stay at his home while in Wychwood (Luke tells everyone he is writing a book on witchcraft), and it is there he meets and becomes smitten with Easterfield's beautiful secretary, Bridget Conway, who also

▲ Lavinia Fullerton (Helen Hayes) tells Luke Williams (Bill Bixby) about the Wychwood murders in *Murder is Easy*.

▲ The stars of *Murder is Easy*: (clockwise from left) Olivia de Havilland as Honoria Waynflete, Bill Bixby (Luke Williams), Lesley Ann Down (Bridget Conway), and Helen Hayes (Lavinia Fullerton).

▲ A publicity shot of Bill Bixby and Lesley Ann Down as Luke Williams and Bridget Conway in *Murder is Easy*.

happens to be engaged to Easterfield.

Bridget introduces Luke to Miss Waynflete, who had been engaged to Easterfield many years before. She is now the curator of Easterfield's museum. Invited to tea at Miss Waynflete's, Luke discovers the body of her maid Amy, who has died from a heroin overdose.

Luke points out to Bridget that there have certainly been an unusual number of sudden deaths in the small village, and confides to her Miss Fullerton's suspicions. The two exchange theories on the crimes, and Luke tells her, 'Unless we do something, the killer will keep on killing.'

Investigating the vairous deaths, Luke discovers that a number of the suspects in the case had motives for more than one of the victims, including Bridget. With the aid of a computer, Luke feeds in data concerning the crime: victims, methods of death, motives, means and opportunity. When the computer comes up with Bridget as the killer, Luke tries to pass it off as a joke.

When he finally is convinced of who the killer is, he goes to see local police Constable Reed, who informs him that theory is nice but 'in England we require evidence'.

By this time Luke is deeply romantically inclined towards Bridget, who returns his affections. When Easterfield's chauffer Rivers is murdered, Reed informs Luke that his chief suspect is now clearly innocent.

Just when Luke thinks he knows for sure this time, he is proved wrong once again, as Bridget gets an important clue that helps her solve the case, but not before she has put herself in great danger.

*Murder is Easy* is a good mystery, and this film remains fairly faithful to the novel. Aside from updating the tale (which does not really hurt the story) the only differences are some character changes, notably the absence in the film of Superintendant Battle.

Lesley Ann Down is lovely as ever as Bridget, and Bill Bixby gives a competent performance as Luke Williams. Olivia DeHavilland also does well in a change-of-pace role. Helen Hayes, later to star as Miss Marple in *A Caribbean Mystery* and *Murder With Mirrors*, offers a nice acting job in the relatively small role of Miss Fullerton.

Best in the cast is Timothy West as Lord Easterfield; he had appeared in another Christie film, *Agatha,* in 1979 and four years later, in 1986, appeared in *A Pocket Full of Rye*. Other notable performances include Patrick Allen as the dog-loving Major Horton, Jonathan Pryce as the enigmatic Mr Ellsworthy, Anthony Valentine as solicitor Abbott, and Shane Briant as the good Doctor Thomas.

The *New York Times* television reviewer enjoyed the 'nice bits and pieces along the way', and *Murder is Easy* was generally well received. Carmen Culver adapted the script.

# ≡ 1982 ≡

## Witness For the Prosecution (TV)

### Made in England. Directed by Alan Gibson.

CAST

| | |
|---|---|
| Sir Ralph Richardson | Sir Wilfred Robarts |
| Deborah Kerr | Nurse Plimsoll |
| Diana Rigg | Romaine |
| Beau Bridges | Leonard Vole |
| Dame Wendy Hiller | Janet Mackenzie |
| Donald Pleasence | Mr Myers |
| David Langton | Mr Mayhew |
| Richard Vernon | Mr Brogan-Moore |
| Michael Gough | Judge |
| Peter Sallis | Carter |
| Peter Copley | Dr Harrison |
| Aubrey Woods | Tailor |
| Frank Mills | Chief Inspector Hearne |
| Michael Nightingale | Clerk of the Court |
| Patricia Leslie | Mrs French |
| John Kidd | Court Usher |
| Ken Kitson | Policeman |
| Wilfred Grove | Photographer |
| Primi Townsend | Diana |
| Andrew MacLachlan | Jury Foreman |
| Zulema Dene | Miss Johnson |
| Barbara New | Miss O'Brien |
| Jenny Donnison | First Nurse |
| Ceri Jackson | Second Nurse |

Based on the short story *Witness For the Prosecution* (1933). 101 minutes.

Norman Rosemont, who was responsible for a number of excellent television films, was producer of this 1982 television remake. John Gay wrote the screenplay, which he adapted faithfully from the original Christie play as well as Billy Wilder's 1957 film.

A marvellous cast was chosen for this film, including Sir Ralph Richardson, Dame Wendy

▲ Sir Wilfred Robarts (Sir Ralph Richardson) confronts a witness in court with a vital piece of evidence in *Witness for the Prosecution.*

Hiller, Deborah Kerr and Diana Rigg.

The story has the likeable Leonard Vole (Beau Bridges, the only poor job of casting in this film) being accused of the murder of Emily French, a wealthy widow with whom he had formed a seemingly innocent relationship. Vole's solicitor Mr Mayhew enlists the aid of Sir Wilfred Robarts, a distinguished barrister who is recouperating from recent heart ailments and is advised for health reasons not to take the case. However he is most interested and, despite the protests of Nurse Plimsoll, decides to take it on.

Vole's wife Romaine seems curiously disinclined to be of any real help, which is puzzling. Research into her background shows that she was married once before and never got a divorce. The rule of law that a wife may not be called to give evidence against her husband therefore no longer applies, and she is called as a prosecution witness.

Circumstantial evidence is building up against Vole; meanwhile through a woman who obviously has a grudge against Romaine certain letters come into the hands of the defence that shed an entirely new light on the case.

The ending Christie wrote for the stage, also used in the 1957 film, is used here.

Sir Ralph Richardson, a consummate professional, is outstanding in the role of Sir Wilfred, playing it with the charm and a certain whimsicality that was his trademark. Deborah Kerr,

as Nurse Plimsoll, complements his performance and they are especially good when working in the same scenes.

Diana Rigg is fine as Romaine (the character's name has been restored to that of the story and play) as well as Dame Wendy Hiller as Janet Mackenzie.

The legal profession is well represented by the excellent Donald Pleasence as Mr Myers (he would appear in two Christie films in 1989 as Jason Rafiel in *A Caribbean Mystery* and Judge Wargrave in *Ten Little Indians*), David Langton as Mr Mayhew, Richard Vernon as Brogan-Moore and Michael Gough as the Judge.

The producers apparently followed the tradition of the previous version of this film, casting an American actor, Beau Bridges, in the role of Leonard Vole. This seems odd because in Christie's original story there is no mention of Vole being American (just like Tyrone Power in the 1957 film) and Bridges' performance, which can be described only as adequate, is swallowed up by the talents of the other actors. This is just one example of producers changing a character in order to have a particular actor in a film: fortunately this is the only error of casting, unlike some of the films, in which locations and characters were changed with disastrous results.

All in all, 1982's *Witness For the Prosecution* is an excellent production, with the direction and photography certainly assets. The *New York Times*, in reviewing the film on December 3, 1982, praised it by saying: '*Witness For the Prosecution* still works wondrously well, its twists and turns devised to the point of perfection. It's still a great deal of fun.'

▲ Romaine (Diana Rigg) assures her husband Leonard Vole (Beau Bridges) that all will be well in *Witness for the Prosecution.*

# ≡ 1982 ≡

## The Agatha Christie Hour (TV series)

Made in England. Directed by Michael Simpson (3 episodes), Brian Farnham (2 episodes), John Frankau (2 episodes), Cyril Coke, Desmond Davis, Christopher Hodson.

Based on short stories found in the collections *The Hound of Death* (1933), *The Listerdale Mystery* (1934), *Parker Pyne Investigates* (1934), *The Regatta Mystery* (1939), *Witness For the Prosecution* (1948) and *The Golden Ball* (1971). Each episode one hour.

Ten hour-long dramas based upon various short stories by Agatha Christie were presented by Thames Television of London in 1982. Pat Sandys was the producer; executive producer was John Frankau (who also directed two of the stories).

None of the stories featured Hercule Poirot or Miss Marple; two of them did, however, include another of Christie's lesser-known detectives, Mr Parker Pyne (the only appearance he has made to date). Other than this, there is no connection between any of the tales except that they were featured in the same short story collections.

Following is a list of each episode with a brief synopsis; Christie's fans were generally pleased to note that careful attention was given to the original works and contained good period flavour.

## The Case of the Middle-Aged Wife

Directed by Michael Simpson. Cast: Maurice Denham, Gwen Watford, Peter Jones, Kate Dorning, Rupert Frazer, Angela Easterling, Brenda Cowlihg, Monica Grey, Linda Robson, Nick Curtis, Malcolm Hebden, Nicholas Cook.

Appearing in the short story collection *Parker Pyne Investigates* (1934), *The Case of the Middle-Aged Wife* concerns Mrs Packington, a woman who has long been married to a husband who now seems to be more attentive to his young secretary that to his wife. After reading an advertisement in *The Times* by Mr Parker Pyne ('Are You Happy? If Not, Consult Mr Parker Pyre'), Mrs Packington is able to get her husband back with the assistance of Claude Luttrell, one of Mr Pyne's operatives.

◀ Businessman Peter Jones slips his secretary (Kate Dorining) a little something extra in *The Case of the Middle-Aged Wife*.

# In a Glass Darkly

Directed by Desmond Davis. Cast: Nicholas Clay, Emma Piper, Shaun Scott, Jonathon Morris, Paul Williamson, Elspeth Gray, Nicholas Le Prevost, Marjorie Bland, David Cook, John Golightly, John Wheatley, Brian Anthony, Kenneth Midwood, Valerie Lush, Eileen Davies, Elizabeth Benson, Sarah-Jane Bickerton.

Based on the short story of the same title that appears in the 1939 collection *The Regatta Mystery*, this story concerns a young man who sees a strange reflection in his bedroom mirror while a guest at his friend's country home. The vision is of a scar-faced man strangling a fairhaired young woman. The doorway to the adjoining room, where the murder took place, is blocked by a dressing table. The young man is later shocked when he goes down to dinner to discover that both the victim and the murderer are also guests at the house.

▶ Sylvia Arslake (Emma Piper) and Matthew Armitage (Nicholas Clay) fall in love at first sight in *In a Glass Darkly*.

# The Girl in the Train

Directed by Brian Farnham. Cast: Osmond Bullock, Sarah Berger, Ron Pember, Ernest Clark, James Grout, Roy Kinnear, David Neal, Arthur Blake, Glyn Baker, Richard Bartlett, Matyelok Gibbs, Jo Warne, Bill Treacher, Harry Fielder, Cherith Mellor, Debbie Farrington.

Recently disinherited by his uncle, idle George Rowland boards a train for London; a young girl suddenly bursts into his compartment imploring him to hide her. When the girl's 'uncle' comes to look for her, George gets rid of him. Elizabeth, the girl, then entrusts him with secret documents involving a Grand Duchess and spies. This story was originally published in *The Listerdale Mystery* (1934).

▶ Osmund Bullock finds romance and adventure with Sarah Berger in *The Girl in the Train*.

# The Fourth Man

Directed by Michael Simpson. Cast: John Nettles, Prue Clark, Fiona Mathieson, Michael Gough, Roy Leighton, Alan MacNaughtan, Geoffrey Chater, Frederick Jaeger, Barbara Bolton, Eric Richard, Christopher Wren, Stuart Fell, Cy Town.

Based on a short story encompassed in 1933's *The Hound of Death*, *The Fourth Man* concerns three fellow train-travellers who are discussing the remarkable multiple-personality case of a slow-witted 21-year-old Brittainy peasant. The men find her death even more remarkable, until the fourth man in the compartment, who has been unobtrusive and self-effacing, offers an explanation.

◄ Young lovers: Raoul Letardeau (Roy Leighton) and Annette (Prue Clark) in the occult tale, *The Fourth Man*.

# The Case of the Discontented Soldier

Directed by Michael Simpson. Cast: Maurice Denham, Lally Bowers, William Gaunt, Patricia Garwood, Angela Easterling, Lewis Fiander, Veronica Strong, Derek Smee, Karen Mount, Jason Norman, Paul Dadson, Barbara New, Peter Brayham, Terry Plummer.

Another case featuring sleuth Mr Parker Pyne, *The Case of the Discontented Soldier*, taken from the *Parker Pyne Investigates* book, also has Mrs Ariadne Oliver, who sometimes worked in association with Pyne (and also Hercule Poirot). The story concerns Major Wilbraham, who is bored after having retired from the army and consults Mr Parker Pyne, who soon has the Major searching for buried treasure and rescuing damsels in distress.

◄ William Gaunt and Patricia Garwood in *The Case of the Discontented Soldier*.

# Magnolia Blossom

Directed by John Frankau. Cast: Ralph Bates, Ciaran Madden, Jeremy Clyde, Brian Oulton, Jack May, Charles Hodgson, Graham Seed, Alexandra Bastedo, Keith Marsh, Philip Cade, Jane Laurie, Sarah-Jane Varley, Jennifer Croxton, Derek Fuke.

Found in *The Golden Ball and Other Stories* (1971), *Magnolia Blossom* concerns the wife of a wealthy man who is running away to South Africa with a business associate of her husband's, with whom she has fallen in love. Learning of her husband's impending financial ruin, her loyalty to him is rekindled and she returns, only to discover further perfidy.

▲ Ciaran Madden as Theo in *Magnolia Blossom*.

▲ Ciaran Madden explains to Ralph Bates why she must not go with him in *Magnolia Blossom*.

# The Mystery of the Blue Jar

Directed by Cyril Coke. Cast: Michael Aldridge, Robin Kermode, Isabelle Spade, Derek Francis, Hugh Walters, Glynis Brooks, Ivor Roberts, Philip Bird, Robert Austin, Tara Ward.

Another short story featured in *The Hound of Death* (1933), this story involves Jack Hartington, who hears cries of 'murder' several consecutive days while playing golf. A French girl, weeding her garden at a nearby cottage has heard nothing, and after consulting a mystic, Jack discovers that the incident is connected with events at the cottage, as well as an antique Chinese jar.

▲ Isabelle Spade, Robin Kermode and friend in *The Mystery of the Blue Jar*.

▲ Michael Aldridge, Robin Kermode and Isabelle Spade in *The Mystery of the Blue Jar*.

# The Red Signal

Directed by John Frankau. Cast: Richard Morant, Joanna David, Christopher Cazenove, Alan Badel, Ewan Roberts, Michael Denison, Rosalie Crutchley, Carol Drinkwater, Hugh Sullivan, Robert Keegan, David Rolfe, Michael Mellinger, Christopher Wren, Andrew McCulloch.

After accepting an invitation to dinner at the home of his friends the Trents, Dermot West admits that he gets what he terms 'The Red Signal', a sixth sense that tells him of impending danger. He does not however tell them that he is getting it at that very moment. Later during a seance, which is attended by an eminent psychiatrist, the medium announces that Dermot's signal is not letting him down. This was another tale appearing in 1933's *The Hound of Death*.

◀ The stars of *The Red Signal*. Above: Christopher Cazenove, Joanna David. Below: Richard Morant, Carol Drinkwater.

# Jane in Search of a Job

Directed by Christopher Hodson. Cast: Elizabeth Garvie, Amanda Redman, Andrew Bicknell, Tony Jay, Stephanie Cole, Geoffrey Hinsliff, Helen Lindsay, Julia McCarthy, Neville Phillips, Robert MacBain, Richard Tate, Tex Fuller, Mac Andrews.

Dramatized by Gerald Savory, *Jane in Search of a Job* (from *The Listerdale Mystery*, 1934) concerns a young woman who, responding to a newspaper advertisement, finds herself in grave danger when she is hired to masquerade as a foreign dignitary, the Grand Duchess of Ostrovia.

◀ L-R: Tony Jay, Amanda Redman, Stephanie Cole and Geoffrey Hinsliff in *Jane in Search of a Job*.

# The Manhood of Edward Robinson

Directed by Brian Farnham. Cast: Nicholas Farrell, Cherie Lunghi, Ann Thornton, Margery Mason, Patrick Newell, Tom Mannion, Sally Anne Law, Bryan Coleman, Rupert Everett, Nicholas Bell, Fiona Hendley, Rio Fanning, Frank Duncan, Simon Green, Georgina Coombs, Julian Wadham.

The last in the series, *The Manhood of Edward Robinson* has Nicholas Farrell perfectly cast as the proper, wimpish character of the title, who is engaged to a domineering woman. After Win- ning £500 in a newspaper contest, he undergoes a personality change (for the better), purchasing an expensive sports car and getting himself involved with a beautiful adventuress.

▲ Adventuress, working man and fiancée: Cherie Lunghi, Nicholas Farrell, and Ann Thornton in *The Manhood of Edward Robinson*.

▶ Cherie Lunghi as the socialite Nicholas Farrell gets involved with, at the party in *The Manhood of Edward Robinson*.

# ≡ 1983 ≡

## A Caribbean Mystery (TV)

Made in Hollywood. Directed by Robert Lewis.

CAST

| | |
|---|---|
| Helen Hayes | Miss Jane Marple |
| Maurice Evans | Major Geoffrey Palgrave |
| Barnard Hughes | Jason Rafiel |
| George Innes | Edward Hillingdon |
| Jameson Parker | Tim Kendal |
| Season Hubley | Molly Kendal |
| Swoozie Kurtz | Ruth Walters |
| Cassie Yates | Lucky Dyson |
| Brock Peters | Dr Graham |
| Zakes Mokae | Captain Daventry |
| Stephen Macht | Greg Dyson |
| Beth Howland | Evelyn Ellingdon |
| Lynne Moody | Victoria |
| Mike Preston | Arthur Jackson |
| Bernard McDonald | Minister |
| Santos Morales | Miguel |
| Sam Scarber | Sergeant |
| Cecil Smith | Hotel Guest |

Based on the novel *A Caribbean Mystery* (1964). 97 minutes.

Warner Brothers' *A Caribbean Mystery*, based on the 1964 novel of the same title, was shot on location, produced by Stan Margulies and directed by Robert Lewis.

The story opens with Miss Marple, on holiday on the Caribbean island of St Honore, at the Golden Palm Hotel. There she meets the dull but garrulous Major Palgrave, a retired military

▲ A toast to crime: Miss Marple (Helen Hayes) and Major Palgrave (Maurice Evans) in *A Caribbean Mystery.*

man. The Major peaks Miss Marple's curiosity when he mentions murder, and asks her if she would like to see a picture of a murderer. Before he can show it to her, he is distracted and hurriedly returns the photo to his wallet.

The next morning Miss Marple learns that the Major has died in his bed, apparently from complications having to do with his blood pressure medicine. In the light of what Palgrave had told her, Miss Marple's curiosity is aroused, and she's doubly convinced of foul play when Dr Graham tells her the photograph she is looking for has disappeared. Miss Marple still faces the problem of just who the killer in the photograph was – this is what she has to discover.

Since the Major did not suffer from high blood pressure, Dr Graham goes to the local police, Captain Daventry, who is reluctant to do anything as yet, because, as he tells the good doctor, 'there is no proof – only rumour and speculation'.

Invalid Jason Rafiel warns Miss Marple not to 'stick your neck out', but Miss Marple is not one to be put off the scent. Everyone on the island exhibits suspicious behaviour, from amorous to schizophrenic. When servant Victoria is bludgeoned to death, it is clearly murder this time and the police step in. However, it is Miss Marple who (as usual) solves the case, but not before the killer claims another victim.

This is a typical example of a film hindered by the casting of 'name' performers (in this case, most of them are American television actors).

Helen Hayes, who was to play Miss Marple one more time in 1985's *Murder With Mirrors*, is just adequate as Miss Marple; she had a better role as Lavinia Fullerton in *Murder is Easy*.

There are two good performances in the film; the first by Maurice Evans as Major Palgrave, and the second by the excellent Brock Peters as Dr Graham.

Most of the others in the film were obviously selected because they were appearing on television in some series or other in America, and this film was made expressly for CBS television. Their performances, with the exception of George Innes,

▲ Barnard Hughes as Jason Rafiel and Helen Hayes as Miss Marple in *A Caribbean Mystery*.

are lacklustre and do nothing for the film.

Fortunately six years later, in 1989, an excellent version of *A Caribbean Mystery* was produced by the BBC in England, starring Joan Hickson, Donald Pleaseance, and Frank Middlemass.

# ≡ 1983 ≡

## Sparkling Cyanide (TV)

Made in Hollywood. Directed by Robert Lewis.

### CAST
▼

| | |
|---|---|
| Anthony Andrews | Tony Browne |
| Deborah Raffin | Iris Marle |
| Harry Morgan | Captain James Kemp |
| Barrie Ingham | Eric Kidderminster |
| Josef Sommer | George Barton |
| Pamela Belwood | Ruth Lessing |
| Nancy Marchand | Lucilla Drake |
| David Huffman | Stephen Farraday |
| Christine Belford | Rosemary Barton |
| June Chadwick | Mrs Kidderminster |
| Anne Rogers | Sandra Ferraday |
| Michael Woods | Victor Drake |
| Shera Danese | Patricia |
| Ismael Carlo | Medical Examiner |
| Linda Hoy | Boat Manager |
| Abby Haman | Cabaret Singer |
| Juan Fernandez | Busboy |
| Eric Sinclair | Charles |

Based on the novel *Sparkling Cyanide* (1945). 94 minutes.

▲ Ruth Lessing (Pamela Bellwood) and Tony Browne (Anthony Andrews) at the fatal party in *Sparkline Cyanide*.

Some critics were quite taken with Christie's 1945 novel *Sparkling Cyanide*, singling out her deft handling of the psychological insights she used in the work.

Nearly 40 years later, *Sparkling Cyanide* was made as a television film in Hollywood by the same group of people responsible for the 1983 version of *A Caribbean Mystery*.

The film, which has been updated to Los Angeles of the 1980s, begins with hedonistic Rosemary Barton caught up in an affair with a married man, Stephen Ferraday. Stephen wants to break it off, but Rosemary tells him her husband George would kill them both if he found out.

At a fashionable party, Rosemary dies after taking a drink of champagne. Police pathologists determine the cocktail she drank had been liberally laced with cyanide, and it is up to Captain Kemp to determine whether it was self-administered or otherwise.

Investigations into the victim's character reveal Rosemary was a somewhat nasty person, and plenty of people had reasons to wish her dead.

Before long, husband George receives letters in the mail to the effect that his wife was murdered, and asking whether or not he has the guts to do anything about it.

George keeps the letters from the police, hoping to use them as a trap for the killer. Since Rosemary's sister Iris is having a bithday next week, George intends to stage a duplicate party, inviting the same guests, in the hope that the killer will give himself away. Unfortunately the strategy backfires, and George is poisoned in exactly the same fashion as his wife.

Tony Browne, an English journalist who also happens to be one of the suspects, investigates the case along with Captain Kemp. Browne is romantically inclined towards sister Iris, and warns her to keep on her guard.

His advice is well-founded; while Iris is out waterskiing, an attempt is made to kill her as a boat nearly runs her down. Browne and the Captain arrive just in time the next day to prevent Iris's murder, this time by gas. Through reconstruction of the crime (and a fortuitous accident), we are shown the identity of the real killer, as well as discovering the fact that George was killed accidentally – the real target was Iris.

*Sparkling Cyanide* is a pretty good story, and is only hurt by the unnecessary updating and change of locale. The wonderful period atmosphere of the novel is lost in this film, but there are some decent performances that make up for it.

Best of these is turned in by Anthony Andrews, who actually solves the case with logic and common sense. At the same time, the makers of the film have thankfully not degraded the role of Captain Kemp, and Harry Morgan plays the role with an earnest type of honesty, and Christine Belford and Deborah Raffin on the distaff side are competent as the bad and good sisters respectively.

Barrie Ingham and Josef Sommer as Eric Kidderminster and George Barton are also effective. All in all, *Sparkling Cyanide* is worth watching, even in a setting that might make Dame Agatha roll over once or twice in her grave.

# ≡ 1983 ≡

## Spider's Web (TV)

### Made in England. Directed by Basil Coleman.

CAST

| | |
|---|---|
| Penelope Keith | Clarissa Hailsham-Brown |
| Robert Flemyng | Sir Rowland Delahaye |
| Thorley Walters | Hugo Birch |
| David Yelland | Jeremy Warrender |
| Elizabeth Spriggs | Mildred Peake |
| Jonathan Newth | Henry Hailsham-Brown |
| John Barcroft | Inspector Lord |
| Holly Aird | Pippa Hailsham-Brown |
| Brian Protheroe | Oliver Costello |
| David Crosse | Elgin |
| Mark Draper | Constable Jones |
| Lee Fox | Doctor |

Based on the original play *Spider's Web* (1954). 105 minutes.

*Spider's Web* was written by Christie as an original stage play in 1954 especially for the star Margaret Lockwood. In 1960 it was made into a film by Danziger Studios starring Glynis Johns. This 1983 film, shot as a television play, starred television comedian Penelope Keith (*Fawlty Towers*) in the key role of Clarissa Hailsham-Brown.

In the story Clarissa, her diplomat husband Henry, and Henry's daughter from a previous marriage Pippa, move into a house owned by a recently deceased antique dealer, who either fell or was pushed down a flight of stairs.

Clarissa has a rather unusual sense of humour, and she is forever imagining or pretending, although she refers to this as 'supposing'. 'Supposing,' she says one day, 'I found a dead body in the living room? What would I do?'

Oliver Costello, the current husband of the former Mrs Hailsham-Brown, appears one evening to tell Clarissa that Pippa's mother now wants her to live with them. She has retained legal

▲ Penelope Keith as Clarissa Hailsham-Brown in *Spider's Web*.

▲ David Yelland as Jeremy Warrender in *Spider's Web*.

Rowland Delahaye, Hugo Birch and Jeremy Warrender, Clarissa attempts to hide the body in a secret panel in the house; later it is transferred to the woods, and subsequently to several other places.

When the doorbell rings, it is not Henry, but the police, who have somehow been tipped off about the murder.

Mysterious clues involve an ace of spades, several pairs of assorted gloves, voodoo books and invisible ink, not to mention the much-travelled body, which appears and disappears with alarming frequency throughout the story.

Penelope Keith is quite good as Clarissa, which is just the sort of role that is especially geared to her talents. Robert Flemyng and Thorley Walters (the latter having appeared as Cedric Ackenthorpe in the 1962 Christie film *Murder She Said*), two very fine character actors, do excellent work here. Other performances are generally good; Jonathan Newth, in the relatively thankless part of Henry, is adequate.

*Spider's Web* is a successful television play – the film techniques are those of a play rather than a film, which works surprisingly well in this story. *Spider's Web*, a story written originally for the medium of the theatre, perhaps works best as a play because of the setting, time frame, and dialogue, and Basil Coleman's direction exemplifies these things, creating an entertaining and enjoyable comedy/mystery.

custody, so why not? But when he attempts to blackmail her, Clarissa points him to the door.

While Clarissa is getting the house in order to prepare for the arrival of Henry's diplomatic colleagues (he has gone to pick them up), she trips over the murdered body of Costello behind the couch.

With the aid of three family friends, Sir

▲ Stars Robert Flemyng (as Sir Rowland Delahaye), Penelope Keith (Clarissa Hailsham-Brown), and Thorley Walters (Hugo Birch) in *Spider's Web*.

# ≡1984≡

## Partners in Crime (TV series)

Made in England. Directed by Tony Wharmby, Paul Annett, others.

### REGULAR CAST

Francesca Annis · · · · · · · · · · · · · · · · · Tuppence Beresford
James Warwick · · · · · · · · · · · · · · · · · ·Tommy Beresford
Reece Dinsdale · · · · · · · · · · · · · · · · · · · ·Albert
Arthur Cox · · · · · · · · · · · · · · · · · · · Inspector Marriott

Based on the short story collection *Partners in Crime* (1929). Each episode 51 mins.

This splendid series, produced by Jack Williams for London Weekend Television, featured ten of the fifteen short stories that can be found in Christie's 1929 Tommy and Tuppence book of the same name.

Each of the story's details of plot and characters are faithfully adhered to, and casting, costumes and photography are done with care. Lovely Francesca Annis, popular recently on television as Lillie Langtry (and who also had appeared in the 1965 Christie film *Murder Most Foul*) played Tuppence; television actor James Warwick was Tommy. The two played splendidly together and looked as if they enjoyed it.

Reece Dinsdale played Albert, the couple's factotum, and Arthur Cox appeared in several episodes as Inspector Marriott.

Fans of Christie and the series had fun trying to guess which fictional detective of the period (and some are pretty obscure) the pair parodied in the different episodes, often relying on the methods they employed.

This was an outstanding feature of the short stories that lost nothing in its translation to television.

Following is a list of each episode with cast credits and a brief synopsis. All of the stories retain their original titles and characters.

▲ James Warwick and Francesca Annis star as Tommy and Tuppence Beresford, the 1920s husband-and-wife detectives, in the *Partners in Crime* series made from ten of the fifteen short stories in Christie's 1929 Tommy and Tuppence book of the same name.

# The Affair of the Pink Pearl

Francesca Annis · · · · · · · · · · · · · · · · Tuppence Beresford
James Warwick · · · · · · · · · · · · · · · · · Tommy Beresford
Reece Dinsdale · · · · · · · · · · · · · · · · · · · · · Albert
Graham Crowden · · · · · · · · · · · · · · Colonel Kingston-Bruce
Arthur Cox · · · · · · · · · · · · · · · · · · Inspector Marriott
Dulcie Gray · · · · · · · · · · · · · · · · · Lady Laura Barton
Noel Dyson · · · · · · · · · · · · · · · · · Mrs Kingston-Bruce
William Hootkins · · · · · · · · · · · · · · · · Hamilton Betts
Lynda Marchal · · · · · · · · · · · · · · · · · · Phyllis Betts
Susannah Morley · · · · · · · · · · · · · Beatrice Kingston-Bruce
Charles Shaughnessy · · · · · · · · · · · · · · · · John Rennie
Ursula Mohan · · · · · · · · · · · · · · · · · · · · · Elsie
Tim Woodward · · · · · · · · · · · · · · · Lawrence St Vincent
Fleur Chandler · · · · · · · · · · · · · · · · · · Janet Smith

When the Beresfords are approached by Mrs Kingston-Bruce and her daughter Beatrice, who are distraught over the theft of a precious pink pearl belonging to their houseguest, Lady Laura Barton, they proceed to investigate. Tommy adopts the guise of Austin Freeman's creation Dr Thorndike, the forensic scientist and attorney who seeks clues from physical entities that will ultimately serve as irrefutable evidence.

◄ Tommy (James Warwick) and Tuppence (Francesca Annis) Beresford in *The Affair of the Pink Pearl*.

# The House of Lurking Death

Francesca Annis· · · · · · · · · · · · · · · · · · Tuppence Beresford
James Warwick · · · · · · · · · · · · · · · · · · ·Tommy Beresford
Reece Dinsdale · · · · · · · · · · · · · · · · · · · · · · · Albert
Joan Sanderson · · · · · · · · · · · · · · · · · · · · · Miss Logan
Liz Smith · · · · · · · · · · · · · · · · · · · Hannah MacPherson
Lynsey Baxter · · · · · · · · · · · · · · · · · · Lois Hargreaves
Louisa Rix · · · · · · · · · · · · · · · · · · · · ·Mary Chilcott
Michael Cochrane · · · · · · · · · · · · · · · · Dennis Radcliffe
Deddie Davies· · · · · · · · · · · · · · · · · · · Mrs Holloway
Anita Dobson · · · · · · · · · · · · · · · · · · · Esther Quant
Kim Clifford · · · · · · · · · · · · · · · · · · · Rose Holloway
Granville Saxton · · · · · · · · · · · · · · · · · · · · · Dr Burton

Shortly after Lois Hargreaves (Lynsey Baxter) inherits a fortune after the death of her spinster aunt, she receives what she believes to be a poisoned box of chocolates.

Tommy and Tuppence are soon on the scene, adopting a straightforward police style detection (a la Sir Alfred Edward Woodley Mason's famous French detective Inspector Gabriel Hanaud of the Surete). Tuppence takes on the role of Hanaud's Watsonian sidekick, Mr Julius Ricardo.

▶ Tommy (James Warwick) and Tuppence (Francesca Annis) Beresford in *The House of Lurking Death*.

# Finessing the King

Francesca Annis· · · · · · · · · · · · · · · · · · Tuppence Beresford
James Warwick · · · · · · · · · · · · · · · · · · ·Tommy Beresford
Reece Dinsdale · · · · · · · · · · · · · · · · · · · · · · Albert
Benjamin Whitrow · · · · · · · · · · · · · · · Sir Arthur Merivale
Peter Blythe · · · · · · · · · · · · · · · · · · Captain Bingo Hale
Arthur Cox· · · · · · · · · · · · · · · · · · · Inspector Marriott
Anna Turner · · · · · · · · · · · · · · · · · · · · · · Widow
Annie Lambert· · · · · · · · · · · · · · · · · Lady Vere Merivale
John Gillett · · · · · · · · · · · · · · · · · · · · Dr Stoughton
Terry Cowling · · · · · · · · · · · · · Detective Sergeant Halliday

One day, as they are reading *The Times*, Tommy and Tuppence come across an unusually cryptic advertisement in the personal column. It reads: 'Three Hearts, Twelve Tricks, Ace of Spades, finesse the King.'

When Tuppence cleverly deduces the similarity between the advert and the Three Arts Ball (three hearts), to be held at midnight (twelve tricks) at the Ace of Spades Cafe, they decide to investigate.

Although they do not as yet understand the 'finesse the king' message, they soon discover that it leads to murder. Knowledgeable viewers will be able to identify the couple's disguises: the little-known Isabel Ostrander creations, McCarty and Riordan.

▲ Tuppence (Francesca Annis) gets a clue while Tommy (James Warwick) looks pensive in *Finessing the King.*

# The Clergyman's Daughter

## CAST

| | |
|---|---|
| Francesca Annis | Tuppence Beresford |
| James Warwick | Tommy Beresford |
| Reece Dinsdale | Albert |
| Jane Booker | Monica Deane |
| Geoffrey Drew | Norman Partridge |
| Bill Dean | Mr Hove |
| Elspeth MacNaughton | Mrs Hove |
| Pam St Clement | Crockett |
| Alan Jones | Gerald Bush |
| David Delve | O'Neill |
| Ben Stevens | Mr Cockwell |
| Janet Hampson | Mrs Cockwell |
| George Malpas | Frank Mulberry |

When Monica Deane's aunt dies leaving her a large house, she has no alternative but to take in lodgers, as her aunt has left no means by which to maintain the house.

The lodgers begin to complain of ghostly apparitions; it is decided the house must be sold, but when a prospective buyer appears too anxious to buy, Tommy and Tuppence are called in, and discover the buyer's motive as well as the truth behind the spirits.

▶ Gerald Bush (Alan Jones) and Monica Deane (Jane Booker) outside the haunted house in *The Clergyman's Daughter*.

# The Sunningdale Mystery

## CAST

| | |
|---|---|
| Francesca Annis | Tuppence Beresford |
| James Warwick | Tommy Beresford |
| Reece Dinsdale | Albert |
| Dennis Lill | Hollaby Jr |
| Emily Moore | Doris Evans |
| Edwin Brown | Hollaby Sr |
| Terence Conoley | Major Barnard |
| Denis Holmes | Mr Lecky |
| Robin Parkinson | Landlord |
| Dorothea Phillips | ABC Waitress |
| Martin Rutledge | Cyril |
| Vivienne Ritchie | Girl |
| Jim Wiggins | Ticket Collector |

While playing golf on the Sunningdale links, Captain Sessle is found stabbed through the heart with a hatpin. A young girl is arrested and charged with his murder; a red piece of cloth found in Sessle's hand matches a wool coat she owns.

Tommy impersonates armchair detective The Old Man in the Corner, created by Baroness Orczy (creator of the Scarlet Pimpernel), Tuppence dons the guise of Polly Burton, the young newspaper reporter who brings the Old Man his information while he solves crimes from the comfort of a tea shop chair, tying and untying knots in an old piece of string.

▶ Tommy (James Warwick) and Tuppence (Francesca Annis) Beresford on the links in *The Sunningdale Mystery*.

# The Ambassador's Boots

CAST

| | |
|---|---|
| Francesca Annis | Tuppence Beresford |
| James Warwick | Tommy Beresford |
| Reece Dinsdale | Albert |
| Jeannie Linden | Cicely Marsh |
| T.P. McKenna | Randolph Wilmot |
| Arthur Cox | Inspector Marriott |
| Clive Merrison | Richards |
| Moira Brooker | Tilly |
| Michael Carter | Rodriguez |
| Tricia George | Bobby St Albans |
| Norma West | Estelle Blaney |
| Jo Ross | Gwen Forster |
| Catherine Schell | Virna La Strange |
| Vera Jakob | Manners |
| Anna Sharkey | Madame Beatrice |
| Judy Gridley | Nightclub Dancer |
| Linda Sands | Girl on Bridge |
| Stephen Rashbrook | Boy on Bridge |

When American Ambassador Randolph Wilmot's bag is mistakenly exchanged for another, he consults Tommy and Tuppence; they learn that a mysterious, unknown valet has switched the bags. Tuppence adopts the role of Dr Reggie Fortune, a middle-class doctor who is also a consultant to Scotland Yard (created by H.C. Bailey).

◀ Tuppence Beresford (Francesca Annis) in *The Ambassador's Boots*.

# The Man in the Mist

## CAST

| | |
|---|---|
| Francesca Annis | Tuppence Beresford |
| James Warwick | Tommy Beresford |
| Reece Dinsdale | Albert |
| Anne Stallybrass | Mrs Honeycott |
| Constantine Gregory | Bulger Estcourt |
| Tim Brierley | Reilly |
| Linda Marlowe | Gilda Glen |
| Christopher Johnston | Police Constable |
| Valerie Lilley | Ellen |
| Roger Kemp | Detective Inspector Jeavons |
| Paddy Ward | Bartender |
| Patrick Marley | Lord Leconbury |
| Geoffrey Greenhill | Police Sergeant |
| Mark Farmer | Page Boy |

In the guise of G.K. Chesterton's Father Brown (which was itself an interesting television series in 1973 with Kenneth More), Tommy, along with Tuppence, encounters a mysterious police-man, an elderly woman, murderers bogus and genuine, while on their way to see glamorous actress Gilda Glen (Linda Marlowe).

▲ L-R: Tuppence Beresford (Francesca Annis), Gilda Glen (Linda Marlowe), Reilly (Tim Brierley) and Tommy Beresford (James Warwick) in *the Man in the Mist*.

# The Case of the Missing Lady

Francesca Annis · · · · · · · · · · · · · · · · · · Tuppence Beresford
James Warwick · · · · · · · · · · · · · · · · · · · Tommy Beresford
Reece Dinsdale · · · · · · · · · · · · · · · · · · · · · · · · Albert
Rowena Cooper · · · · · · · · · · · · · · · · · · · · · Irma Kleber
Ewan Hooper · · · · · · · · · · · · · · · · · · · · · Dr Horriston
Elspeth March · · · · · · · · · · · · · · · · Lady Susan Clonray
Jonathan Newth · · · · · · · · · · · · · · Gabriel Stavansson
Tim Pearce · · · · · · · · · · · · · · · · · · · · · · · Muldoon
Mischa De La Motte · · · · · · · · · · · · · · · · · Manservant
Susie Fairfax · · · · · · · · · · · · · · · · · · · · · Girl in Shop
Elizabeth Murray · · · · · · · · · · · · · · · · Mrs Leigh Gordon

When Tommy and Tuppence are consulted by famous arctic explorer Gabriel Stavansson (Jonathan Newth) in order to find his missing fiancée, their investigation leads then to a sanitorium headed by a doctor whose credentials and practices are suspicious.

Tuppence infiltrates the place in a ballerina disguise, while Tommy adopts the guise of the famous sleuth from Baker Street, Sherlock Holmes.

◄ L-R: Gabriel Stavansson (Jonathan Newth), and Tuppence (Francesca Annis) and Tommy (James Warwick) Beresford in *The Case of the Missing Lady*.

# The Unbreakable Alibi

Francesca Annis · · · · · · · · · · · · · · · · · · Tuppence Beresford
James Warwick · · · · · · · · · · · · · · · · · · · Tommy Beresford
Reece Dinsdale · · · · · · · · · · · · · · · · · · · · · · · · Albert
Anna Nygh · · · · · · · · · · · · · · · · · · · · Una/Vere Drake
Tim Meats · · · · · · · · · · · · · · · · · · Montgomery Jones
Michael Jayes · · · · · · · · · · · · · · · · Peter LeMarchant
Ellis Dale · · · · · · · · · · · · · · · · · · · · · · · · · · Henri
Gay Soper · · · · · · · · · · · · · · · · · · Hotel Receptionist
Elaine Wells · · · · · · · · · · · · · · · · · · · Chambermaid
Preston Lockwood · · · · · · · · · · · · · · · · · Head Waiter
Stephen Wale · · · · · · · · · · · · · · · · Dining Car Attendant

Scotland Yard Detective Inspector Joseph French, a creation of author Freeman Willis Crofts, is the subject of parody in this Christie short tale.

The story concerns Mr Montgomery Jones, whose fiancée (Anna Nygh) challenges him to ascertain how she can be in two different places at the same time.

Fearing she will break their engagement if he is unable to solve the riddle, he seeks the advice of Tommy and Tuppence to crack 'the unbreakable alibi'.

▶ Tuppence (Francesca Annis) and Tommy (James Warwick) Beresford in *the Unbreakable Alibi*.

# The Crackler

## CAST

| | |
|---|---|
| Francesca Annis | Tuppence Beresford |
| James Warwick | Tommy Beresford |
| Reece Dinsdale | Albert |
| Shane Rimmer | Hank Ryder |
| Arthur Cox | Inspector Marriott |
| Carolle Rosseau | Marguerite Laidlaw |
| Christopher Scoular | Captain Jimmy Faulkener |
| David Quilter | Major Laidlaw |
| Lawrence Davidson | Monsieur Heroulabe |
| Patrick Godfrey | Maybrick |
| Stan Pretty | Harry |
| Terence Hillyer | Chauffer |

Edgar Wallace, certainly one of the most popular mystery writers of all time, was at his apex when Christie wrote *The Crackler*, which is done in the Wallace style and tradition (at one point in the story Tuppence actually mentions Wallace, who is said to have written a book a week during the 1920s).

Inspector Marriott (Arthur Cox) seeks the help of the Beresfords, this time to help catch a counterfeiter who has been at work in France as well as England: Tommy helps to trap the counterfeiter with a dose of catnip.

▶ Tommy (James Warwick) and Tuppence (Francesca Annis) Beresford in *The Crackler*.

# ≡1984≡

## Ordeal By Innocence

Made in England. Directed by Desmond Davis.

CAST

| | |
|---|---|
| Donald Sutherland | Dr Arthur Calgary |
| Christopher Plummer | Leo Argyle |
| Sarah Miles | Mary Durrant |
| Ian McShane | Philip Durrant |
| Diana Quick | Gwenda Vaughan |
| Faye Dunaway | Rachel Argyle |
| Annette Crosbie | Kirsten Lindstrom |
| Michael Elphick | Inspector Huish |
| George Innes | Archie Leach |
| Valerie Whittington | Hester Argyle |
| Phoebe Nicholls | Tina Argyle |
| Michael Maloney | Mickey Argyle |
| Cassie Stuart | Maureen Clegg |
| Anita Carey | Martha Jessup |
| Ron Pember | Ferryman |
| Kevin Stoney | Solicitor |
| Brian Glover | Executioner |
| Billy McColl | Jack Argyle |
| Rex Holdsworth | Police Doctor |
| John Bardon | Night Porter |
| Martyn Townsend | Detective |
| Doel Luscombe | Prison Governor |
| Alex Porwal | Young Policeman |
| Robert McBain | Hotel Manager |

Based on the novel *Ordeal By Innocence* (1958). 90 minutes.

▲ Dr Arthur Calgary (Donald Sutherland) questions suspect Mary Durrant (Sarah Miles) in *Ordeal by Innocence*.

*Ordeal By Innocence*, written in 1958, was one of Christie's favourite books. The story is set in Devonshire, where Christie lived when she wrote it.

The 1984 film, which was shot in and around Dartmouth, Devon, begins with paleontologist Dr Arthur Calgary returning from a two-year Antarctic research trip. He goes to the home of Jack Argyle, who had left an address book in his keeping the night Calgary left on his voyage; it is the first chance he has had to return it.

Calgary is shocked to learn that young Jack is dead; he was hanged for the murder of his mother. The trouble is, Calgary tells Leo Argyle (Jack's father) that his son was with him at the time he was supposed to have committed the crime.

Calgary wants to go to the police to clear the

young man's name, but meets with indifference and even resistance on the part of the Argyle family. They really just want to forget it all – it seems Jack was not exactly loved by his family.

Since Calgary knows Jack could not have done the murder, he goes to the police himself, but they tell him the case cannot be reopened without the approval of the Home Secretary. Calgary meets with resistance from every side, so, knowing the lad to have been innocent, he takes it upon himself to investigate the crime. 'The trouble with capital punishment,' Calgary tells Leo, 'there's no room for error.'

With the aid of Jack's address book, which he has hung onto, Calgary looks up other family members, who are equally reticent about helping him, since one of them must be the real killer.

Suspects include Jack's sister Mrs Durrant and her wheelchair-bound husband Philip, brother Mickey and sister Tina. There is no love lost in the Argyle family, and it is from Tina that Calgary learns all the siblings are adopted, as the late Mrs Calgary was unable to have children.

One night after interviewing some suspects, Calgary is nearly deliberately run down in the street; Inspector Huish, who was in charge of the Argyle case, advises him to pack his bags and

▲ Christopher Plummer as Leo Argyle, one of the murder suspects in *Ordeal by Innocence*.

▲ Leo Argyle (Christopher Plummer) demonstrates his prowess with small arms to Dr Calgary (Donald Sutherland) in *Ordeal by Innocence*.

▲ Paleontologist Dr Arthur Calgary (Donald Sutherland) in an introspective pose in *Ordeal by Innocence*.

leave town. Villagers are also reluctant to offer Calgary any assistance.

Philip Durrant tells Calgary that Jack was blackmailing someone at the house, and also that Tina was there on the night of the murder. But Tina is murdered herself before she can tell Calgary what she knows.

When Philip is found murdered in the hothouse, Calgary is close to the solution. By eliminating the innocent through their alibis, Calgary is finally able to come up with the right answer.

*Ordeal By Innocence* is an interesting film that adheres closely to the original novel. The action keeps moving along and there are no lags or dull spots.

Reconstruction of the original murder and events leading up to it are interspersed throughout the film with black-and-white flashbacks. The photography by Bill Williams is first-rate, and there is some excellent jazz music throughout by Dave Brubeck.

Donald Sutherland is earnest as Dr Calgary, portraying him as honest and determined. Christopher Plummer is also good as the head of the Argyle family whose 'innocent' son may have got what he deserved. Faye Dunaway is seen only in the flashback scenes, and does little other than adding her name to the cast list; she would have a bit more to do in the 1985 film *13 at Dinner*.

Sarah Miles as tipsy Mrs Durrant, Ian McShane as her invalid husband, and Michael Elphick as the policeman who resents his case reopened are all fine. Also offering good performances are Phoebe Nicholls as Tina, Cassie Stuart as the amorous wife of the hanged man, and Michael Maloney as the brother who is wrongfully held. Kevin Stoney, who had a small part as Dr Markwell in *Murder at the Gallop*, has an even briefer one here as a solicitor.

# The Secret Adversary (TV)

Made in England. Directed by Tony Wharmby.

## CAST

▼

| | |
|---|---|
| Francesca Annis | Tuppence Cowley |
| James Warwick | Tommy Beresford |
| Alec McCowen | Sir James Peel Edgerton |
| Peter Barkworth | Mr Carter |
| George Baker | Whittington |
| Honor Blackman | Rita Vandemeyer |
| John Fraser | Kramenin |
| Donald Houston | Boris |
| Gavan O'Herlihy | Julius P. Hersheimmer |
| Toria Fuller | Jane Finn |
| Reece Dinsdale | Albert |
| Gabrielle Blunt | Annie |
| Joseph Brady | Dr Hall |
| Wolf Kahler | The German |
| Peter Lovstrom | Henry |
| Matthew Scurfield | Conrad |
| Holly Watson | Child on Beach |
| Phyllida Hewat | Woman in Tea Shop |
| James Walker | First Clerk |
| Mike Elles | Second Clerk |
| Norman Hartley | Florist |
| Roger Ostime | Ritz Receptionist |
| Nicholas Geake | Watson |
| Simon Watkins | Man at Astley Priors |
| Steve Fletcher | Messenger Boy |

Based on the novel *The Secret Adversary* (1922). 107 minutes.

Agatha Christie's 1922 novel *The Secret Adversary* was the first of her works to be filmed. A German-made version of the story, called *Die Abenteuer GMBH* (Adventurers Inc.) had been made in 1928. Some 57 years later, a marvellous film was made for television under the story's original title. Although filmed at the same time as the *Partners in Crime* series, *The Secret Adversary* was released the following year.

The story takes place shortly after the end of the First World War; childhood friends Tommy and Tuppence are reunited after a long separation. Both find themselves out of work, and over tea they discuss ways and means of putting an end to this situation.

Tuppence comes up with the idea of advertising in the newspaper, and soon afterwards is approached by Mr Whittington, who has overheard their conversation.

Whittington wants to hire Tuppence to travel abroad, masquerading as someone else. When she gives the name of Jane Finn as her own, Whittington becomes alarmed, telling Tuppence to return the following day. When she does, she finds that Mr Whittington has vanished.

She and Tommy decide to place a further advert asking for any information on Jane Finn, a name that Tommy had heard someone use in casual conversation, which had so upset Whittington.

Two people respond to the advert. The first, a Mr Carter, is a member of British Intelligence,

▲ The distinguished stars of *The Secret Adversary* include (L-R, above) Honor Blackman as Rita Vandemeyer, George Baker (Whittington), (L-R, below) Alec McCowan (Sir James Peel Edgerton), Peter Barkworth (Mr Carter), and Donald Houston (Boris).

▲ (Above) Toria Fuller stars as Annette, Donald Houston as Boris, (below) John Fraser as Kramenin, and Honor Blackman as Rita Vandemeyer in *The Secret Adversary*.

▲ Francesca Annis (left), who starred as Tuppence Beresford in *The Secret Adversary*, is seen here with Gabrielle Blunt (Annie) and Joseph Brady (Dr Hall).

who decides to hire the two young people to find Jane Finn, warning them at the same time against a mysterious arch-criminal known only as 'Mr Brown'. It seems that Jane Finn may be in possession of a secret political treaty whose ramifications involve national security.

The other respondent is American Juilus P. Hersheimmer, who tells the pair that he is Jane's cousin and also 'the third richest man in America'.

Tommy and Tuppence recruit Hersheimmer into the operation; his money will turn out to come in handy and, anyway, he is Jane's only relative, as far as they know.

Whittington is seen and leads Hesheimmer to a nursing home in Bournemouth, while Tommy tracks Boris, Whittington's partner, to a lonely house where a mysterious meeting is taking place. He is discovered listening and is imprisoned in the house.

Meanwhile Tuppence, in disguise, has secured a position as a maid in the home of Mrs Rita Vandermeyer, where Whittington was seen.

It is here that Tuppence first encounters Sir James Peel Edgerton, who is also apparently on the trail of Mrs Vandermeyer. Mrs Vandermeyer is no fool, however, and merely traps Tuppence, but the resourceful young woman is able to turn the tables on her – but not before Mrs Vandermeyer is murdered under her very nose.

Tommy, who is making his escape with the aid of a girl who turns out to be Jane Finn, gets back to Mr Carter, who has met with Edgerton to discuss the situation.

Returning to the Ritz Hotel, Tommy finds Julius, who had given him up for dead. Tuppence, it seems, has gone to Yorkshire in response to Tommy's telegram – one he never sent.

Tracking the trail to Yorkshire, Tommy and Julius discover clues to show that she has been at a lonely home, but her clothing found by a little girl on the beach gives the appearance that she has been drowned.

Through further detecting, Tuppence is found very much alive, although a prisoner; Julius comes to the rescue and Tommy also pops up, never really believing Tuppence dead.

Jane Finn, who has hidden the secret document, reveals its whereabouts, and this is the key to Tommy and Tuppence's unmasking of 'Mr Brown', who swallows a poison capsule rather than stand trial.

*The Secret Adversary* is a wonderful blend of suspense, mystery, and romance, produced by Jack Williams for London Weekend Television.

▲ James Warwick (left) as Tommy Beresford and Gavan O'Herlihy as Julius P. Hersheimmer in *The Secret Adversary*.

Penny Lowe's period costumes deserve special recognition, as well as the wonderful casting by Corinne Rodriguez. Francesca Annis is wonderful as Tuppence, and she and James Warwick (Tommy) work very well together here. Reece Dinsdale, who played the couple's man-of-all-duties Albert in the series, is also on hand here.

Performances by Alec McCowen, Peter Barkworth, George Baker, Honor Blackman and Gavan O'Herlihy are all first-class, as is the production, which was directed with style and skill by Tony Wharmby.

# Murder With Mirrors (TV)

Made in England. Directed by Dick Lowry.

## CAST

Sir John Mills · · · · · · · · · · · · · · · · · · · · · · · · Lewis Serrocold
Helen Hayes · · · · · · · · · · · · · · · · · · · · · · · · · · Miss Marple
Bette Davis · · · · · · · · · · · · · · · · · · · · Carrie Louise Serrocold
Leo McKern · · · · · · · · · · · · · · · · · · · · · · · Inspector Curry
Dorothy Tutin · · · · · · · · · · · · · · · · · · · · · · Mildred Strete
Anton Rodgers · · · · · · · · · · · · · · · · · · · · Dr Max Hargrove
John Woodvine · · · · · · · · · · · · · · · · · Christian Gulbrandsen
Frances De La Tour · · · · · · · · · · · · · · · · · · Juliet Bellever
Liane Langland · · · · · · · · · · · · · · · · · · · · · Gina Markham
John Laughlin · · · · · · · · · · · · · · · · · · · · Walter Markham
James Coombes · · · · · · · · · · · · · · · · · · Stephen Restarick
and: Tim Roth, Christopher Fairbank, Amanda Maynard.

Based on the novel *Murder With Mirrors* (1952). 96 minutes.

▲ Miss Marple (Helen Hayes) and Lewis
Serrocold (Sir John Mills) in *Murder with Mirrors*.

*Murder With Mirrors* was written by Christie during a visit to Iraq in 1952. The film begins with Miss Jane Marple alighting from a train in London; she is there to pay a visit to Christian Gulbrandsen. He is the stepson of Carrie Louise Serrocold, a friend of Miss Marple's who she has not seen for years.

Gulbrandsen asks her if she could renew her friendship with Carrie Louise and pay her a visit, as he is convinced there is 'something serious' going on down there.

It seems that Stonygates, Carrie's home, is being used as a rehabilitation centre for juvenile delinquents. After arriving in granddaughter Gina Markham's speeding car, Miss Marple is reunited with Carrie, and meets her husband Lewis (this is Carrie's third marriage).

Lewis is very concerned with the problem of juvenile delinquency and, along with psychologist Dr Max Hargrove, has started a foundation that reforms the young offenders.

Taking Miss Marple aside that evening, Lewis tells her that his wife 'isn't terribly well', and goes on to tell her that he has reason to believe someone is trying to poison Carrie. Miss Marple finds some of the characters a bit odd, especially the youths; everyone reminds her of someone she has come across before.

Christian Gulbrandsen arrives and while Lewis is having words with one of the wayward lads in the study, is murdered upstairs. Everyone appears to have an alibi, but Inspector Curry of Scotland Yard is determined to find the guilty party with, of course, the help of Miss Marple, who he has heard a great deal about from one of his colleagues. The colleague, he tells her, has described Miss Marple as 'meddlesome' but also 'intuitive and bloody useful'.

An attempt is made on Miss Marple's life when she is (apparently) alone in a deserted theatre; the rope holding the heavy stage prop that narrowly missed her head was deliberately cut through. The principals do not have very good alibis for the time of the attempt, and of course there are about 200 boys, who have committed various offences, nearby.

When Carrie receives an anonymous box of chocolates, Lewis takes them to the police for analysis, and it turns out that they were loaded with poison. Fortunately for Carrie, she did not eat any of them.

Meanwhile, Stephen Restarick has grown tired of it all and decides to leave, only to be brought back when he is caught at a London train station. When Miss Marple confronts Dr Hargrove, she arouses his fear to the point that he too leaves – only he is not caught, instead he meets a fiery death when his car explodes after crashing into the gates. Miss Marple warns the Inspector that the murderer is still at large.

After one of the boys attempts to flee and is drowned in a nearby lake, Miss Marple comes up with the solution. Gathering the suspects in the drawing room, she explains. 'Go ahead Miss Marple,' says Inspector Curry. 'It's your show.'

*Murder With Mirrors* was a fairly well-done mystery. Helen Hayes was an adequate, if not exceptional, Miss Marple. Bette Davis, looking emaciated after a recent stroke, has little to do – in essence a very sick, old lady playing a very sick, old lady.

Best performances in the film come from Sir John Mills as Lewis Serrocold and Leo McKern as Inspector Curry. Dorothy Tutin, Anton Rodgers and John Woodvine also offer good portrayals.

Dick Lowry's direction is competent, and there is good photography by Brian West, editing by Richard Bracken, and music by Richard Rodney Bennett. Richard Eckstein adapted the script; casting was by Maud Spector and Ann Stanborough.

▲ Miss Marple (Helen Hayes, left) with Carrie Louise Serrocold (Bette Davis) in *Murder with Mirrors*.

## Thirteen at Dinner (TV)

Made in England. Directed by Lou Antonio.

### CAST

| | |
|---|---|
| Peter Ustinov | Hercule Poirot |
| Jonathan Cecil | Captain Arthur Hastings |
| Faye Dunaway | Jane Wilkinson |
| Lee Horsley | Bryan Martin |
| David Suchet | Inspector Japp |
| Allan Cuthbertson | Sir Montague Corner |
| John Barron | Lord Edgware |
| Benedict Taylor | Donald Ross |
| Bill Nighy | Ronnie Marsh |
| John Stride | Film Director |
| Avril Elgar | Housekeeper |
| David Frost | Himself |

and: Amanda Pays, Diane Keen, Glyn Baker, Peter Clapham, Leslie Dunlop, Orianne Grieve, Russell Keith-Grant, Roger Milner, David Neville, Geoffrey Rose, John Quarmby, Pamela Salem, Jean Sincere.

Based on the novel *Lord Edgware Dies* (1933). 95 minutes.

*Thirteen at Dinner*, based on the 1933 novel *Lord Edgware Dies*, had been filmed 51 years before in 1934 under its original title, starring Austin Trevor as Hercule Poirot.

In this 1985 television film, made in England as a British-American co-production for CBS Television, Peter Ustinov starred as Poirot, a role he had played in two previous cinema films, *Death On the Nile* in 1978 and *Evil Under the Sun* in 1982.

The film, which has been updated to modern times, begins with American actor Bryan Martin and the Belgian sleuth being interviewed on television by David Frost.

When Bryan's co-star in the film he is doing appears on the programme, no one is more surprised than the actress herself, one Jane Wilkinson, who happens to be at home watching the programme on television. Frost reveals that she is merely an impersonator, and Jane is amused enough to invite her (as well as Poirot and Hastings) to her home for dinner.

During cocktails, Jane tells Poirot she wants to 'get rid of her husband' and asks him if he will consent to visit Lord Edgware to discuss a divorce.

Poirot agrees, and makes an appointment with Lord Edgware's secretary to visit him the following day. When he arrives and talks to Lord Edgware, he is surprised to learn that Edgware has already consented to grant his wife a divorce; in fact, he had written to her six months before to tell her of his decision.

The following day, Scotland Yard Inspector Japp visits Poirot to impart the news that Lord Edgware has been murdered, apparently by his wife. But Jane was attending a dinner party at the home of Sir Montague Corner at the time her husband was murdered, although Edgware's servants swear that she was at Edgware's home.

This leads Poirot to the conclusion that the double, one Carlotta Adams, was involved in the deception, but upon seeking an interview with her, he instead finds her corpse, the victim of a drug overdose he believes 'was not self-induced'.

The updating of the film to modern times certainly only makes this production suffer; it is absolutely unnecessary and only serves to taint the tale. Faye Dunaway, who had appeared in a small role in *Ordeal by Innocence* the previous year, seems out of place, and Lee Horsley, a popular television star, adds nothing to the film; these

▲ Hercule Poirot (Peter Ustinov, left) looks on while Jane Wilkinson (Faye Dunaway) signs an autograph in *13 at Dinner*.

▲ Hercule Poirot (Peter Ustinov, left) and Sir Montague Corner (Allan Cuthbertson) share a friendly game of croquet in *13 at Dinner*.

two were obviously added for their name value to American audiences.

Ustinov plays Poirot for the third time, and is competent in the part (which he would play three more times).

Jonathan Cecil plays Hastings as shy and rather bumbling, a type of character he has made a career out of.

The best performances in *Thirteen at Dinner* are offered by the versatile David Suchet as Inspector Japp (several years later he would be the definitive Hercule Poirot in television films

for London Weekend Television) and Allan Cuthbertson as the titled fellow who cheats at croquet.

Clever visual devices are used when Poirot has assembled the suspects in the end scene while Ustinov narrates, a technique that had been effectively employed previously in *Death On the Nile* and *Murder on the Orient Express*.

All in all, *Thirteen at Dinner* is pleasant and entertaining, with John Addison's music a definite asset. Rod Browning adapted the script from the original work.

# ≡ 1985 ≡

## The Body in the Library (TV)

Made in England. Directed by Silvio Narizzano.

### CAST
▼

| | |
|---|---|
| Joan Hickson | Miss Jane Marple |
| Moray Watson | Colonel Bantry |
| Gwen Watford | Dolly Bantry |
| David Horovitch | Detective Inspector Slack |
| Andrew Cruickshank | Conway Jefferson |
| Jess Conrad | Raymond Starr |
| Keith Drinkel | Mark Gaskell |
| Valentine Dyall | Lorrimer |
| Frederick Jaeger | Colonel Melchett |
| Anthony Smee | Basil Blake |
| Raymond Francis | Sir Henry Clithering |
| Ian Brimble | Detective Constable Lake |
| Sarah Whitlock | Woman Police Constable |
| John Moffat | Edwards |
| Ciaran Madden | Adelaide Jefferson |
| Trudie Styler | Josie Turner |
| Sally Jane Jackson | Ruby Keene |
| Martyn Read | Hugo McLean |
| Andrew Downer | Peter Carmody |
| Debbie Arnold | Dinah Lee |
| Astra Sheridan | Pamela Reeve |
| Karen Seacombe | Florrie Small |

Based on the novel *The Body in the Library* (1942). 158 minutes.

▲ Miss Marple (Joan Hickson, left) investigates *The Body in the Library* at the request of her friend Dolly Bantry (Gwen Watford).

Agatha Christie was very pleased with the opening sequence of her 1942 novel *The Body in the Library*, a story that marked the return of the character of Miss Jane Marple, the shrewd observer of human nature, after an absence of ten years.

The story opens at Gossington Hall at the village of St Mary Mead (Gossington Hall was also used as the setting for *The Mirror Crack'd*). A platinum blonde is found murdered in the library of Colonel and Mrs Bantry, strangled with the sash of a dress.

Police begin by questioning the household servants, as well as the family, with little result. Mrs Dolly Bantry enlists the aid of her friend, local resident Miss Jane Marple, who has something of a reputation for solving murders. Miss Marple arrives, studies the scene, but does not attempt to offer an explaination forthwith.

While Miss Marple agrees to look into the matter, police inquiries lead them to discover the victim was an 18-year-old reported missing the previous evening from the nearby Majestic Hotel. Miss Marple, accompanied by Mrs Bantry, takes up residence at the hotel in order to further her investigation.

A photo was found in the victim's purse; it is identified as that of Basil Blake, an ill-mannered idler who knew Ruby Keene, the dead girl. Elderly, wealthy, semi-invalid Conway Jefferson was fond of Ruby, who reminded him of his dead daughter. Josephine Turner, a dance hostess and entertainer at the hotel, is also among the suspects, as are gambler Mark Gaskell, tennis pro Raymond Starr, and George Bartlett, who was infatuated with Ruby.

As the police routinely and methodically gather evidence in the case, Miss Marple sifts through the clues to trap the killer in her usual inimitable style, drawing on parallels of the events and everyday occurrences she has witnessed.

Christie, who once stated that *The Body in the Library* was 'the best opening I ever wrote', would doubtless have been pleased at the care taken by Guy Slater, who produced this film for the BBC.

The casting of 79-year-old Joan Hickson, a British character actress who had appeared on stage since 1927 and in over 100 motion pictures (she was often seen in dithery or eccentric parts), was a stroke of genius. Critics and public alike hailed Miss Hickson's portrayal of the elderly crime solver as the definitive Miss Jane Marple, and plans were already under way to film more of the stories. *The Body in the Library* is, in fact, the first of ten television films made by the BBC between 1985 and 1989 starring Joan Hickson as Miss Marple.

The nuances of the story are well captured in this flavourful adaptation, and *The Body in the Library*, while not one of Christie's best-known stories, was still a very good choice here – definitely vintage Marple.

Others among the notable cast (again, a wonderful job of casting was an enormous asset in these adaptations) included Gwen Watford as Dolly Bantry, Moray Watson as the Colonel, David Horovitch as Detective Inspector Slack (a characterization that would be repeated several times), Frederick Jaeger as Colonel Melchett, and Valentine Dyall as Lorrimer. Andrew Cruickshank, who appeared as the acidulous judge in *Murder Most Foul* in 1965, gives a marvellous performance as Conway Jefferson, evoking a deep emotion of feeling.

A good period atmosphere was created, and other technical credits, including sets, photography, costumes and lighting, are all impressive.

The following year (1986), Joan Hickson was awarded an OBE for her long and distinguished career; certainly the accolades she received playing Miss Marple gave added recognition to this talented actress.

▲ Aged Conway Jefferson (Andrew Cruickshank) and his protege Ruby Keene (Sally Jane Jackson), who gets murdered in *The Body in the Library*.

# The Moving Finger (TV)

Made in England. Directed by Roy Boulting.

CAST

▼

| | |
|---|---|
| Joan Hickson | Miss Jane Marple |
| Michael Culver | Edward Symmington |
| Richard Pearson | Mr Pye |
| John Arnatt | Reverend Guy Calthrop |
| Gerald Sim | Coroner |
| Andrew Bicknell | Gerry Burton |
| Martin Fisk | Owen Griffith |
| Sandra Payne | Eryl Griffith |
| Sabina Franklyn | Joanna Burton |
| Dilys Hamlett | Maud Calthrop |
| Patsy Smart | Mrs Cleat |
| Deborah Appleby | Megan Hunter |
| Hilary Mason | Emily Barton |
| Penelope Lee | Partridge |
| Victor Maddern | Police Constable Johnson |
| Juliet Waley | Beatrice |
| Imogen Bickford-Smith | Elsie Holland |
| Geoffrey Davion | Superintendant Nash |
| Roger Ostime | Detective Inspector Crawford |
| Ninka Scott | Miss Ginch |
| Gordon Rollings | Mr Cleat |
| Catherine Owen | Rose |
| Carol Gleeson | Contralto |
| John Keenan | Pianist |

Based on the novel *The Moving Finger* (1942). 98 minutes.

Written in 1942 and published immediately after *The Body in the Library*, *The Moving Finger* was the second story to be filmed for television with Joan Hickson as Miss Marple.

Young airman Gerry Burton, recovering from a bad flying crash, rents Little Furze, a house in the small community of Lymstock. His sister Joanna is with him to minister to his needs.

After various members of the community come over to introduce themselves, an anonymous 'poison pen' letter arrives, intimating that Gerry and Joanna are not brother and sister.

Joanna is initially outraged, then amused, and Gerry burns the letter. When local doctor Owen Griffith arrives to look in on Gerry, he tells the doctor about the letter. To his surprise, the doctor tells him that he has received a similar letter, as had lawyer Edward Symmington and middle-aged Miss Ginch.

In each case, the *Moving Finger* accuses the letter recipients of illicit sexual behaviour, and rumour among the locals has it that several of the letters hit very close to the mark.

When one of the recipients commits suicide (or was it murder?) Maud Calthrop gets in touch with her old friend Jane Marple, who comes to the village to stay with the Calthrops and sort out the mystery.

Leading characters in the drama include attorney Edward Symmington and his wife,

▶ Joan Hickson, the quintessential Miss Marple, in *The Moving Finger*.

Reverend Guy Calthrop and his wife Maud, refined and gentle spinster Emily Barton, and local physician Owen Griffith and his sister Eryl.

Once again, Joan Hickson shines as Miss Marple – although in *The Moving Finger* a great deal of the story takes place before she becomes involved.

Richard Pearson, who played Dr Haydock in *The Mirror Crack'd*, is cast as Mr Pye in this film, the man to whom beauty is 'the goal of mankind'. John Arnatt, who was well-known as the Deputy Sheriff in the 'Robin Hood' television series of the fifties, is also well cast as the thoughtful reverend.

The music, photography and other technical credits are all up to par. The able direction is by Roy Boulting.

◄ Maud Calthrop (Dilys Hamlett, left) invites Miss Marple (Joan Hickson) to investigate a series of poison pen letters in *The Moving Finger*.

# 1986

## A Pocket Full of Rye (TV)

Made in England. Directed by Guy Slater.

### CAST

| | |
|---|---|
| Joan Hickson | Miss Jane Marple |
| Timothy West | Rex Fortescue |
| Fabia Drake | Miss Henderson |
| Martyn Stanbridge | Vivian DuBois |
| Clive Merrison | Percival Fortescue |
| Stacy Dorning | Adele Fortescue |
| Rachel Bell | Jennifer Fortescue |
| Peter Davison | Lance Fortescue |
| Frances Low | Patricia Fortescue |
| Frank Mills | Mr Crump |
| Selina Cadell | Mary Dove |
| Merelina Kendall | Mrs Crump |
| Annette Badland | Gladys Martin |
| Tom Wilkinson | Detective Inspector Neele |
| John Glover | Detective Sergeant Hay |
| Charles Pemberton | Sergeant Rose |
| Laurin Kaski | Police Constable White |

Based on the novel *A Pocket Full of Rye* (1953). 102 minutes.

▲ Miss Marple (Joan Hickson) uses a Mother Goose nursery rhyme to solve the murder of financier Rex Fortescue (Timothy West) in *A Pocket Full of Rye.*

Rex Fortescue, the wealthy patriarch of Yew Tree Cottage, is found dead at his counting house shortly after drinking a cup of tea. The police pathologists report, however, that the poison used is a kind that takes several hours to kill, therefore it could not have been in the tea, but must have been in his breakfast marmalade. The police do not have a clue to the motive and even less an explanation as to why rye was found in the dead man's pocket.

Rex's young wife Adele is the most likely suspect, and Inspector Neele launches into his investigation. But when Adele is murdered by cyanide in her tea (right after eating a meal of bread and honey) the Inspector has to look elsewhere.

Miss Marple gets involved in the case when Gladys Martin, an adenoidal, simple-minded parlourmaid, is found strangled when hanging up the washing; a clothes pin has been placed on her nose as a gruesome touch by the murderer.

Inspector Neele, who is anxious to get to the bottom of the mystery, does not resent Miss Marple entering into the case. In fact, she is the one who points out to him the similarity between the murders and the Mother Goose nursery rhyme.

'Sing a song of sixpence, a pocket full of rye . . . The king was in his counting house, counting out his money . . .' Well, after all, was not Rex Fortescue sort of a king? He certainly ruled his family, and was the head of a financial empire. And he died in his counting house, with rye in his pockets . . .

'The queen was in the parlour eating bread and honey . . .' Clearly Adele. 'The maid was in the garden hanging up the clothes, when a blackbird came by and nipped off her nose.' Gladys, of course, replete with clothespin.

The servants are flustered by the murders, but Miss Henderson (she and Rex had referred to each other as 'sister-in-law' and 'brother-in-law' at the breakfast table) is only surprised that something of the sort had not happened before!

Miss Marple puts it all together as usual, and there is an interesting clue about the old Black-bird Mine (Rex had been given a 'present' of dead blackbirds before he was murdered).

Joan Hickson is up to her usual standard, and is ably assisted by the other members of the cast. Tom Wilkinson, who plays Inspector Neele here, gives a good performance as a frustrated, and at times, reluctant official.

Timothy West, who played the policeman in charge of looking for Agatha Christie in the 1979 film *Agatha* is fine as the first of the victims. Fabia Drake is also impressive as Miss Henderson.

Peter Davison, who would later star as the gentlemanly sleuth Albert Campion in his own television series, does well as Lancelot Fortescue, and he is matched by Clive Merrison playing his brother Percival.

Annette Badland also is good as Gladys Martin; the audience, just like Miss Marple, feels genuine outrage and anger when this harmless, slow-witted character is done in (a Christie characteristic employed on a number of occasions in her work). This, after all, is the reason Miss Marple determines to solve the case, just as the murder of the innocent, kindly Dora Bunner ruffled her feathers in *A Murder is Announced.*

## A Murder is Announced (TV)

Made in England. Directed by David Giles.

### CAST

▼

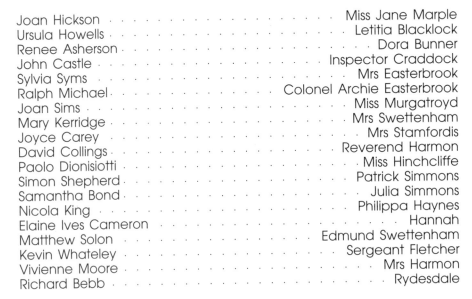

| | |
|---|---|
| Joan Hickson | Miss Jane Marple |
| Ursula Howells | Letitia Blacklock |
| Renee Asherson | Dora Bunner |
| John Castle | Inspector Craddock |
| Sylvia Syms | Mrs Easterbrook |
| Ralph Michael | Colonel Archie Easterbrook |
| Joan Sims | Miss Murgatroyd |
| Mary Kerridge | Mrs Swettenham |
| Joyce Carey | Mrs Stamfordis |
| David Collings | Reverend Harmon |
| Paolo Dionisiotti | Miss Hinchcliffe |
| Simon Shepherd | Patrick Simmons |
| Samantha Bond | Julia Simmons |
| Nicola King | Philippa Haynes |
| Elaine Ives Cameron | Hannah |
| Matthew Solon | Edmund Swettenham |
| Kevin Whateley | Sergeant Fletcher |
| Vivienne Moore | Mrs Harmon |
| Richard Bebb | Rydesdale |

Based on the novel *A Murder is Announced* (1950). 156 minutes.

Thirty years previously, *A Murder is Announced* had been made into a television film for NBC-TV as an episode of the Goodyear Television Playhouse. It had the problem of trying to tell a story in 55 minutes. Here, the BBC gave us another television version, this time running 156 minutes, and much more detail was paid to story line and characterization.

People in the village of Chipping Cleghorn discover a strange advert in the local newspaper; there is to be a murder at Little Paddocks, the home of Letitia Blacklock. A few people decide to show up out of curiosity, thinking it a party invitation.

Nobody, including the hostess, quite knows what to make of the situation; all of a sudden the lights go out and a voice says 'Hands up or I'll shoot', followed by three shots.

Some of the guests, who were amused by the whole thing, became shocked and confused when the lights came back on and the mysterious intruder is found dead on the floor. Miss Blacklock

has been wounded, and her friend Miss Bunner recognizes the dead man as someone who had tried to extort money from Miss Blacklock.

Police Detective Inspector Craddock is soon on the scene, interviewing members of the household as well as the guests. Opinions vary regarding accident, from suicide to murder. Craddock learns from the Swiss police that the victim, Rudy Sherz, had a criminal record. Craddock and his superior disagree about certain aspects of the crime, and the latter suggests the Inspector pay a visit to Miss Marple, who happens to be staying at a nearby hotel 'taking the spa waters for rheumatism'.

Miss Marple has had an encounter with the victim herself; he changed the amount on a check she had written. She also tells Craddock that she is sure the crime is one of murder. 'Turn over a rock,' she says, 'and you will never know what's likely to crawl out.'

The dead man's girlfriend, who works at the local hotel, informs Craddock that her boyfriend

▲ Miss Marple (Joan Hickson) contemplates the situation in *A Murder is Announced.*

had been hired by someone to go to the place where he was killed as a joke.

Further investigations lead Craddock to the opinion that Miss Blacklock is marked for murder, as she is soon to come into a large sum of money.

Miss Marple is angered by the subsequent murder of Dora Bunner, a completely harmless, trusting person, and she resolves to solve the crime (which she does in her usual able manner), but not before Miss Murgatroyd too meets her fate.

*A Murder is Announced* is another in the excellent Miss Marple series produced by the BBC. As was true of the series, particular details were adhered to in this film, with a faithfulness to the original work. The long running time is necessary for the story's plot, which never drags or becomes overlong.

Performances are first rate by everyone. Joan Hickson, playing Miss Marple for the fourth time (she has played Miss Marple twelve times so far) is, as usual, superb. Miss Hickson is unquestionably the closest thing to the Christie character ever to be seen on the screen, and is an absolute joy.

She is backed up by some very fine performances by a cast including John Castle as Inspector Craddock, Renee Asherson as Miss Bunner, Ursula Howells as Letitia Blacklock, and Ralph Michael and Sylvia Syms as the Easterbrooks. Joan Sims, a comedy actress who was one of the mainstays of the *Carry On* films, evokes the audiences compassion as the slow-witted Miss Murgatroyd.

Period atmosphere and music are also well handled in this production.

# ≡1986≡

## Dead Man's Folly (TV)

Made in England. Directed by Clive Donner.

CAST
▼

| | |
|---|---|
| Peter Ustinov. | Hercule Poirot |
| Jonathan Cecil | Captain Hastings |
| Tim Pigott-Smith | Sir George Stubbs |
| Jean Stapleton | Ariadne Oliver |
| Constance Cummings | Amy Folliat |
| Kenneth Cranham | Inspector Bland |
| Susan Wooldridge | Amanda Brewis |
| Ralph Arliss | Michael Wayman |
| Christopher Guard | Alec Legge |
| Caroline Langrishe | Sally Legge |
| Jeff Yeager | Eddie South |
| Nicolette Sheridan | Lady Stubbs |
| Sydney Bromley | Old Murdell |

and: Fanny Carby, Marjorie Yates.

Based on the novel *Dead Man's Folly* (1956). 95 minutes.

▲ Hercule Poirot (Peter Ustinov) plays the murder game at Nasse House created by Ariadne Oliver (Jean Stapleton) in *Dead Man's Folly*.

Filmed in England, as a British/US co-production for Warner Brothers Television, *Dead Man's Folly* begins with Hercule Poirot bumping into writer Ariadne Oliver, who informs him she is in charge of putting together a murder game for an upcoming fair at Nasse House, owned by Sir George Stubbs.

Mrs Oliver asks Poirot if he can come down to lend a hand; he and Captain Hastings consent. Arriving at the sprawling estate, Poirot learns that Sir George has completely restored Nasse House to all its past glory and splendour.

After meeting Sir George and his young, attractive and vacuous wife, he and Hastings are introduced to some of the guests staying at the large estate. These include secretary Amanda Brewis, architect Michael Wayman, and a young couple, Alec and Sally Legge. He later also meets Amy Folliat, former owner of Nasse House, who now resides in a small cottage on the property.

Mrs Oliver goes over the details of her 'game' with the guests while Poirot and Hastings are shown to their rooms.

Poirot makes the acquaintance of Old Murdell, the elderly ferryman who suffers from the combination of senility and inebriation. Shortly after Poirot leaves, the old man is deliberately drowned, although his body is not discovered for a while and it is not clear at this point why he has been killed.

A young girl named Marlene is selected to play the victim in the murder game, which is held during a fair on the grounds of Nasse House. Naturally, Poirot and Hastings get the jump on everyone else playing the game. They are able to find the clues easier than the others, but the trail eventually leads them to an unexpected conclusion: Marlene is not the pseudo-victim but a real one, having been strangled to death in the boathouse.

Inspector Bland is soon on the scene; he remembers Poirot's brilliant solving of the ABC murders 15 years previously, and gives Poirot carte blanche to investigate the crime, so the official and the private detective work alongside.

Nobody can think of any reason why anyone would want to kill Marlene, and now there is an added wrinkle in the case to contend with: Lady Stubbs has disappeared.

Poirot believes that the victim either knew or recognized her killer, and also that the missing Lady Stubbs has been murdered. Sir George, on the other hand, is convinced that his wife is alive, and begs Poirot to try and find her.

It is clear that Poirot has done his homework on the suspects: when one points out that he knows quite a bit about her, he replies: 'Oh, I keep my ears open.'

At this point Lady Stubbs' hat is found floating in the river. But that is not all – the body of Old Murdell is discovered there too.

Poirot tells Hastings that Mrs Folliat, the former owner of Nasse House, knows more than she is telling about the business and is keeping something back. But when Poirot confronts her, she refuses to tell him anything. But he warns her: 'Hercule Poirot never gives up.'

The dead girl's mother gives Poirot what turns out to be a vital piece of intelligence – Old Murdell happened to be Marlene's grandfather. Could the two deaths then be tied together in some way? Double identities and disguises also turn out to be vital in helping Poirot uncover the truth in this case.

*Dead Man's Folly* was fairly well done. The direction by Clive Donner is good, as is Curtis Clark's photography, Donald R. Rode's crisp editing and the music of John Addison.

Ustinov plays Poirot a bit too tongue-in-cheek at times, and Jean Stapleton, best known for the long-running comedy series *All in the Family*

makes a very poor Mrs Oliver, overacting with exaggerated gestures (and she also pronounces Poirot's first name 'Her-cu-lee').

Tim Pigott-Smith and Constance Cummings offer the best acting, and there is also fine work by the players in smaller parts.

▲ Ariadne Oliver (Jean Stapleton), Hercule Poirot (Peter Ustinov, centre), and Captain Hastings (Jonathan Cecil) in *Dead Man's Folly*.

## Murder in Three Acts (TV)

Made in Hollywood. Directed by Gary Nelson.

CAST

▼

| | |
|---|---|
| Peter Ustinov | Hercule Poirot |
| Jonathan Cecil | Captain Hastings |
| Tony Curtis | Charles Cartwright |
| Emma Samms | Jennifer Eastman (Egg) |
| Dana Elcar | Dr Wally Strange |
| Diana Muldaur | Angela Stafford |
| Nicholas Pryor | Freddie Dayton |
| Lisa Eichhorn | Cynthia Dayton |
| Fernando Allende | Ricardo Montoya |
| Pedro Armendariz | Colonel Mateo |
| Frances Lee McCain | Miss Milray |
| Marian Mercer | Daisy Eastman |
| Concetta Tomei | Janet Crisp |
| Jacqueline Evans | Mrs Babbington |
| Angeles Gonzales | Housekeeper |
| Philip Guilmant | Reverend Babbington |
| Claudia Guzman | Rosa |
| Rodolfo Hernandez | Miguel |
| Martin Lassalle | Doctor |
| Alma Levy | Nurse |
| Julio Monterde | Manager |
| Rene Pereyra | Waiter |
| Jose Chavez Trowe | Watchman |

Based on the novel *Murder in Three Acts* (1935). 97 minutes.

*Murder in Three Acts*, written in 1935, was the first of Agatha Christie's novels to surpass the 10,000 mark in sales in its first year of publication, thus firmly establishing Christie as a best-selling author. It also did much to increase her popularity.

This film, which has been updated and transplanted to an Acapulco setting, begins with Hastings meeting his friend Hercule Poirot, the world-famous detective, at the airport in Acapulco. Poirot has travelled there to do some work on his memoirs, and reluctantly agrees to be a guest at a house party.

The enormous house, which belongs to their host Charles Cartwright, an American actor, overlooks the sea on three sides of a cliff. The guests include neurologist Dr Strange, Broadway actress Angela Stafford, playwright Janet Crisp,

Daisy Eastman and her daughter Jennifer (known as 'Egg'), Mr and Mrs Dayton, and the Reverend and Mrs Babbington.

While drinking a toast to their host, Reverend Babbington crumples to the floor, dead. Cartwright believes he may have been poisoned but, as Poirot asks, 'Who would want to kill an innocent old clergyman at a cocktail party?' and, anyway, analysis of his glass shows there was only gin and tonic in it.

After Charles leaves for his home in Los Angeles, Poirot does likewise to return to his memoirs, which he is having quite a time writing. Meanwhile, back in Acapulco, Dr Strange invites all those from the previous party to dinner. Dr Strange meets the same fate as the Reverend, choking to death after taking a drink.

Poirot and Charles Cartwright return, visiting

▲ Poirot on holiday: Peter Ustinov in Acapulco, Mexico, in *Murder in Three Acts*.

Colonel Mateo of the Acapulco Police. He informs them that Dr Strange was poisoned by a derivative of an orchid pesticide. But how it got into his body is another mystery, as analysis of his glass showed it to have contained only wine.

Snooping around in Strange's house, Poirot and Hastings come across a secret passage in the library; perhaps this is how the missing butler disappeared. But all they find is a servant girl on her way to an assignation.

As exhumation of Reverend Babbington reveals that he was also murdered by the same poison found in the Doctor's body. It is obvious to Poirot that the two crimes are merely two halves of the same crime, although he later realizes this is a false assumption. Poirot also thinks that Babbington's murder may have been committed in error.

Gathering the suspects together, Poirot serves cocktails and this time it is Cartwright who falls choking to the floor. But he is all right – it was simply Poirot's collaboration with the actor in order to prove the point that the glasses of the two victims could easily have been switched.

Clues that finally help Poirot to solve the case include a murdered old lady in a sanitorium, a poisoned box of chocolates (a favourite Christie device), a happy family deck of cards, and the dress rehearsal of a play.

With the exception of Hercule Poirot, there is a complete change of characters in the film of *Murder in Three Acts*. Even Captain Hastings has replaced the Mr Satterthwaite who appeared in the novel; this is the only change on the positive side.

An unnecessary updating of the story, and change of location and nearly every character are the kind of things likely have Agatha Christie turning over in her grave.

Unlike *Ten Little Indians*, which has been filmed five times all in different settings, *Murder in Three Acts* as a story is not anywhere in the same class, and such bastardization of Christie's original work is only a disservice to this mediocre film.

Filmed in and around Acapulco, Mexico, *Murder in Three Acts* has some beautiful location photography, one of the few things of note in the film. Scott Swanton's writing, and direction by Gary Nelson, are nothing to brag about.

Ustinov plays Poirot with his usual panache, and Jonathan Cecil once more plays Hastings, taking down copious notes at every opportunity during the investigation.

The casting is uninspired. Tony Curtis, who offered a decent performance in *The Mirror Crack'd*, looks silly at times in his white curly wig, knee socks and short pants. The other performers, made up of television performers to cater to Warner Brothers television fans, add little. Typical Mexican cliches are invoked, such as 'It's not my job, I don't know,' in answer to Poirot's questioning of a Mexican menial.

# ≡1986≡

## Murder by the Book (TV)

Made in England. Directed by Lawrence Gordon Clark.

### CAST
▼

| | |
|---|---|
| Dame Peggy Ashcroft | Dame Agatha Christie |
| Ian Holm | Hercule Poirot |
| Richard Wilson | Sir Max Mallowan |
| Michael Aldridge | Edmund Cork |
| Dawn Archibald | Sally |
| John Atkinson | Edgecomb |
| Chico | Bingo |

Based on characters created by Agatha Christie. 51 mins.

▲ Poirot (Ian Holm) asks Christie (Dame Peggy Ashcroft) to shoot him rather than kill him off the way she has planned in *Murder by the Book*.

▲ Hercule Poirot (Ian Holm) must solve his own murder in *Murder by the Book*.

*Murder by the Book* is an odd little television film about the conflict between Agatha Christie and Hercule Poirot.

The film has Christie in a cat-and-mouse game with Poirot, her famous literary creation who first appeared in *The Mysterious Affair at Styles* in 1920.

While Christie's gardener Edgecomb busies himself with poisoning moles on the property, publisher Edmund Colt pays Christie a visit, urging her to allow publication of *Curtain*, a book written in about 1940 in which Hercule Poirot dies. As Christie is 85 years old and in failing health, her output of work has diminished, but the public is still clamoring for a new book.

Agatha begins to read the manuscript, which she last read 35 years ago; her dog Bingo senses something and begins to bark. Rushing to the front door, Christie flings it open to reveal none other than the one and only Hercule Poirot.

Poirot tells Christie that he has come to investigate a murder that has not yet occurred, further telling her that he knows not only the identity of the victim, but the killer as well. What he does not know is the time the crime will take place, or as yet the motive behind it.

After he discloses that it is himself that is to be murdered, he further tells Christie that she is his 'killer'. Poirot reveals how he has made his deductions, while Christie at first denies that she wants to get rid of him.

When Christie finally admits what he already knows, Poirot remarks that it is her jealousy of him that has driven her to kill him. 'You owe everything to me,' he quips.

While Christie goes to the kitchen to make cocoa, Poirot finds the manuscript. After a cat-and-mouse game involving a revolving table (readers of *Curtain* will be familiar with this), Christie notices Poirot sitting on the manuscript, which scatters all over the floor when she tries to grab it from him.

Poirot reads a few pages and is enraged at the way Christie has written of him, aged and arthritic. He is further outraged to learn that he simply dies of a heart attack at the end of the book.

▲ Ian Holm as Hercule Poirot and Dame Peggy Ashcroft as Agatha Christie in the ingenious *Murder by the Book*.

Christie is awakened by Sir Max; it seems that she had fallen asleep and spent the night in a chair – the Poirot confrontation was just a dream.

Made in 1986, the film was first shown in the US in 1990, concurrently with a television documentary marking the 100th anniversary of Christie's birth.

Dame Peggy Ashcroft, always the professional, and Ian Holm likewise, give excellent performances in this offbeat little production. John Price's editing is commendable, as does Peter Jessop's photography. Nick Evans produced; Howard Goodall did the music.

# ≡1987≡

## Sleeping Murder (TV)

Made in England. Directed by John Davies.

### CAST

| | |
|---|---|
| Joan Hickson | Miss Jane Marple |
| Frederick Treves | Dr James Kennedy |
| John Moulder-Brown | Giles Reed |
| Geraldine Alexander | Gwenda Reed |
| Jack Watson | Mr Foster |
| Esmond Knight | Mr Galbraith |
| John Bennett | Richard Erskine |
| Jean Anderson | Mrs Fane |
| Kenneth Cope | Jackie Afflick |
| Sheila Raynor | Shop Assistant |
| Terence Hardiman | Walter Fane |
| Joan Scott | Mrs Crocker |
| Geraldine Newman | Janet Erskine |
| Jean Hayward | Edith Paget |
| Eryl Maynard | Lily Kimble |
| Peter Spraggon | Detective Inspector Last |
| Ken Kitson | Jim Kimble |

Based on the novel *Sleeping Murder* (1976). 104 minutes.

Like *Curtain*, which was published in 1975, Agatha Christie wrote *Sleeping Murder* during the Second World War. These two novels were to be the final cases for Christie's most celebrated characters, although Miss Marple does not suffer the same fate as Hercule Poirot.

Christie, who was in failing health the last two years of her life, did not write any further novels after *Postern of Fate* in 1973. Realizing this, her publishers put together some previously published short stories and offered them under the title *Poirot's Early Cases* in 1974.

The problem of having no new Christie stories was certainly a daunting one to them, and they exerted considerable pressure on Christie to get her to release the novels they knew she was saving until after her death (they were successful in 1975, when she allowed *Curtain* to be published). However, *Sleeping Murder* would have to await the demise of the author (she died on January 12, 1976) before it saw the light of day.

The story concerns young Gwenda Reed and her husband Giles. The couple have been married for three months when they decide to return to England; they had met and married in New Zealand.

▲ Dr James Kennedy (Frederick Teves) has a vital clue that will help Miss Marple (Joan Hickson) solve the case in *Sleeping Murder*.

As Giles has a few business matters he wishes to attend to, Gwenda returns to England ahead of him. She comes across a charming villa in the seaside community of Dillworth, and decides to take up residence.

After settling in, she has a sense of *déjà vu*, coupled with a sensation of horror. These feelings disappear however and she gets on with the job of redecoration.

Going over the house and grounds, Gwenda discovers that a number of her remodelling ideas are in fact things that were previously there, i.e. she is simply changing some things back to the way they were.

These coincidences get to be too much for Gwenda to cope with, so she takes a little trip to the home of Mr and Mrs Raymond West, who are friends of Giles. It is there that she meets Miss Jane Marple, the shrewd, insightful spinster aunt of novelist Raymond. Raymond suggests they all go see a play, and it is in the theatre that Gwenda becomes hysterical upon hearing certain lines, although she cannot explain why.

The next morning she confides to Miss Marple that the lines of the play brought back to her a horrible memory of when she was a tiny child. She had seen a body lying at the foot of a staircase, and heard the same words that were spoken in the play. She also tells Miss Marple about the strange occurrences at her new home.

Giles now returns, and Gwenda seeks to find an answer to the problem. With Miss Marple's help, she is able to unlock the secrets of her memory, solving a mystery nearly 20 years old, as well as a murder that has resulted from their current investigations.

Critics were generally pleased with *Sleeping Murder*, but some wondered why Christie had held back its release for more than 30 years. *Curtain*, it is believed, was definitely held back as Hercule Poirot meets with death himself, and it was written as his final case. But Jane Marple triumphs once again in *Sleeping Murder*, and one has the feeling that she went on to solve further cases.

Joan Hickson's performance was up to its usual high standard here, and Geraldine Alexander and John Moulder-Brown are effective as Gwenda and Giles Reed. There is especially fine work from Frederick Treves and Jack Watson, as well as Esmond Knight, playing the small role of the retired land agent.

The remainder of the cast, along with direction by John Davies, and the other technical credits, is topnotch.

# ≡ 1987 ≡

## At Bertram's Hotel (TV)

Made in England. Directed by Mary McMurray.

CAST

| | |
|---|---|
| Joan Hickson | Miss Jane Marple |
| George Baker | Chief Inspector Fred Davy |
| James Cossins | Colonel Derek Luscombe |
| Joan Greenwood | Selina Hazy |
| Caroline Blakiston | Bess Sedgwick |
| Preston Lockwood | Canon Pennyfather |
| Edward Burnham | Dr Whittaker |
| Helena Michell | Elvira Blake |
| Philip Bretherton | Detective Inspector Campbell |
| Irene Sutcliffe | Miss Gorringe |
| Neville Phillips | Henry |
| Robert Reynolds | Ladislaus Malinowski |
| Peter Baldwin | Mr Humfries |
| Brian McGrath | Michael Gorman |
| Randal Herley | Richard Egerton |
| Kate Duchene | Rose |
| Helen Horton | Mrs Cabot |
| Henrietta Voigts | Alice |

Based on the novel *At Bertram's Hotel* (1965). 105 minutes.

▲ Miss Marple (Joan Hickson) discusses the case *At Bertram's Hotel* with Chief Inspector Davy (George Baker) as Michael Gorman (Brian McGrath) looks on.

Bertram's Hotel, the fictional hotel in the Christie novel, was based on the real-life Brown's Hotel in London, an establishment originally opened in 1837 that catered to the nobility and upper classes.

Raymond West, Miss Marple's successful novelist nephew, had already sent his aunt Jane on a holiday in the Caribbean the previous year; this time he leaves the choice up to her. She selects for her holiday a trip to Bertram's Hotel in London, a place where she had spent a few days when she was a teenager.

The return to the hotel is a nostalgic one for Miss Marple. It seems that she is in a time warp; everything is just as she remembers. Although she cannot pinpoint it however, she nonetheless has a feeling that things are not quite right somehow.

Enter Chief Inspector Davy of Scotland Yard, who unofficially observes the goings-on of suspects in several spectacular robberies who have been traced to the hotel.

One of the hotel's guests is Bess Sedgwick, the oft-married, do-everything celebrity, certainly a personality incongruous with the usual type of Bertram's guest.

One day Miss Marple accidentally learns the reason Bess is at the hotel: she had a daughter from one of her many marriages who is also staying at the hotel with her guardian, Colonel Derek Luscombe. Bess tells Luscombe that he ought to take the girl away from the hotel. But Miss Marple is not the only one who overhears this conversation; Elvira, the daughter, is nearby and disappears shortly after hearing this startling news.

Meanwhile, hotel commissionaire Michael Gorman, who happened to have once been married to Bess Sedgwick, is murdered. Now Chief Inspector Davy launches his investigation openly. Right before the murder, elderly Canon Penny-father, a guest at the hotel, was struck over the head entering a room and woke up elsewhere. Could the two events be related?

While Inspector Davy is running his investigation, Miss Marple discovers the true identities of a number of the staff and guests of Bertram's, and solves the case in her usual shrewd and inimitable style.

Once again, Joan Hickson's performance as Miss Marple is a joy to Christie fans (as well as anyone who appreciates great acting). George Baker, as the Inspector, is also fine, as is Joan Greenwood, in one of her last roles as Miss Marple's friend Selina Hazy. Nice work too by James Cossins as Colonel Luscombe, and Caroline Blakiston as the madcap society woman Bess Sedgwick.

▲ (Above) Joan Hickson as Miss Marple, George Baker (Chief Inspector Davy), (below) Caroline Blakiston (Bess Sedgwick) and Brian McGrath (Michael Gorman) in *At Bertram's Hotel*.

# ≡ 1987 ≡

## Nemesis (TV)

Made in England. Directed by David Tucker.

CAST

| | |
|---|---|
| Joan Hickson | Miss Jane Marple |
| John Horsley | Professor Wanstead |
| Margaret Tyzack | Clothilde Bradbury-Scott |
| Peter Copley | Archdeacon Brabazon |
| Helen Cherry | Miss Temple |
| Anna Cropper | Anthea Bradbury-Scott |
| Peter Tilbury | Lionel Peel |
| Bruce Payne | Michael Rafiel |
| Roger Hammond | Mr Broadribb |
| Liz Fraser | Mrs Brent |
| Valerie Lush | Lavinia Glynne |
| Joanna Hole | Madge |
| Jane Booker | Miss Cooke |
| Alison Skilbeck | Miss Barrow |
| Patrick Godfrey | Mr Schuster |
| Ann Queensbury | Miss Wimpole |
| Marlene Sidaway | Miss Trollope |
| Jonathan Stephens | Policeman |
| Diana Agnew | Receptionist |
| Roger Booth | Mr Pelham |
| Reginald Stewart | Mr Hallowes |

Liz Adams, Maraquita Annis, Lesley Burt, Jack Crosbie, Jeremy Davies, Jack Frost, Eileen Matthews, Mary Maxfield, Bette Shawe, Cy Town · · · · · · · Members of the Coach Party.
and: Frank Gatliff.

Based on the novel *Nemesis* (1971). 104 minutes.

*Nemesis*, written in 1971, was the last story Agatha Christie wrote about the observant spinster of St. Mary Mead, Miss Jane Marple. *Sleeping Murder*, written in the 1940s, was the last published Miss Marple book, appearing just after Christie's death in 1976.

The film opens with Miss Marple observing the obituaries in the newspaper; the name Jason Rafiel strikes a chord with her. Rafiel had appeared in the book (and two television film versions of) *A Caribbean Mystery*.

Rafiel, a great admirer of the shrewdness and capabilities of Miss Marple, has left the old lady £20,000 in his will, providing of course that she can investigate and solve a certain crime.

The problem is, at least temporarily, that Miss

Marple has no idea just which crime it is, as it is not specifically detailed. This causes Miss Marple a certain degree of consternation until a month after Rafiel's death, when a letter arrives informing her the late Mr Rafiel had booked her on a tour of famous homes and gardens.

Boarding the tour bus with nothing to go on but her wits and powers of observation, Miss Marple takes in her fellow passengers. She wonders whether the crime she has been commissioned to investigate is one that has already taken place or one that will take place.

She strikes up conversations with her fellow travellers, paying attention at the same time to the tour locations for insight to any clues. Only one person admits to even having heard of Jason Rafiel.

▲ Miss Marple (Joan Hickson) must solve a ten-year-old mystery in *Nemesis*. L-R: Clothilde Bradbury-Scott (Margaret Tyzack), Lavinia Glynne (Valerie Lush), Anthea Bradbury-Scott (Anna Cropper) and Miss Jane Marple (Joan Hickson).

After several days, Miss Marple is approached by a woman who tells her that Rafiel had wanted Miss Marple to come to the family home, so naturally she accepts.

Arriving there, she meets the Bradbury-Scott sisters, Clothilde, Anthea, and Lavinia. Lavinia is a widow; the other two are spinsters.

Miss Marple discovers that ten years before, Rafiel's son Michael was convicted of murder: this must be what she has been commissioned for.

Returning to the town hotel, she is approached by Professor Wanstead, another friend of Rafiel, who has been instructed to tell something to Miss Marple. His information consists of the reiteration of a belief held by several important people that Michael Rafiel was innocent.

A dying clue from Miss Temple proves to be the linchpin in the case; she knows something of the victim of the ten-year-old crime. The tenacious Miss Marple comes through once again with the solution. Returning home, she picks up the paper and returns to her perusal of the obituaries.

Production by George Gallaccio (with some splendid photography), dramatization by T.R. Bowen, and direction by David Tucker are all done with the usual high standards by the BBC.

Joan Hickson, who by now has developed quite a following, shines once again as Miss Marple, and she is joined by some fine actors including John Horsley, Margaret Tyzack, Peter Copley and Helen Cherry, all professionals of the first rank whose performances give an added lustre to the production.

## Murder at the Vicarage (TV)

Made in England. Directed by Julian Amyes.

CAST

| | |
|---|---|
| Joan Hickson | Miss Jane Marple |
| Paul Eddington | Reverend Leonard Clement |
| Cheryl Campbell | Griselda Clement |
| Robert Lang | Colonel Lucius Protheroe |
| David Waller | Colonel Melchett |
| Norma West | Mrs Lestrange |
| James Hazeldine | Lawrence Redding |
| Rosalie Crutchley | Mrs Price-Ridley |
| Polly Adams | Ann Protheroe |
| Tara MacGowran | Lettice Protheroe |
| Christopher Good | Christopher Hawes |
| Michael Browning | Dr Haydock |
| David Horovitch | Detective Inspector Slack |
| Ian Brimble | Detective Sergeant Lake |
| Jack Galloway | Bill Archer |
| Rachel Weaver | Mary Wright |
| Barbara Hicks | Mrs Hartnell |
| Deddie Davies | Mrs Salisbury |

Based on the novel *Murder at the Vicarage* (1930). 94 minutes.

▲ The Reverend Leonard Clement (Paul Eddington) and his wife Griselda Clement (Cheryl Campbell) blissfully unaware of the murder about to happen in their home in *Murder at the Vicarage*.

*Murder at the Vicarage*, written in 1930, was the first of Agatha Christie's stories to introduce the wise, watchful spinster Miss Jane Marple, and the fictional village of St Mary Mead. Although Miss Marple would develop quite a following over the years, Christie did not write another Miss Marple novel for 12 more years (the character did, however, appear in the short story collection *The Thirteen Problems* in 1932).

*Murder at the Vicarage*, adapted by Moie Charles and Barbara Toy, was an extremely successful play; it opened at the London Playhouse on December 14, 1949, produced by and starring Reginald Tate. The play, which was praised by critics and the public alike, ran for nearly five years.

The London *Times*, reviewing the play the day after it opened, stated: 'Everyone has a motive for killing. Nobody, unhappily, has any good stage reason for living. It is not until the final scene – the pressure of events then forcing two of the characters into melodramatic life – that we become aware that there was, after all, an effective

▲ Colonel Lucius Protheroe (Robert Lang), his daughter (Tara MacGowan) and wife (Polly Adams) in *Murder at the Vicarage.*

one-act play in Mrs Christie's novel.' The play was revived quite successfully in 1975 starring Barbara Mullen as Miss Marple.

For the film, which remains faithful to the original novel, Joan Hickson is once again cast as the spinster who takes parallels from everyday life and ordinary people in her small village to help her solve crimes.

The story centres on Colonel Lucius Protheroe, an unpopular magistrate and churchwarden in the village of St Mary Mead. Even the vicar, Leonard Clement, remarks to his wife one day that the world would be done a favour should someone decide to do away with the Colonel.

Gossip among the villagers reveals that there are others who feel the same way about the Colonel, so it comes as no great surprise to anyone when Protheroe is murdered.

It seems the Colonel had an appointment with the vicar, hence the place of discovery of his body. The vicar, however, was not there, as a bogus telephone message got him out of the way.

Miss Marple, who happens to live next door to the vicarage, is naturally in on the case, and

it is up to her to separate the clues and solve the crime. Was it the Colonel's unfaithful wife and/ or her lover, Lawrence Redding? Was it daughter Lettice Protheroe, who was waiting for her father to die to inherit his money? Or what about poacher Bill Archer, who had been dealt with rather severely by the Colonel?

There are certainly an abundance of suspects and motives in *Murder at the Vicarage,* a popular Christie device, although in this story the victim is more unpleasant than usual.

Lawrence Redding confesses to the crime, but Miss Marple is unconvinced; he may be only trying to shield someone. Or is it a clever way of throwing off suspicion?

While Inspector Slack and Dr Haydock take up the case officially, Miss Marple manages to sift through the labyrinthine plot, evidence, suspects, etc., and comes up with the right answer: a trap that the killer will fall into.

Joan Hickson again deserves our applause as Miss Marple; Paul Eddington and Cheryl Campbell are also in good form as the Clements, and there is a beautiful performance from Robert Lang as the unpopular Colonel Protheroe.

*Murder at the Vicarage* was the first and probably best Miss Marple story, and fans of Christie should be delighted at the tastefulness and style that went into this production.

## 4.50 From Paddington (TV)

### Made in England. Directed by Martyn Friend.

CAST

| | |
|---|---|
| Joan Hickson | Miss Jane Marple |
| Maurice Denham | Luther Crackenthorpe |
| Joanna David | Emma Crackenthorpe |
| David Horovitch | Detective Inspector Slack |
| David Waller | Chief Inspector Duckham |
| Andrew Burt | Dr John Quimper |
| Jill Meager | Lucy Eyelsbarrow |
| John Hallam | Cedric Crackenthorpe |
| David Beames | Bryan Eastley |
| Bernard Brown | Harold Crackenthorpe |
| Robert East | Alfred Crackenthorpe |
| Mona Bruce | Elspeth MacGillicuddy |
| Juliette Mole | Anna Stravinska |
| Ian Brimble | Detective Sergeant Lake |
| Pamela Pitchford | Mrs Kidder |
| Rhoda Lewis | Mrs Brogan |
| Leslie Adams | Desk Sergeant |
| Nicholas Blane | Paddington Porter |
| Katy Jarrett | Mary |
| Alan Penn | Patmore |
| Christopher Haley | Alexander Eastley |
| Daniel Steel | James Stoddart-West |

Based on the novel *4.50 From Paddington* (1957). 103 minutes.

Agatha Christie's 1957 novel, *4.50 From Paddington*, had been turned into the first of a series of several films starring Dame Margaret Rutherford by British MGM Studios in 1962.

This television film, made in 1988, restored the character of Elspeth MacGillicuddy, who had been replaced by Miss Marple in the 1962 film.

The film opens at London's Paddington Station with the London *Times* carrying the headline 'Russians in Space'. Elspeth MacGillicuddy is returning to her home in St Mary Mead, travelling by train. After waking from a nap, she witnesses the strangling of a woman on a train travelling the same direction on adjacent tracks.

When she arrives in her village, she goes directly to the home of that shrewd, observant little old lady with the fondness for knitting, Miss Jane Marple. Miss Marple, an old friend, listens to Elspeth's story and the two women set off for the local police station.

Detective Inspector Slack, who has encountered Miss Marple in the past, takes the trouble to have a search made of the train and areas through which it had travelled, but no body can be found and he thinks that perhaps this time Miss Marple is off on a wild goose chase.

Miss Marple, however, tells him that 'Elspeth MacGillicuddy may not be a sophisticated person, but she saw what she saw', and decides to tackle the investigation herself.

Miss Marple enlists the aid of young Lucy Eyelsbarrow, who secures a position as a domestic at Rutherford Hall, home of the Crackenthorpe family. Since the Hall and its estate are a likely place to drop a body (Miss Marple took the same train trip that her friend did, and deduced the body is somewhere around the grounds), she wants Lucy on the spot to look for clues.

▲ Miss Marple (Joan Hickson) assists Detective Inspector Slack (David Horovitch, left) and Sergeant Lake (Ian Brimble) in *4.50 from Paddington*.

tian sarcophagus, which leads her to the theory that the murderer was someone familiar with Rutherford Hall. No one admits to knowing the dead woman, and it takes an additional two murders of members of the Crackenthorpe family before Miss Marple is able to solve the crimes, with the aid of Elspeth MacGillicuddy.

Martyn Friend's direction in *4.50 From Paddington* is first rate, and there is a fine period atmosphere of the late 1950s created here.

There are also some fine performances. Joan Hickson, who played Mrs Kidder in the 1962 film of this story, *Murder She Said*, turns in another of her splendid renditions of Miss Marple; by now she had been widely acknowledged as the genuine article. Maurice Denham, who played Inspector Japp in *The Alphabet Murders* and also Mr Parker Pyne in two television films in the 1982 Thames TV Christie series, lends his professionalism to the role of the difficult Luther Crackenthorpe.

Repeating their roles in earlier productions are David Horovitch and Ian Brimble as Detective Inspector Slack (the novel featured Inspector Craddock) and Detective Sergeant Lake, respectively. David Waller, who portrayed Colonel Melchett earlier in 1988 in *Murder at the Vicarage*, is fine here as Chief Inspector Duckham.

Joanna David, Andrew Burt, John Hallam and Jill Meager are also winning in their respective parts, and the technical credits are up to the usual high standards of this wonderful BBC series.

This she does while ostensibly practicing golf on the estate; she finds a clue when she is pretending to look for a lost ball. Miss Marple is pleased.

She has reason to be pleased further when Lucy discovers the missing corpse in an Egyp-

▲ The stars of *4.50 from Paddington*. L-R.: Joan Hickson as Miss Jane Marple, David Waller (Chief Inspector Duckham) and Joanna David (Emma Crackenthorpe).

# ≡ 1988 ≡

## Appointment With Death

### Made in England. Directed by Michael Winner.

CAST

| | |
|---|---|
| Peter Ustinov | Hercule Poirot |
| Sir John Gielgud | Colonel Carbury |
| Lauren Bacall | Lady Westholme |
| David Soul | Jefferson Cope |
| Piper Laurie | Emily Boynton |
| Carrie Fisher | Nadine Boynton |
| Jenny Seagrove | Dr Sarah King |
| Hayley Mills | Miss Quinton |
| Nicholas Guest | Lennox Boynton |
| John Terlesky | Raymond Boynton |
| Valerie Richards | Carol Boynton |
| Amber Bezer | Ginevera Boynton |
| Michael Craig | Lord Peel |
| Douglas Sheldon | Captain Rogers |
| Michael Sarne | Healy |
| Rupert Horrox | British Official |
| Hugh Brophy | British Official |
| Mohammad Hirzalla | Hassan |
| Marcel Solomon | Ship Captain |
| Danny Muggia | Italian Policeman |
| Ruggero Comploy | Tourist Guide |
| Lutuf Nuayser | Boynton Driver |
| Babi Neeman | Vendor |

Based on the novel *Appointment With Death* (1938). 102 minutes.

Like so many of Agatha Christie's filmed novels, *Appointment With Death* had been a stage play, opening on March 31, 1945, at the Piccadilly Theatre in London. It was produced by Terence De Marney, who had starred in *Ten Little Indians* in 1943. Christie adapted the play herself, making several changes – the most noticeable being the absence of Hercule Poirot.

Happily, for the 1988 motion picture, which was splendidly photographed on location by David Gurfinkel, the Poirot character was restored in the person of Peter Ustinov, making his sixth appearance as the Belgian detective.

The film concerns the wealthy but unhappy Boynton family, whose centre of focus revolves around the unscrupulous matriarch Emily Boynton; her power and personality dominate her entire family, as well as others with whom they come in contact.

The family takes a holiday, and it is on board ship heading for Jerusalem that Poirot first encounters them. He overhears a conversation in which someone utters 'You see don't you, that she's got to be killed?' and immediately he is in his element.

Aside from the Boynton family, there are American Lady Westholme, who has married into the British aristocracy, her companion Miss Quinton, an impressionable and easily influenced young woman, the Boynton family lawyer Jefferson Cope, who has been carrying on an affair with Nadine, and Dr Sarah King, who had

▶ Peter Ustinov as Hercule Poirot in *Appointment with Death*.

▲ Colonel Carbury (Sir John Gielgud) meets Poirot (Peter Ustinov) and Dr Sarah King (Jenny Seagrove) as their ship docks in Palestine in *Appointment with Death*.

assisted Mrs Boynton earlier on and who is interested in son Raymond.

After landing, Poirot is met by Colonel Carbury, head of the police force and the two men reminisce about old times, while the family and others head for a campsite at Petra.

While the principal characters go off in different directions, certain sub-plots are introduced that may be relevant to the upcoming murder or merely red herrings.

Mrs Boynton had expressed a desire to be left alone, and surprisingly permitted the others out of her sight. She is left sitting in a chair in the sun; when the others come back several hours later, she is just where they left her – except now she is no longer breathing.

▲ The cast of the 1988 version of *Appointment with Death*. L-R, back: John Terlesky as Raymond Boynton, Nicholas Guest (Lennox Boynton), Sir John Gielgud (Colonel Carbury) and David Soul (Jefferson Cope). L-R, front: Amber Bezer (Ginevera Boynton), Valerie Richards (Carol Boynton), Piper Laurie (Emily Boynton), Carrie Fisher (Nadine Boynton), Peter Ustinov (Hercule Poirot, sitting), Lauren Bacall (Lady Westholme), Jenny Seagrove (Dr Sarah King) and Hayley Mills (Miss Quinton).

The official investigation of the cause of her death reveals she was murdered by a fatal dose of digitoxin, injected by syringe into her wrist. As Poirot happens to be in the right place at the right time, he undertakes the case. There are a surfeit of suspects, as Mrs Boynton was not only a sadist but a blackmailer as well.

But Poirot is able to get his famous little grey cells into high gear and clear up the matter, even giving the killer a way to save further disgrace.

*Appointment With Death* has quite a few high points. Firstly, the excellent location photography by David Gurfinkel is an asset, as well as Arnold Crust's crisp editing and fine clear sound by Eli Yarkoni.

Anthony Shaffer, who adapted the screenplays for *Death On the Nile* and *Evil Under the Sun*, wrote the screenplay for this film, with assistance from director Michael Winner and Peter Buckman.

The costumes by John Bloomfield, as well as Pino Donaggio's music, help to create a good period atmosphere for the film.

Peter Ustinov gives a good performance as Poirot. This was his first cinema Poirot film since *Evil Under the Sun* although he had played the Belgian sleuth in three television films for Warner Brothers CBS Television in the mid-1980s.

Some Christie alumni also turn in fine portrayals – Lauren Bacall, who had appeared in *Murder On the Orient Express* in 1974 as Lady Westholme, Sir John Gielgud, who also appeared in *Murder On the Orient Express*, as Colonel Carbury and is always a joy to watch, and Hayley Mills, who starred in the 1972 film *Endless Night*, as Miss Quinton.

Others in the cast of note are David Soul as the family lawyer, Carrie Fisher as daughter Nadine, and Jenny Seagrove as the earnest young Doctor Sarah King. Piper Laurie is also quite effective, although perhaps not quite as old and ugly as the character in Christie's novel.

The direction by Michael Winner is effective, keeping up a good degree of suspension and maintaining a smooth pace throughout.

# 1989

## Ten Little Indians

Made in England. Directed by Alan Birkinshaw.

### CAST

| | |
|---|---|
| Donald Pleasence | Mr Justice Lawrence Wargrave |
| Herbert Lom | General Branko Romensky |
| Frank Stallone | Captain Philip Lombard |
| Sarah Maur Thorp | Vera Claythorne |
| Brenda Vaccaro | Marion Marshall |
| Warren Berlinger | William Henry Blore |
| Neil McCarthy | Anthony James Marston |
| Yehuda Efroni | Dr Hans Werner |
| Moira Lister | Ethel Rodgers |
| Paul Smith | Elmo Rodgers |

Based on the novel *Ten Little Niggers* (1939). 100 minutes.

This fifth screen version of Agatha Christie's classic story was filmed on location. Previously, it had been a highly successful play in England and the United States, and is probably the Christie story familiar to most people. Former film versions were done in 1945 with Barry Fitzgerald and Walter Huston, in 1949 with John Stuart and John Bentley, in 1965 with Wilfrid Hyde-White and Dennis Price, and in 1975 with Sir Richard Attenborough and Oliver Reed.

Like its three film predecessors, this version of *Ten Little Indians* features still another change of location – this time it is a safari in Africa.

The invitees to Mr U.N. Owen's little party board the train, then disembark to meet Philip Lombard who, along with a group of tongue-clicking natives, is to lead them to their destination. One of the guests, Anthony Marston, arrives by plane; the Rodgers' are already waiting at the camp.

The group is cut off when natives cut the rope of the basket used to transport the guests across a chasm.

Aside from Lombard and young Marston, the guests include Judge Wargrave, Hollywood-type Marion Marshall, Mr William H. Blore, lovely Vera Claythorne, Russian General Romensky, Dr Hans Werner, and American couple Ethel and

▲ The cast of the 1989 version of *Ten Little Indians* includes (L-R) Herbert Lom as General Romensky, Warren Berlinger (Mr Blore), Brenda Vaccaro (Marion Marshall), Yehuda Efroni (Dr Werner), Donald Pleasence (Judge Wargrave), Neil McCarthy (Anthony Marston), Frank Stallone (Captain Lombard) and Sarah Maur Thorp (Vera Claythorne).

Elmo Rodgers – he is a large, surly fellow who does the cooking.

Following the first night dinner, a gramophone record is put on by Rodgers that accuses each person of a past crime. Some of the guests want to turn it off, but Rodgers, who put it on in the first place, insists that it be played to its conclusion.

Shortly afterwards, Anthony Marston drinks a poisoned cocktail, and Mrs Rodgers is killed not long afterwards. The following morning, the guests decide to search for Mr Owen, who may be in hiding, and the General is pushed off a cliff to his death.

Other murders follow rapidly according to the nursery rhyme; the massive Rodgers is found with an axe in his skull, and soon there are only two guests left alive. Which can it be? Those unfamiliar with the story will be in for a surprise.

This film was not critically praised by a great number of people. *Variety*, in its review of May 17, 1989 stated: 'The filmmakers convey little sense of danger, with characters often seen in exaggerated long reaction shots.' They also noted the fact that this motion picture was based on Agatha Christie's play, which they termed a 'curious credit'. However, one must certainly appreciate that all the films made of this story contained the same ending as the play, not the novel, so in essence this is the only film that got that detail correct!

There are a number of interesting details in this motion picture. While not the classic or definitive film the first two versions of the story are, the 1989 version of *Ten Little Indians* nevertheless is the only one of the films to be set in the time period of the original work, and there is some good camerawork by Arthur Lavia and period costumes by Dianna Villiers.

Sir Noel Coward's *Mad Dogs and Englishmen*, a popular song in the thirties, is used to good advantage in several instances.

Casting for this film is not without interest. Donald Pleasence, a first-rate actor, makes a good judge; this is the only film where the character's name is the same as the Christie novel. Herbert Lom, the only actor to appear in a remake of a remake of a Christie film (he played Dr Armstrong in the 1975 *Ten Little Indians*) gives a decent performance as the Russian General.

Newcomer Sarah Maur Thorp does a very fine job as Miss Claythorne. *Variety* said: 'The Lovely Sarah Maur Thorp brings passion to her part as an English governess whose crime was that she accidentally caused a boy's death.' Neil McCarthy also scores – here again the character's name from the novel is used for the first time in a film.

Frank Stallone, brother of the better-known Sylvester Stallone, shows little emotion in the role of Lombard. Brenda Vaccaro's character has been changed to that of a middle-aged Hollywood actress, who admits to a past lesbian affair, and Yehuda Efroni's Doctor is now a German.

Although the surname of Rodgers (a 'd' has been added) returns, they are now an American couple. Paul Smith, the enormous villain of the 1980 film *Popeye*, seems miscast here.

The Cannon Group produced this film for Breton Films; Jackson Hunsicker and Gerry O'Hars adapted the script. This film was produced by Harry Alan Towers, who also did the marvellous 1965 version.

Following is a list of all five films including the character names and the actors who played them. It is interesting to note that Blore and Lombard are the only names that remain the

▲ General Romensky (Herbert Lom) confronts Marion Marshall (Brenda Vaccaro) in *Ten Little Indians*.

same throughout, and only in 1989 were two of the novel's characters names used. The General, called MacArthur in the novel, was never so named in any film (and on stage he was called MacKenzie).

▲ L-R: Captain Lombard (Frank Stallone), Vera Claythorne (Sarah Maur Thorp), Judge Wargrave (Donald Pleasence), Mr Blore (Warren Berlinger) and Dr Werner (Yehuda Efroni) examine the poem *Ten Little Indians*, which was conspicuously left in the main tent in the 1989 version of *Ten Little Indians*.

| 1945 | 1949 | 1965 | 1975 | 1989 |
|---|---|---|---|---|
| Barry Fitzgerald (Judge Francis J. Quincannon) | Bruce Belfrage (Sir Lawrence Wargrave) | Wilfrid Hyde-White (Judge Arthur Cannon) | Sir Richard Attenborough (Judge Arthur Cannon) | Donald Pleasence (Judge Lawrence Wargrave) |
| Walter Huston (Dr Edward Armstrong) | John Stuart (Dr Edward Armstrong) | Dennis Price (Dr Edward Armstrong) | Herbert Lom (Dr Edward Armstrong) | Yehuda Efroni (Dr Hans Werner) |
| Louis Hayward (Philip Lombard) | John Bentley (Philip Lombard) | Hugh O'Brian (Hugh Lombard) | Oliver Reed (Hugh Lombard) | Frank Stallone (Philip Lombard) |
| Roland Young (William Henry Blore) | Campbell Singer (William H. Blore) | Stanley Holloway (William Henry Blore) | Gert Frobe (Wilhelm Blore) | Warren Berlinger (William Henry Blore) |
| June Duprez (Vera Claythorne) | Sally Rogers (Vera Claythorne) | Shirley Eaton (Ann Clyde) | Elke Sommer (Vera Clyde) | Sarah Maur Thorp (Vera Claythorne) |
| Sir C. Aubrey Smith (General Sir John Mandrake) | Arthur Wontner (General Mackenzie) | Leo Genn (General Sir John Mandrake) | Adolfo Celi (General Andre Salve) | Herbert Lom (General Branko Romensky) |
| Dame Judith Anderson (Emily Brent) | Margery Bryce (Emily Brent) | Daliah Lavi (Ilona Bergen) | Stephane Audran (Ilona Morgan) | Brenda Vaccaro (Marion Marshall) |
| Mischa Auer (Prince Nikita Starloff) | Douglas Hurn (Antony Marston) | Fabian (Mike Raven) | Charles Aznavour (Michel Raven) | Neil McCarthy (Anthony Marston) |
| Richard Haydn (Thomas Rogers) | Stanley Lemin (Thomas Rogers) | Mario Adorf (Josef Grohmann) | Alberto DeMendoza (Otto Martino) | Paul Smith (Elmo Rodgers) |
| Queenie Leonard (Ethel Rogers) | Elizabeth Maude (Ethel Rogers) | Marianne Hoppe (Elsa Grohmann) | Maria Rohm (Elsa Martino) | Moira Lister (Ethel Rodgers) |
| Harry Thurston (Boatman) | Barry Steele (Fred Narracot, Boatman) | — | — | — |

# ≡ 1989 ≡

## A Caribbean Mystery (TV)

Made in England. Directed by Christopher Petit.

### CAST

| | |
|---|---|
| Joan Hickson | Miss Jane Marple |
| Donald Pleasence | Jason Rafiel |
| Frank Middlemass | Major Palgrave |
| T.P. McKenna | Dr Grahame |
| Adrian Lukis | Tim Kendal |
| Sophie Ward | Molly Kendal |
| Michael Feast | Edward Hillingdon |
| Sheila Ruskin | Evelyn Hillingdon |
| Robert Swan | Greg Dyson |
| Sue Lloyd | Lucky Dyson |
| Barbara Barnes | Esther Walters |
| Stephen Bent | Jackson |
| Joe Mydell | Inspector Weston |
| Valerie Buchanan | Victoria |
| Isabelle Lucas | Auntie Johnson |
| Shaughan Seymour | Napier |
| Trevor Bowen | Raymond West |
| James Curran | Piers Musgrave |

Based on the novel *A Caribbean Mystery* (1964). 95 minutes.

*A Caribbean Mystery*, taken from the 1964 Christie novel, was the tenth of the splendid BBC adaptations of the Miss Marple television films, starring the wonderful Joan Hickson. A mediocre television film of the story had been produced in 1983.

Raymond West, the novelist nephew of Miss Jane Marple, convinces his aunt to take a Caribbean holiday, for which he will pay. Miss Marple takes him up on the offer, and finds herself on the sunny isle of St Honore.

There, at the Golden Palm Hotel, she encounters Major Palgrave, a retired army officer whose verbosity bores Miss Marple and the other guests. But when his talks get around to murder, the sharp spinster pricks up her ears. Just when he is about to show her a photograph of a killer, his sees something and hurriedly puts it back in his wallet.

Miss Marple's curiosity is aroused; she wants to see the picture but there is no opportunity for her to do so – the Major succumbs in the night and it is put down to high blood pressure.

Now Miss Marple is really interested, especially when Dr Grahame tells her he cannot find the picture she so desperately wants to see.

When it is shown that Palgrave did not suffer from high blood pressure, Miss Marple is convinced it was murder, and only a preamble of something yet to come.

Not surprisingly, she is proved right, and the police get on the ball when Victoria, the servant who discovered Palgrave's body, is also murdered. As Miss Marple investigates, she discovers most of the guests have something to hide (a common Christie trait).

Before she can solve the case however, Lucky Dyson is killed – the killer mistakes her for the real victim. Returning to her rainy little village, Miss Marple is glad to be back home.

*A Caribbean Mystery* was produced and presented with the same tastefulness and style that marked all the BBC's Christie productions. Christopher Petit does a good job handling the direction, and a splendid cast is on hand.

There is Joan Hickson – by now the quintessential Miss Jane Marple, going about her business in a capable, thoughtful way; Donald Pleasence as the invalid Jason Rafiel, especially good in scenes of conspiratorial delight with Miss Marple; Frank Middlemass as the glass-eyed, garrulous Major; and T.P. McKenna as the good Dr Graham.

Other members of the cast, who are primarily British theatre and television actors, do very well in their parts and are far more believeable than the actors who were cast in the same parts six years previously.

This is a good example of the right way to cast a film – choosing the right person for the role rather than relying on a performer's name or current popularity.

Location filming in Barbados, West Indies, also enhances this film, as does Ken Howard's music (he did it for all the Hickson-Marple television films).

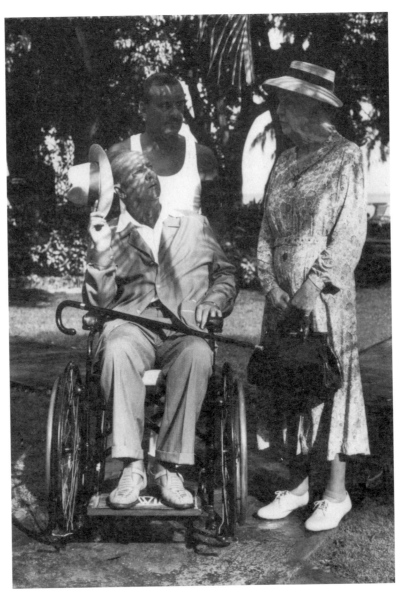

▲ Jason Rafiel (Donald Pleasence, seated), Jackson (Stephen Bent) and Miss Jane Marple (Joan Hickson) in *A Caribbean Mystery*.

## The Man in the Brown Suit (TV)
### Made in Hollywood. Directed by Alan Grint.

CAST

| | |
|---|---|
| Edward Woodward | Sir Eustace Pedlar |
| Tony Randall | Reverend Chichester |
| Stephanie Zimbalist | Anne Beddingfield |
| Nickolas Grace | Guy Underhill |
| Ken Howard | Gordon Race |
| Rue McClanahan | Susan Blair |
| Simon Dutton | Harry Lucas |
| Jack Taylor | Police Inspector |
| Maria Casal | Anita |
| Federico Luciano | Leo Carton |
| Rose McVeigh | Valerie |
| Jorge Bosso | Businessman |
| Jose Canalejas | First Arab |
| Tiby Costa | Second Arab |
| Robert Case | Ship Captain |
| James Duggan | Steward |
| Gabriel Edu | Shop Clerk |
| Bill Holden | John Eardsley |
| Charley Mahdy | First Taxi Driver |
| Aldo Sambrell | Second Taxi Driver |
| Alito Rodgers | Third Taxi Driver |
| Elias Mayali | Policeman |
| Antonio Ross | Concierge |
| Claudio Vicente | Pianist |

Based on the novel *The Man in the Brown Suit* (1924). 95 minutes.

Agatha Christie found her 1924 novel *The Man in the Brown Suit* a rather difficult one to write. Her hard work evidently paid off, as this, her fifth novel, was critically praised, as well as appreciated by the public.

The 1989 television film, which, like many others, has been updated, begins in Cairo with the shooting of a cabaret singer at a villa. The action then cuts to Cairo Airport, where American traveller Anne Beddingfield witnesses a man run over by automobile. A man in a brown suit claiming to be a doctor attempts to pick the pocket of the dead man, and Anne finds herself under arrest.

Gordon Race of the United States Embassy comes to Anne's aid in response to her call, bailing her out of trouble and suggesting that she go back home.

But Anne has other ideas; she is seeking adventure and would like to get to the bottom of this mystery. It may all revolve around a cruise ship, so Anne turns in her plane ticket and exchanges it for a ticket on the *Kilmorden Castle*.

On board she encounters Sir Eustace Pedlar, the wealthy man at whose villa the cabaret singer was murdered, often-married Susan Blair, eccentric Reverend Chichester, Guy Underhill, Pedlar's secretary, and Gordon Race.

The first evening out, a wounded man stumbles into Anne's cabin, and she recognizes him as the man in the brown suit who tried to pick the pocket of the man killed at the airport. Something about him makes her want to trust him, but after she ministers to his wound, he vanishes.

▲ Cast members of *The Man in the Brown Suit* include (L-R) Stephanie Zimbalist as Anne Beddingfield, Edward Woodward (Sir Eustace Pedlar), Tony Randall in disguise (Minks), Rue McClanahan (Suzy Blair) and Ken Howard (Gordon Race).

Later on Anne's cabin is ransacked, but she has no clue as to why or by whom, only that everyone seemed to want that particular cabin. During the ship's ball, a costume affair, Anne decides to take Susan Blair into her confidence, telling her everything she knows.

The two women search their own cabins, and in Susan's discover four pink diamonds hidden in the wall behind some tiles. The diamonds may have been those taken in a spectacular robbery at the Kimberley Mines in South Africa.

While on deck that night, a mysterious figure tries to push Anne overboard, but she is rescued in the nick of time by the man in the brown suit. Since the authorities are looking for him, he jumps ship at the first chance he gets, diving into the Mombasa harbour.

Going into the city, Anne is kidnapped in the market place and taken to a villa where she is held captive. Effecting an escape, she notices the Reverend Chichester, who she overhears works for the mysterious man known only as 'The Colonel'.

Several further attempts are made on Anne's life, the last by luring her away from her hotel with a note allegedly written to her by the man in the brown suit (who saves her life a second time). When the principals in the case return to Cairo, the mystery is finally resolved after many moves and countermoves.

Changing the location of the action to Cairo does not hurt *The Man in the Brown Suit*, in fact, Ken Westbury's beautiful photography of cascading waterfalls and other lush scenery is certainly an asset (the film was actually shot in Madrid and Cadiz). Producer Alan Shayne's high production values make the film worth watching, and there is a fairly well-written script by Carla Jean Wagner.

The best performance in the film is given by Edward Woodward as Sir Eustace Pedlar. Woodward, a versatile actor well known in England for the long-running *Callan* series, had just finished a five-year run as Robert McCall in *The Equalizer* for CBS Television.

Tony Randall, who had starred in 1966 as Hercule Poirot in *The Alphabet Murders*, is also good as an actor who plays several different parts. Simon Dutton, who was starring on British television as 'The Saint' at this time, is also effective as 'The Man in the Brown Suit'.

American television actors Ken Howard and Rue McClanahan are mediocre at best and certainly were cast for their tie-ins with CBS Television (both had been on CBS series). Stephanie Zimbalist, daughter of actor Efrem Zimbalist, shows a modicum of talent, but Warner Brothers Television's policy of casting performers for their appeal rather than talent is to the detriment of the film. They would do well to take a lesson from London Weekend Television and the BBC, who have flawlessly cast their actors to reflect the characters they portray, thus capturing the wonderful flavour of the manner in which Christie devised and created them.

# ≡ 1989 ≡

## The Adventure of the Clapham Cook (TV)

### Made in England. Directed by Edward Bennett.

CAST

| | |
|---|---|
| David Suchet | Hercule Poirot |
| Hugh Fraser | Captain Hastings |
| Philip Jackson | Chief Inspector Japp |
| Pauline Moran | Miss Lemon |
| Brigit Forsyth | Mrs Todd |
| Dermot Crowley | Arthur Simpson |
| Freda Dowie | Eliza Dunn |
| Antony Carrick | Mr Todd |
| Katy Murphy | Annie |
| Daniel Webb | Porter |
| Richard Bebb | Mr Cameron |
| Brian Poyser | Salvation Army Speaker |
| Frank Vincent | Purser |
| Philip Manikum | Police Sergeant |
| Jona Jones | Constable |
| Nicholas Coppin | Constable |

Based on the short shory *The Adventure of the Clapham Cook* (1951). 50 minutes.

London Weekend Television's first of over 30 stories featuring Hercule Poirot. *The Adventure of the Clapham Cook* first appeared in the short story collection entitled *The Under Dog & Other Stories* in 1951.

David Suchet, a versatile actor who had appeared as Inspector Japp in the 1985 television film *13 at Dinner*, is splendidly cast here as the Belgian detective.

The story opens as Hastings is reading a newspaper account of various crimes to Poirot, who admits he is more concerned with his wardrobe and taking care of his moustache than anything he has heard so far.

Just then a Mrs Todd calls on Poirot, asking him to find her missing cook. At first Poirot is insulted, but Mrs Todd's remarks seem to convince him that a good cook is just as important to some as jewels.

While accompanying Mrs Todd to her home at 88 Albert Street, Clapham, Poirot warns Hastings not to let Inspector Japp know about this case, as he is a bit sensitive about the interpretations put on searching for a missing domestic.

Questioning the housemaid, Poirot learns that the missing cook later sent for her things, although she had given no indication of leaving. Mr Todd believes there has been no crime, but he is still miffed at the loss of the cook.

The Todd's lodger, Arthur Simpson, apparently does not even realize the cook is gone, and can shed no light on the mystery. 'It is a curious case,' remarks Poirot, 'full of contradictory features.'

Poirot is outraged when he receives a note from the Todds, dismissing him from the case and offering one guinea for his time. Insulted, he determines to solve the problem.

After running into Inspector Japp, who is working on another case, Poirot realizes that the Inspector's case and that of the missing domestic are tied together. He places an advert in the papers, and gets a response from the missing cook.

Travelling to Carlisle in the north of England, he and Hastings discover that the servant was deliberately got out of the way by means of a ruse; she was to inherit a legacy and house, but only if she left immediately, hence her 'disappearance'.

▲ David Suchet stars as Hercule Poirot in *The Adventure of the Clapham Cook,* along with Hugh Fraser as Captain Hastings (top right), Pauline Moran as his loyal secretary Miss Lemon, and Philip Jackson as Inspector Japp.

Poirot learns from Annie, the Todd's maid, the real reason for the subterfuge, and is able to solve a murder as well as foil a robbery involving £90,000 of negotiable securities.

Commendations to all at London Weekend Television for this marvellous production, happily the first of many they have produced featuring Hercule Poirot.

David Suchet is outstanding as Poirot, capturing all the subtle nuances and eccentricities of the character. Hugh Fraser, Philip Jackson and Pauline Moran are all excellently cast, and there are flawless performances from every actor.

Clive Exton did the dramatization, and Christopher Gunning's splendid music is an asset to all these productions, which are stylishly, faithfully and beautifully realized by producer Bryan Eastman and the rest of the highly professional crew at London Weekend Television.

# ⚊⚊ 1989 ⚊⚊

## The Adventure of Johnnie Waverly (TV)

Made in England. Directed by Renny Rye.

CAST

| | |
|---|---|
| David Suchet | Hercule Poirot |
| Hugh Fraser | Captain Hastings |
| Philip Jackson | Chief Inspector Japp |
| Pauline Moran | Miss Lemon |
| Geoffrey Bateman | Marcus Waverly |
| Julia Chambers | Ada Waverly |
| Dominic Rouger | Johnnie Waverly |
| Patrick Jordan | Treadwell |
| Carol Frazer | Jessica Withers |
| Sandra Freeman | Miss Collins |
| Robert Putt | Rogers |
| Patrick Connor | Hughes |
| Philip Manikum | Sergeant |
| Jona Jones | Constable |
| Jonathan Magnanti | Policeman |
| Samantha Beckinsale | Barmaid |

Based on the short story *The Adventure of Johnnie Waverly* (1950). 50 minutes.

*The Adventure of Johnnie Waverly*, dramatized for London Weekend Television by Clive Exton, first appeared in the short story collection entitled *Three Blind Mice and Other Stories* in 1950.

It concerns a wealthy couple, Marcus and Ada Waverly, who have received several letters of extortion: unless a large sum of money is paid out, their small son Johnnie will be kidnapped.

Mr Waverly visits the celebrated private detective Hercule Poirot, as the police do not take the matter seriously. The letters have announced the precise day and time of the kidnapping, and Poirot decides to take the case.

When Poirot takes Waverly to Scotland Yard, Chief Inspector Japp tells them: 'We get a hundred of these things every day; we don't have the manpower to deal with all of them.' Waverly angrily dismisses the Inspector as a fool, and Poirot accompanies him to his country home.

Hastings has already arrived by car, and Poirot begins to familiarize himself with the house and grounds in order to aid him in forestalling the crime. Hastings tells Poirot he believes the letters to be the work of 'a gang of foreigners'.

Poirot wonders why the kidnappers should bother to announce the exact moment they will abduct the child; perhaps this is merely a red herring.

The evening before the scheduled day, Mrs Waverly is taken ill with dreadful cramps; she is still weak on the following morning. Meanwhile, Mr Waverly has discovered a handwritten note pinned to his pillow reminding him of the events.

▲ Julia Chambers and Dominic Rougere as mother and son in *The Adventure of Johnnie Waverley*.

He feels sure the note is the work of a disloyal servant, and decides to sack the lot of them. Poirot however tells him such action is 'the height of folly'.

Everyone receives a surprise when Chief Inspector Japp shows up. He has had a change of heart, and brings a number of policemen as a guard against anything happening to the boy. While Japp is positioning his men about the house and grounds, Poirot and Hastings take off to a nearby village to have a meal.

On the way back to the Waverly estate, Hastings' car breaks down. Poirot sets off on foot as he is determined to be back before twelve o'clock. As the clock in the Waverly study strikes twelve, a tramp is found outside on the grounds with chloroform and a note, but this turns out to be a diversion when a car speeds away with Johnnie seen in the back seat.

The clock in the study was put ahead ten minutes to confuse matters, but Poirot guarantees the safety of the boy to his grieving mother. 'Poirot shall act,' he tells her. And indeed he does, using his little grey cells to bring about the safe return of the boy and uncovering the kidnappers.

This is another marvellous production by the people at London Weekend Television. Renny Rye's direction (he directed half of the first ten films) is splendid, and the other technical work is skilfully handled.

Commendations to the entire cast: Suchet is the definitive Poirot, and again captures all the character's fussy mannerisms; Fraser is a stoic Hastings, refusing to believe an Englishman would perpetrate such a crime; Philip Jackson portrays Japp with a solidity of presence and professionalism; and the other performers are well cast.

# ≡ 1989 ≡

## Murder in the Mews (TV)

### Made in England. Directed by Edward Bennett.

### CAST
▼

| | |
|---|---|
| David Suchet | Hercule Poirot |
| Hugh Fraser | Captain Hastings |
| Philip Jackson | Chief Inspector Japp |
| Pauline Moran | Miss Lemon |
| James Faulkner | Major Eustace |
| David Yelland | Laverton West |
| Juliette Mole | Jane Plenderleith |
| Gabrielle Blunt | Mrs Pierce |
| John Cording | Inspector Jameson |
| Barrie Cookson | Dr Brett |
| Christopher Brown | Golfer |
| Bob Bryan | Barman |
| Beccy Wright | Maid |
| Nicholas Delve | Freddie |
| Moya Ruskin | Singer |

### Based on the short story *Murder in the Mews* (1937). 50 minutes.

*Murder in the Mews*, which was the title story of the 1937 short story collection, begins on Guy Fawkes' night.

Poirot, Hastings and Japp are enjoying the festivities when Hastings remarks that it would be a good night for a murder, as the noise of rockets and fireworks would mask the sound of a gunshot.

▲ Captain Hastings (Hugh Fraser, left) and Hercule Poirot (David Suchet) observe a suspect in *Murder in the Mews*.

His remarks turn out to be prophetic: a woman is discovered dead of a gunshot wound in Bardsley Garden Mews next morning. Her roommate, Jane Plenderleith, was away the previous evening and can offer no explanation.

As the room where the victim was killed was locked (the windows as well as the door), Inspector Japp concludes that suicide is probable; he calls in Poirot and the two work on the case together.

A disturbing feature is that the key to the door is missing and cannot be found; also there is part of a man's broken cufflink and nine cigarettes in the ashtray.

Freddie, a small boy, saw a man enter and leave the mews the previous evening – this man may or may not be Mr Laverton West, a rather stuffy MP who was engaged to the dead woman. Upon learning of her death, he does not display any emotion, but is extremely concerned with the notoriety and possible bad publicity that may damage his career and reputation. 'A stiff upper lip, that's the British way,' he tells Poirot.

Japp tells Poirot that Laverton West is a 'stuffed fish' and is now convinced there is a definite case of murder.

After uncovering the fact that the victim withdrew a large sum of money the day she died, as well as the fact she was not left-handed (the gun was found in her left hand), inquiries lead Inspector Japp to Major Eustace, who may have been blackmailing the victim. Eustace admits to having been in the victim's house on the night of her death, and also happens to smoke the same type of cigarettes found in the ashtray. His broken cufflink matches the piece found in the murder room too.

With the circumstantial evidence against the Major, Japp arrests him for the crime and takes him off to jail. But Poirot has other ideas, eventually getting to the crux of the crime and confronting the suspect directly, telling exactly how he arrived at the solution. 'He has his methods,' says Japp. 'Better humour him.'

*Murder in the Mews* is a wonderful television film, expertly directed by Edward Bennett, who alternated with Renny Rye during 1989.

Poirot's prowess on the golf links is charmingly exhibited by David Suchet, who is a joy to watch. Hugh Fraser is also good, showing Hastings' enthusiasm for automobiles, also innocently needling Poirot ('Why don't you get some turned down collars? They're the thing, you know').

Philip Jackson makes a fine Japp, and works well with Suchet, mixing the right amount of respect and friendly antagonism. The rest of the cast excels, especially James Faulkner as the Major from India, and David Yelland as the pompous, impersonal Member of Parliament.

# ≡1989≡

## Four and Twenty Blackbirds (TV)

Made in England, Directed by Renny Rye.

CAST

| | |
|---|---|
| David Suchet | Hercule Poirot |
| Hugh Fraser | Captain Hastings |
| Philip Jackson | Chief Inspector Japp |
| Pauline Moran | Miss Lemon |
| Philip Locke | Cutler |
| Richard Howard | George Lorrimer |
| Denys Hawthorne | Bonnington |
| Clifford Rose | Makinson |
| Hilary Mason | Mrs Hill |
| Tony Aitken | Tommy Pinner |
| Charles Pemberton | Stooge |
| Geoffrey Larder | Harry Clarke |
| Holly De Jong | Dulcie Lang |
| Cheryl Hall | Molly |
| Marjie Lawrence | Irene Mullen |
| Su Elliott | Edith |
| John Bardon | Toilet Attendant |
| Peter Waddington | Forensic |
| Guy Standeven | Vicar |
| Andrew Mackintosh | Doctor |
| Stephen Pruslin | Pianist |
| John Sessions | Radio Announcer |

Based on the short story *Four and Twenty Blackbirds* (1950). 51 minutes.

▲ Poirot (David Suchet, left) is dining with his dentist (Denys Hawthorne) when Molly (Cheryl Hall) tells them about a regular customer suddenly ordering something he has never has before in *Four and Twenty Blackbirds*.

*Four and Twenty Blackbirds* first appeared as a short story in the *Three Blind Mice and Other Stories* collection in 1950.

The film opens with Poirot dining at a restaurant with his dentist. They are exchanging small talk on habits when their waitress tells them something that intrigues Poirot. It seems an elderly man, who has been coming to the restaurant for years, suddenly orders something he has never had before.

When Poirot visits the dentist to have his teeth attended to, he is told that the elderly man from the restaurant was found dead in his home, having broken his neck falling down stairs.

Still curious over the old man's deviation from a years-long norm in his eating habits, Poirot begins to ask questions. He discovers the old man was a painter, also that he had a twin brother who had not spoken to him for many years.

Poirot soon becomes convinced that the man's death was not an accident. With the help of Chief Inspector Japp's forensic department, he learns that the contents of the corpse's stomach do not reflect the meal Poirot had seen him eat with his own eyes!

Poirot and Hastings attend an art exhibit; an invitation was found on the dead man and this may be a clue. Makinson, the dead man's agent, tells them that he was never allowed to sell any of the deceased's paintings, but now the works will appreciate and anyone who has them possesses a valuable commodity.

Poirot attempts to see the old man's nephew, George Lorrimer, but is told he is in Brighton taking care of the funeral arrangements for his uncle, who was the twin brother of the late artist. Poirot tells Hastings that the artist was murdered, and it was the murderer he had seen in the restaurant impersonating his victim.

Poirot realizes the brothers' wills and which of them died first has a vital bearing on the case. 'Mon ami,' he tells Hastings, 'We have been running up the wrong tree.'

*Four and Twenty Blackbirds* is well made, and mystery fans may note the similarity between this story and Dorothy L. Sayers' *Unpleasantness at the Bellona Club.*

Suchet once again shines as Poirot, showing off his culinary skills as well as an acquired knowledge of cricket, and other cast members are faultless, as is Renny Rye's direction.

# ≡ 1989 ≡

## The Third Floor Flat (TV)

### Made in England. Directed By Edward Bennett.

CAST

| | |
|---|---|
| David Suchet | Hercule Poirot |
| Hugh Fraser | Captain Hastings |
| Philip Jackson | Chief Inspector Japp |
| Pauline Moran | Miss Lemon |
| Suzanne Burden | Patricia Matthews |
| Nicholas Pritchard | Donovan |
| Robert Hines | Jimmy |
| Amanda Elwes | Mildred |
| Josie Lawrence | Mrs Grant |
| Alan Partington | Inspector Flint |
| Susan Porrett | Trotter |
| James Aidan | Major Sadler |
| Norman Lumsden | Vicar |
| George Little | Dicker |
| Jona Jones | Police Constable |
| John Golightly | Removal Man |
| Peter Aubrey | Removal Man |
| Helena McCarthy | Coffee Stall Owner |

Based on the short story *The Third Floor Flat* (1950). 50 minutes.

The film of *The Third Floor Flat*, based on the short story of the same title contained in *Three Blind Mice & Other Stories*, starts off at White-haven Mansions, the large block of flats where Hercule Poirot resides. Hercule is suffering from a bad cold, as well as depression as a result of having had no cases for three weeks. He tells Miss Lemon that if this continues his little grey

▲ Nicholas Pritchard as Donovan in *The Third Floor Flat*.

cells will 'starve and die'.

In an attempt to cheer up his friend, Captain Hastings invites Poirot to the theatre to see a new murder mystery, affectionately wagering the great detective will be unable to solve the stage murder. Poirot accepts, but his incorrect deduction only adds to his depression. First calling the playwright an imbecile, he then reconsiders and comes to the conclusion that his mental powers might be slipping.

Returning to his flat, he and Hastings hear some odd noises. It seems that a tenant of his building, Patricia Matthews, has misplaced her key and two of her friends have taken the dumbwaiter used for the dustbins in an attempt to gain entry to her flat.

The two young men, Donovan and Jimmy, get off on the wrong floor and find themselves in a strange flat. But that is not all they find – in the flat is the murdered body of a woman, who turns out to be a Mrs Grant.

Since the world-famous Hercule Poirot lives on the premises, his aid is enlisted by the young people. When Inspector Japp arrives, Poirot informs him that the victim only moved into the flat that day.

Mrs Grant was shot with a small-calibre handgun, and Poirot finds it curious that the murderer moved her body in an attempt to forestall its discovery. A handkerchief monogramed J.F. and a letter signed simply 'Frazer' are two clues found in the murder room.

After he has another look at the dead woman's flat, Poirot announces: 'The case is finished – I now know everything.'

Through a clever ruse, Poirot is able to scare the killer to take flight; unfortunately Hastings' car is stolen and wrecked in the abortive escape. The remainder of the film has Poirot explaining everything, including the motive, which involves a bigamous marriage.

Suchet has indeed captured the essence of the little Belgian, even playing matchmaker in this film, and the rest of the cast, as well as the direction and technical aspects of *The Third Floor Flat* are up to the usual high standards set by London Weekend Television.

▶ Hercule Poirot (David Suchet) enjoys a cup of tea in *The Third Floor Flat*.

# Triangle at Rhodes (TV)

Made in England. Directed by Renny Rye.

CAST

▼

| | |
|---|---|
| David Suchet | Hercule Poirot |
| Hugh Fraser | Captain Hastings |
| Frances Low | Pamela Lyall |
| Jon Cartwright | Commander Chantry |
| Annie Lambert | Valentine Chantry |
| Peter Settelen | Douglas Gold |
| Angela Down | Majorie Gold |
| Timothy Kightley | Major Barnes |
| Patrick Monckton | Hotel Manager |
| Al Fiorentini | Police Inspector |
| Anthony Benson | Skelton |
| Dimitri Andreas | Greek Cashier |
| Georgia Dervis | Greek Girl |
| Sophia Olympiou | Good Woman |
| Tilemanos Emanuel | Customs Officer |
| Yannis Hadjiyannis | Purser |
| Stephen Gressieux | Italian Policeman |
| George Little | Dicker |
| Martyn Whitby | Postman |

Based on the short story *Triangle at Rhodes* (1937). 51 minutes.

In *Triangle at Rhodes*, Poirot goes it solo as he is on holiday alone; Hastings is on a shooting holiday in England, while Miss Lemon is visiting relatives. In Rhodes, Poirot makes the acquaintance of several English travellers: Pamela Lyall,

▲ Douglas Gold (Peter Settelen) and Valentine Chantry (Annie Lambert) enjoy a cocktail in *Triangle at Rhodes*.

Commander and Valentine Chantry, Douglas and Marjorie Gold, and Major Barnes.

Observing a colourful snake, Poirot remarks: 'If every killer was as clearly marked, I would be out of a job.'

Beautiful, flirtatious Valentine Chantry appears to be openly toying with Douglas Gold, to the annoyance of her husband and his wife. Poirot advises Mrs Gold to 'leave this place before it is too late. Leave this island if you value your life.'

Gossip now has it that Valentine will divorce Chantry and marry Douglas, but before that can happen she is murdered, choking on a poisoned drink. Chantry believes that Gold put poison in the glass, which had been intended for him.

Poirot, who has missed his ship, is summoned back from the dock to investigate the crime. Douglas Gold, who was found to have poison on his person, has been arrested and held in jail. But after visiting him, Poirot is convinced of his innocence, and assures him that he will be released.

The police do not share the Belgian's view at this juncture; nevertheless Poirot assures Marjorie Gold that her husband will soon be out of jail.

With his customary inimitable style in this colourful and unusual setting, Poirot is able to get his little grey cells to come up with the right answer, identifying the culprit whose crimes include more than murder.

Rebecca Howard has done another excellent job of assembling the cast, all of whom perform well. Stephen Wakelam did the dramatization, Clive Exton was the story consultant, and there is lavish photography by Peter Jessop.

▲ Captain Hastings (Hugh Fraser, left), Hercule Poirot (David Suchet) and Pamela Lyall (Frances Low) in *Triangle at Rhodes.*

# ≡1989≡

## Problem at Sea (TV)

Made in England. Directed by Renny Rye.

CAST

| | |
|---|---|
| David Suchet | Hercule Poirot |
| Hugh Fraser | Captain Hastings |
| John Normington | Colonel John Clapperton |
| Sheila Allen | Mrs Clapperton |
| Roger Hume | General Forbes |
| Ann Firbank | Ellie Henderson |
| Ben Aris | Captain Fowler |
| Colin Higgins | Skinner |
| James Ottaway | Mr Russell |
| Geoffrey Beevers | Mr Tolliver |
| Kitty Mooney | Melissa Greenwood |
| Victoria Hastead | Pamela Cregan |
| Dorothea Phillips | Nelly Morgan |
| Sheri Shepstone | Emily Morgan |
| Louisa James | Ismene |
| Jack Chissick | Bates |
| Caroline John | Mrs Tolliver |
| George Kotanidis | Photographer |
| Panayotis Kaldis | First Hawker |
| Stathis Mauropoulos | Second Hawker |

Based on the short story *Problem at Sea* (1939). 50 minutes.

▲ Hercule Poirot (David Suchet), with the aid of a doll, demonstrates a clue to the murder in *Problem at Sea*.

*Problem at Sea*, originally published in *The Regatta Mystery* (1939), finds Poirot and Hastings on a sea voyage. While Hastings amuses himself with skeet shooting, Poirot spends his time indoors.

Fellow travellers include Colonel and Mrs John Clapperton, General Forbes, Mr and Mrs Tolliver, and Ellie Henderson. Mrs Clapperton browbeats her husband and is rude about the other guests, some of whom provide amateur entertainment. 'Many odious women have devoted husband – it is an enigma of nature,' comments Poirot.

Colonel Clapperton tries to keep his sense of humour, amusing fellow passengers with card tricks; he had been in the music halls before joining the army.

As the ship docks in Alexandria, Clapperton goes into the city with two young women from the ship; his wife does not feel well and remains in her cabin. Poirot and Hastings also go ashore, trying to avoid, as Hastings puts it, 'the usual tourist things'.

After everyone returns to the ship several hours later, Mrs Clapperton is found stabbed to death in her cabin by her husband and a steward, the door having been locked. It looks like an outsider did it, as money and jewellery have been stolen and other clues left in the murder room indicate a stranger.

Medical evidence cannot pinpoint the exact time of death, which makes Poirot's job of investigation the more difficult. The most likely suspect would seem to be the Colonel, who nonetheless has an airtight alibi for every minute since he left the ship.

Hastings catches someone trying to sell the dead woman's jewellery, but this turns out to be unconnected with the murder. Poirot then puts on a little demonstration as an entertainment. 'I can assure you that behind my madness, as you English say, is method,' he informs them. Proceeding with props that include a suitcase and a doll, he is able to prove just how Mrs Clapperton was killed.

Suchet is once again brilliant, also Hugh Fraser as Hastings, believing in his countrymen and thinking the murder must be the work of 'foreign devils'. John Normington, Roger Hume and Ann Firbank are also notable in this splendidly cast film, well directed by Renny Rye.

# ≡ 1989 ≡

## The King of Clubs (TV)

Made in England. Directed by Renny Rye.

CAST

| | |
|---|---|
| David Suchet | Hercule Poirot |
| Hugh Fraser | Captain Hastings |
| Philip Jackson | Chief Inspector Japp |
| Niamh Cusack | Valerie Saintclair |
| David Swift | Henry Reedburn |
| Jonathan Coy | Bunny Saunders |
| Jack Klaff | Prince Paul of Maurania |
| Rosie Timpson | Miss Deloy |
| Gawn Grainger | Ralph Walton |
| Mark Culwick | Young Man |
| Avril Elgar | Mrs Oglander |
| Vass Anderson | Frampton |
| Abigail Cruttenden | Miss Oglander |
| Sean Pertwee | Ronnie Oglander |
| Cathy Murphy | Maid |

Based on the short story *The King of Clubs* (1951). 48 minutes.

*The King of Clubs*, which first appeared in *The Under Dog* short story collection, opens on a film set at the mythical Parade Studios. Poirot and Hastings are visiting the set; Hastings and assistant director Bunny Saunders are old friends. Poirot tells Hastings: 'Films are very boring, but the actors who are paid to deceive us, they are interesting.'

Director Henry Reedburn is interesting, if only for the fact that he is universally despised; he rages on the set, fires actors indiscriminately, and makes improper advances to the leading lady. Prince Paul of Maurania, the principal backer of the film, seeks Poirot's help with a problem connected with the filmmaker.

One stormy night, Chief Inspector Japp of Scotland Yard arrives at Reedburn's home in response to a telephone report of 'a disturbance'. What he discovers is the murdered body of Reedburn, bludgeoned to death in his library.

As police search the house and grounds for clues, Poirot arrives with Hastings to conduct his own investigation. Japp tells Poirot that he is close to cracking the case, but the little Belgian has his own ideas. 'A man like Reedburn has enemies,' Poirot tells Hastings. 'Too many enemies.'

Poirot continues his inquiry at 'The Willows', home of Reedburn's neighbours, the Oglanders. It seems the family had been playing bridge on the night of the murder, when actress Valerie Saintclair, who discovered the body, arrived to seek help.

Reconstructing the bridge game, Poirot takes note that there are only 51 cards on the table; the missing card is the king of clubs. He finds the card in the box; it was apparently never

▲ Henry Reedburn (David Swift, left), Ralph Walton (Gawn Grainger) and Valerie Saintclair (Niamh Cusack) in *The King of Clubs*.

taken out. 'To play bridge for over one hour with only 51 cards is not believable,' states Poirot.

It seems that Poirot knows everything now, but because of the severe offensive nature of the victim, informs Hastings that he fears the case will go unsolved.

We can see a parallel between *The King of Clubs* and another Christie story, *Murder on the Orient Express*. In both cases, the murder victim was so odious to Poirot that he makes the moral judgement of allowing the killer(s) to go free.

The acting in the drama is up to standard, and Renny Rye's direction is skilfully handled, making *The King of Clubs* another most enjoyable telefilm produced by London Weekend Television.

# ≡ 1989 ≡

## The Dream (TV)

### Made in England. Directed by Edward Bennett.

CAST

▼

| | |
|---|---|
| David Suchet | Hercule Poirot |
| Hugh Fraser | Captain Hastings |
| Philip Jackson | Chief Inspector Japp |
| Pauline Moran | Miss Lemon |
| Alan Howard | Benedict Farley/Hugo Cornworthy |
| Joely Richardson | Joanna Farley |
| Mary Tamm | Mrs Farley |
| Martin Wenner | Herbert Chudley |
| Paul Lacoux | Dr Stillingfleet |
| Neville Phillips | Holmes |
| Christopher Saul | Mr Tremlett |
| Donald Bisset | Mayor |
| Tommy Wright | Workman |
| Fred Bryant | Workman |
| Arthur Howell | Fencing Instructor |
| George Little | Dicker |
| Christopher Gunning | Bandmaster |
| Richard Bebb | Newsreel Voice |

Based on the short story *The Dream* (1939). 49 minutes.

*The Dream*, originally a short story in 1939 in *The Regatta Mystery* collection, commences with meat pie magnate Benedict Farley addressing his factory workers. Poirot has received a letter from him, signed by his secretary, inviting him to come and call.

That evening Farley tells Poirot that night after night he has the same dream, a nightmare in which he commits suicide by blowing his brains out. Psychiatrists have been no help, and he wants the little Belgian's opinion; however, he does not allow Poirot to examine his bedchamber. 'There

is something wrong in that house, Hastings, badly wrong,' Poirot remarks 'and I haven't the faintest idea what it is.'

The next day secretary Hugo Cornworthy discovers the body of Farley, shot dead in precisely the manner of the dream he related to Poirot. Physical evidence and statements from those on the premises support the suicide theory, however Inspector Japp believes it may be murder, if only for the fact that Poirot is involved.

Farley's daughter Joanna, who stands to inherit the bulk of the fortune, tells Poirot her father was a singularly unpleasant person; among other things he had blacklisted a young man Joanna was going to marry.

'We must give the little grey cells time to do their work,' Poirot tells Japp. Poirot is now convinced that he is matching his wits against a very clever murderer, but he is frustrated by his inability to put it all together.

After Miss Lemon provides him with an insight, Poirot is able to see how it was done. Assembling the entire Farley household, Poirot proceeds to enlighten them all on the manner of murder; the killer is apprehended while trying to run away.

Dramatized by Clive Exton, *The Dream* is yet another faithful adaptation of a Christie short story. Directed with flair by Edward Bennett, it also boasts fine performances from the entire cast.

Versatile Alan Howard, son of Arthur and nephew of Leslie Howard, is excellent in a dual role, and Pauline Moran, who plays Poirot secretary Miss Lemon in these films, is effective. Constantly nagging her employer for a new typewriter, she is momentarily thrilled when Poirot brings in a large box at the conclusion of the case. But it is a clock – given so that she will no longer have to lean out the window to look at the church clock in order to see the time. Poirot tells Hastings he would not make a good millionaire because he is 'too considerate of his employees'.

▲ Poirot explains all in *The Dream*. L-R: Hercule Poirot (David Suchet), Dr Stillingfleet (Paul Lacoux), Hugo Cornworthy (Alan Howard), Joanna Farley (Joely Richardson), and Mrs Farley (Mary Tamm).

# ≡1989≡

## The Incredible Theft (TV)

Made in England. Directed by Edward Bennett.

### CAST
▼

David Suchet · · · · · · · · · · · · · · · · · · · · · · · · · Hercule Poirot
Hugh Fraser · · · · · · · · · · · · · · · · · · · · · · · · Captain Hastings
Philip Jackson · · · · · · · · · · · · · · · · · · · · Chief Inspector Japp
Pauline Moran · · · · · · · · · · · · · · · · · · · · · · · · · Miss Lemon
John Stride · · · · · · · · · · · · · · · · · · · · · · · · Tommy Mayfield
Carmen DuSautoy · · · · · · · · · · · · · · · Mrs Joanna Vanderlyn
John Carson · · · · · · · · · · · · · · · · · · · Sir George Carrington
Ciaran Madden · · · · · · · · · · · · · · · · · · · · Lady Mayfield
Phyllida Law · · · · · · · · · · · · · · · · · · · Lady Carrington
Guy Scantlebury · · · · · · · · · · · · · · · · Reggie Carrington
Albert Welling · · · · · · · · · · · · · · · · · · · · · · · · · · Carlile
Dan Hildebrand · · · · · · · · · · · · · · · · · · · · · · · Chauffer
Philip Manikum · · · · · · · · · · · · · · · · · · · · · · · Sergeant

Based on the short story *The Incredible Theft* (1937). 49 minutes.

▲ Hercule Poirot (David Suchet) helps Lady Mayfield (Ciaran Madden) with a matter of national security in *The Incredible Theft*.

*The Incredible Theft*, taken from the short story collection *Murder in the Mews*, is a very classy television production from London Weekend Television.

The story opens on the eve of the Second World War as the Mayfield Kestrel, a new British aeroplane, is being tested. This plane is technologically superior to the German Messerschmitt, but manufacturer Tommy Mayfield is frustrated by the British government's restrictions regarding their financial support.

At Whitehaven Mansions, Poirot receives a call from a woman refusing to give her name, but telling him her problem concerns national security.

Meeting Poirot in the zoo, the woman tells him she is Lady Mayfield, wife of the plane manufacturer. It seems her husband has invited Mrs Joanna Vanderlyn, a socialite with openly pro-German sentiments to spend the weekend, hoping to expose her as a spy and using the plans of the Kestrel as bait.

Poirot accepts her invitation as a guest and keeps his eyes open, hoping to prevent the possible threat to the country. At Poirot's request, Hastings is staying at the inn at a nearby village. Poirot is especially interested to know why Scotland Yard Chief Inspector Japp just happens to be staying at the very same inn (by coincidence he is also sharing Hastings' room).

On the evening of Poirot's arrival, a key page of the plans for the design of the aeroplane is stolen, and it is up to Poirot to solve this delicate and serious matter. 'It is a small problem merely,' comments Poirot, 'but a problem that will agitate the little grey cells most adequately.'

*The Incredible Theft* is skilfully adapted by dramatists David Reid and Clive Exton, who vividly create the atmosphere of pre-war Britain.

Edward Bennett, who has directed a number of these David Suchet/Hercule Poirot films for London Weekend Television, again does fine work with the excellent cast, which includes regulars Suchet, Fraser, Jackson and Moran, as well as John Stride, John Carson, Carmen DuSautoy and Ciaran Madden (who appeared in *Magnolia Blossom* in 1982).

▲ Sir Tommy Mayfield (John Stride) reassures Lady Mayfield (Ciaran Madden) in *The Incredible Theft.*

# 1990

# The Life of Agatha Christie
# (TV Documentary)

No other technical information available.

*The Life of Agatha Christie* was a 52-minute television documentary that marked the 100th anniversary of Dame Agatha Christie's birth.

The film itself shows photographs of Christie as a child and young woman, and there is a commentary by some less-than-expert Christie fans; there are also a few words here and there by her grandson Matthew Prichard (who was given the rights to *The Mousetrap* as a birthday present when a small boy).

Joan Hickson, who recently appeared as Miss Marple, makes a few comments, and there are clips shown from some of the Hickson-Marple television films.

There is also David Suchet, television's current Hercule Poirot in the series for London Weekend Television.

All in all, a very disappointing tribute to mark the centennial of the greatest mystery writer of all time. Very few of the films are seen; only brief clips of those made for television and only a mere handful at that.

▲ Dame Agatha Christie's likeness in Madame Tussaud's.

# ≡ 1990 ≡

## The Mysterious Affair at Styles (TV)

Made in England. Directed by Ross Devenish.

### CAST

| | |
|---|---|
| David Suchet | Hercule Poirot |
| Hugh Fraser | Captain Hastings |
| Philip Jackson | Chief Inspector Japp |
| Beatie Edney | Mary Cavendish |
| David Rintoul | John Cavendish |
| Gillian Barge | Mrs Inglethorp |
| Michael Cronin | Alfred Inglethorp |
| Joanna McCallum | Evie Howard |
| Anthony Calf | Lawrence Inglethorp |
| Michael Godley | Dr Wilkins |
| Morris Perry | Mr Wells |
| David Saville | Summerhaye |
| Tim Munro | Edwin Mace |
| Tim Preece | Phillips, KC |
| Penelope Beaumont | Mrs Raikes |
| Allie Byrne | Cynthia Murdoch |
| Lala Lloyd | Dorcas |
| Bryan Coleman | Vicar |
| Merilina Kendall | Mrs Dainty |
| Eric Stovell | Chemist |
| Donald Pelmeer | Judge |
| Caroline Swift | Nurse |
| Ken Robertson | Army Officer |
| Michael Roberts | Tindermans |
| Gordon Dulieu | Clerk of the Court |
| Jeffrey Robert | Jury Foreman |
| Robert Vowles | Hire Car Driver |

Based on the novel *The Mysterious Affair at Styles* (1920). 101 minutes.

*The Mysterious Affair at Styles*, published in 1920, was not only Agatha Christie's first novel, it was also the introduction of the endearing little Belgian detective with the waxed moustache, passion for order and symmetry, and brilliant 'little grey cells', Hercule Poirot.

Fans of Christie, Poirot, and the fabulous films made by London Weekend Television will take heart at the faithfulness to Christie's story and characters in this adaptation of *The Mysterious Affair at Styles*.

It begins with Captain Arthur Hastings on a month's sick leave after convalescence during the First World War. Running into his friend John Cavendish, he is invited to the Cavendish country estate in Essex, Styles Court. Cavendish's stepmother, Emily Inglethorp, is now married to one Alfred Inglethorp, a man 20 years her junior and of dubious background and appearance.

Emily runs Styles with an iron hand; even her husband appears obsequious and toadies towards her. But Hastings feels a strong undercurrent of tension at Styles Court.

Mrs Inglethorp has been instrumental in settling a number of Belgian refugees in the nearby village of Styles St Mary. Among them is one

▲ Captain Hastings (Hugh Fraser, left) and Hercule Poirot (David Suchet) in *The Mysterious Affair at Styles*, Christie's first story, which also introduced Poirot.

Hercule Poirot, late of the Belgian police force. While touring the village, Hastings is reunited with his old friend, who is experiencing a sense of boredom coupled with displacement.

Later that evening, Mrs Inglethorp suffers a horrid convulsive death, and subsequent police tests determine she has been poisoned.

Inglethorp seems the most likely suspect, a man universally disliked at Styles Court, referred to on various occasions as a rotten little bounder, a bad lot, a fortune hunter and a sycophant.

Aside from motive, Inglethorp's attitude does not sit well with Chief Inspector Japp of Scotland Yard; Inglethorp is arrested and tried for the murder of his wife. Hastings thinks of Poirot, and requests him to get to the bottom of the mystery, which he does with his usual style and sense of timing.

For Christie to employ the use of poison as a means of murder in her first novel should come as no surprise; certainly she had plenty of practical training and knowledge of toxicology from her wartime experiences serving in a hospital dispensary. Sales of the book on which this film is based were quite good, although Christie received only £25, due to the contractual agreement she had signed. Reviews of the book were

▲ Hercule Poirot (David Suchet, left) expounds his theory on *The Mysterious Affair at Styles* to Captain Hastings (Hugh Fraser).

favourable, and the career of the First Lady of Crime was launched.

*The Mysterious Affair at Styles* was directed with style by Ross Devenish, and producer Brian Eastman, who did the television films for London Weekend Television, cannot be too highly praised for the care and thoughtfulness that went into this and the other productions.

It may seem a bit odd to fans of the series that the producers chose to do this film after a dozen or so other Poirot tales, as we have been used to seeing the character well established in his flat at Whitehaven Mansions.

Nevertheless, *The Mysterious Affair at Styles* is done with a flair and style that captures the atmosphere of post-Edwardian England, not to mention the rich and vivid characters.

David Suchet, who has gathered quite a following, is the essence of Poirot; he is so good we do not even notice that a great deal of action has taken place before he makes his appearance.

Hugh Fraser and Philip Jackson offer crisp, clean performances, while Beatie Edney and Michael Cronin do fine work in this noteworthy production, which shines like a highly polished diamond.

# ≡ 1990 ≡

## Peril at End House (TV)

Made in England. Directed by Renny Rye.

### CAST

▼

| | |
|---|---|
| David Suchet | Hercule Poirot |
| Hugh Fraser | Captain Hastings |
| Philip Jackson | Chief Inspector Japp |
| Pauline Moran | Miss Lemon |
| Geoffrey Greenhill | Wilson |
| Joe Bates | Alfred |
| Mary Cunningham | Ellen |
| Polly Walker | Nick Buckley |
| Christopher Baines | Charles Vyse |
| Jeremy Young | Bert Croft |
| Godfrey James | Inspector |
| Carol Macready | Milly Croft |
| John Harding | Commander George Challenger |
| Alison Sterling | Freddie Rice |
| Jane Eaton | Hotel Receptionist |
| John Crocker | Dr Graham |
| Fergus McLarnon | Hood |
| Jenny Funnell | Nurse Andrews |
| Paul Geoffrey | Jim Lazarus |
| Janice Cramer | Maid |
| Edward Pinner | Page Boy |

Based on the novel *Peril at End House* (1932). 98 minutes.

*Peril at End House*, written in 1932, was a critical success, although Christie stated in her autobiography that 'Peril at End House was another of my books that left so little impression on my mind that I cannot even remember writing it'.

In 1940, *Peril at End House* opened as a play, marking its debut at the Vaudeville Theatre in London on May 1st. Francis L. Sullivan, the distinguished actor who had played Poirot in the stage version of *Black Coffee* in 1930, once again

▲ The stars of *Peril at End House* (clockwise from top left) David Suchet as Hercule Poirot, Pauline Moran (Miss Lemon), Philip Jackson (Inspector Japp), and Hugh Fraser (Captain Hastings).

played the Belgian detective. Ian Fleming, a distinguished character actor who was no relation to the James Bond author of the same name, played Captain Hastings.

Generally critically successful, the London *Times* reviewed the play the day after it opened, particularly praising Francis L. Sullivan: 'Mr Sullivan conspicuously enjoys Poirot's eloquence and handles it skillfully.'

The 1990 television film, directed by Renny Rye for London Weekend Television, is a first-rate production. The story involves Poirot and Hastings spending a week at the Hotel Majestic in St Loo.

Walking along the hotel terrace, Poirot twists his ankle and a young, attractive lady, Nick Buckley, shows concern.

Inviting her for a cocktail, Poirot and Hastings learn that she lives at End House, a rather imposing, run-down place situated on a rocky point that can be seen from the hotel.

Miss Buckley tells Poirot that she leads a charmed life; she has had three brushes with death in as many days and lived to tell the tale. A bee buzzes by her head, and after she leaves, Poirot points out to Hastings that the hole in her abandoned hat was caused by a bullet and not a bee.

Going to End House ostensibly to return the hat, Poirot is concerned with Miss Buckley's safety. Questions regarding the 'accidents' lead him to the conclusion that they were unsuccessful murder attempts.

▲ David Suchet as the famed Belgian sleuth, Hercule Poirot, in *Peril at End House*.

▲ Poirot (David Suchet, right) confers with Captain Hastings (Hugh Fraser) in *Peril at End House*.

The Belgian determines to protect the girl, but it is difficult to identify a murderer from the many suspects at End House. 'Until a murderer has committed his murder,' Poirot tells Hastings, 'his footprints are faint, if they exist at all.'

After another girl is murdered, presumably mistaken for Nick by the killer, Poirot spirits the girl off to the protection and safety of a nursing home, digging deep into the question of who will benefit from her death.

Finally, with the use of his little grey cells, and a bit of help from Chief Inspector Japp, Poirot is able to solve the mystery.

Fans of Christie will certainly applaud London Weekend Television yet again for their faithfulness to the original work.

*Peril at End House* is twice the normal length of most of these Poirot features, as all others, with only the fewest exception, have been taken from short stories.

Renny Rye must be commended for his skillful direction; a tense pace is maintained throughout the film and the acting is superb, especially by David Suchet and Hugh Fraser. Among non-series regulars, Polly Walker, Jeremy Young and John Harding turn in very good work, and the remainder of the cast is more than competent.

▲ Freddie Rice (Alison Sterling, left), Nick Buckley (Polly Walker) and Commander George Challenger (John Harding) in *Peril at End House*.

## The Veiled Lady (TV)

Made in England. Directed by Edward Bennett.

CAST

| | |
|---|---|
| David Suchet | Hercule Poirot |
| Hugh Fraser | Captain Hastings |
| Philip Jackson | Chief Inspector Japp |
| Pauline Moran | Miss Lemon |
| Frances Barber | Lady Millicent |
| Terence Harvey | Lavington |
| Carol Hayman | Mrs Godber |
| Tony Stephens | Sergeant |
| Don Williams | Constable |
| Lloyd Maguire | Museum Guard |
| Peter Geddis | Museum Guard |

Based on the short story *The Veiled Lady* (1924). 49 minutes.

*The Veiled Lady* opens with a jewel robbery in Burlington Arcade. Poirot, meanwhile, is lamenting the lack of criminal activity. Inspector Japp tells him of the robbery – although the thief was caught, examination of the jewels showed they were imitations.

While he was out, Poirot was visited by a lady wearing a heavy black veil. She left no name, but Miss Lemon tells Poirot that she will wait for him at the Athena Hotel.

▲ Captain Hastings (Hugh Fraser, left) and Hercule Poirot (David Suchet) meet the mysterious veiled Lady Millicent (Frances Barber) in *The Veiled Lady*.

Accompanied by Hastings, Poirot finds the lady in question, who tells the two men she is Lady Millicent. She has a difficult problem: it seems a man is attempting to blackmail her over a rather foolish letter she had written as a young girl. 'The ingenuity of Hercule Poirot shall defeat your enemies,' the little detective tells her.

The blackmailer, a chap called Lavington, pays Poirot a visit and delivers an ultimatum. If he does not receive £18,000 by the following Tuesday evening, the letter will be turned over to Lady Millicent's fiancé.

While Lavington is in Paris, Poirot gains access to his Wimbledon house posing as a locksmith, ostensibly to put in a burglar alarm system. Late that same night, Poirot and Hastings return to the house to look for the letter, which is kept in a Chinese puzzle box. Poirot cleverly deduces the hiding place of the box, but the housekeeper has alerted a passing constable, who arrests the detective. Hastings escapes with the box by crashing through a window.

After having spent the night in jail, Poirot is 'rescued' by Chief Inspector Japp, who rubs it in a bit 'We've been after him for months,' Japp tells a policeman. 'Nobody knows his real name, but he's known as "Mad Dog".'

Japp tells Poirot something which comes as a surprise to the Belgian: Mr Lavington had been murdered in Amsterdam several days before he came to see Poirot. Who then impersonated him, and why?

Poirot later discovers that the puzzle box contains not only a letter, but the jewels from the Burlington Arcade robbery, and Lady Millicent as well as Lavington are bogus – in reality they are notorious jewel thieves. After they are apprehended, Poirot remarks to Hastings and Japp, 'Even the criminals employ me when they have nowhere else to turn,' as the film charmingly concludes.

*The Veiled Lady* is an outstanding television film, touchingly and charmingly directed by Edward Bennett. David Suchet displays a skill unknown to any actor who has previously portrayed the Belgian sleuth. This is also the first time we see Poirot employ a disguise.

Philip Jackson is staunch and yet human at the same time, and Hugh Fraser displays charm and virtue in the role of Hastings; the three actors work very well together, establishing a camaraderie that is touching and believable.

# ≡ 1990 ≡

## The Lost Mine (TV)

### Made in England. Directed by Edward Bennett.

### CAST
▼

| | |
|---|---|
| David Suchet | Hercule Poirot |
| Hugh Fraser | Captain Hastings |
| Philip Jackson | Chief Inspector Japp |
| Pauline Moran | Miss Lemon |
| Anthony Bate | Lord Pearson |
| Colin Stinton | Charles Lester |
| Barbara Barnes | Mrs Lester |
| James Saxon | Reggie Dyer |
| John Cording | Jameson |
| Vincent Wong | Chinaman |
| Julian Firth | Bank Teller |
| Richard Albrecht | Lobby Clerk |
| Gloria Connell | Miss Devenish |
| Peter Barnes | Wilkins |
| Hi Ching | Chow Feng |
| Ozzie Yue | Restaurant Manager |
| Christopher Walker | First Officer |
| Joe Frazer | Second Officer |
| Daryl Kwan | Oriental Gentleman |
| Susan Leong | Chinese Tart |
| Nick Gillard | Stunts |

### Based on the short story *The Lost Mine* (1934). 51 minutes.

Set in 1935, *The Lost Mine* was dramatized by Michael Baker and David Renwick. It begins as Poirot and Hastings are playing Monopoly; this reminds Poirot to go to his bank, as there is an error in his account. He is outraged and vows to go to the president.

Later that evening, Lord Pearson, a director

of the bank, calls on Poirot at Whitehaven Mansions, but it is not regarding the matter of his account. A Chinese businessman negotiating with the bank concerning the rights to a valuable 'lost' mine is missing.

Inspector Japp tells Poirot where he can find the missing man: he is in the police morgue, a victim of murder. The map to the mine was not found on his body, so Poirot has the double task of finding the map as well as the murderer.

A subsequent search of the dead man's rooms at the Saint James Hotel fails to reveal the map. Returning to police headquarters, Japp proudly shows Poirot and Hastings the latest in police technology – an operations centre that links field operatives to headquarters by means of radio – something that is put to good use to help them apprehend one of the suspects in the case.

'While the Chief Inspector is frying his important fish,' Poirot says to Hastings, 'let us see what we can catch.'

Inspector Japp's inquiries lead him to Reggie Dyer, a criminal with Chinese connections, eventually run to ground in an opium den in Limehouse.

Wondering why a man with a full box of matches in his suitcase would ask for another, Poirot endeavours to solve the mystery of the cigarettes in the ashtray.

During yet another Monopoly game, Poirot suddenly sees the light, and is able to expose the murderer, who has attempted a clever frame against another person.

*The Lost Mine* is a very faithful, atmospheric account of the Christie short story, with excellent use made of sets, costumes, and lighting.

Acting from the entire cast is splendid, with Anthony Bate standing out among the non-regulars. The smaller parts are impressively cast and Suchet, Fraser, Jackson and Moran give their usual professional performances.

▲ Christopher Walker (left) photographing a suspect in *The Lost Mine* while Joe Frazer looks on.

# ≡ 1990 ≡

## The Cornish Mystery (TV)

### Made in England. Directed by Edward Bennett.

CAST

| | |
|---|---|
| David Suchet | Hercule Poirot |
| Hugh Fraser | Captain Hastings |
| Philip Jackson | Chief Inspector Japp |
| Pauline Moran | Miss Lemon |
| Jerome Willis | Edward Pengelley |
| John Bowler | Jacob Radnor |
| Chloe Salaman | Freda Stanton |
| Amanda Walker | Mrs Pengelley |
| Derek Benfield | Dr Adams |
| John Rowe | Prosecutor |
| Hugh Munro | Judge |
| Richard Brain | Shop Assistant |
| Tilly Vosburgh | Jessie Dawlish |
| Laura Girling | Edwina Marks |
| Graham Callan | Solicitor |
| Edwina Day | Landlady |
| Hugh Sullivan | Vicar |
| Jonathan Whaley | Policeman |

Based on the short story *The Cornish Mystery* (1951). 48 minutes.

Dramatized by Clive Exton for London Weekend Television, *The Cornish Mystery* (originally published in the 1951 collection *The Under Dog*) opens with Poirot meeting a woman from Cornwall who fears that her husband is poisoning her. Mr Pengelley, a dentist, is apparently having an affair with his assistant, so he has a motive. Poirot promises he and Hastings will travel to Cornwall the following day, adding, 'We will be discretion itself.'

Upon arriving at the house, they are told that Mrs Pengelley is dead. Poirot refers to himself as 'a criminal imbecile', and vows to avenge the death of the woman who came to him for help.

Visiting the local the doctor, who attended the dead woman, Poirot is in an extreme state of agitation; the doctor insists the cause of death was acute gastritis. 'A doctor who lacks doubt is not a doctor, he's an executioner,' Poirot tells Hastings. 'We owe it to Madame Pengelley to unmask her murderer.'

At the reading of Mrs Pengelley's will we learn that she has left £2,000 to her neice, Freda

Stanton; the remainder of her estate, which totals £20,000, is left to Edward Pengelley, her husband.

Poirot tells Hastings that Pengelley will soon be in the dock charged with murder, adding that 'it will be up to us to save him from the gallows'.

Exhumation of Mrs Pengelley's body shows traces of poison and, as Poirot foretold, Pengelley is arrested for the murder of his wife. At the trial, circumstantial evidence as well as various motives seems strong against the accused.

Inspector Japp is also on hand, and is disconcerted by Poirot's assurances that the accused is innocent. He tells the little Belgian it is an open and shut case – everyone knows he did it. 'Everyone does not use their grey cells, I think,' replies Poirot.

Realizing who the killer is (but lacking proof), Poirot confronts him directly, forcing him to sign a confession in order to save the wrongly accused husband, but allowing him a 24-hour head start on the police.

The Cornish Mystery is another finely adapted film of the Christie short story. David Suchet is excellent as Poirot, showing a depth of emotion only briefly seen in the Christie works. Hugh Fraser, as Hastings, plays off him well, brilliantly inventing a ruse in order to force the killer's hand, being complimented by the master on the superb use of his grey cells.

Jerome Willis is also excellent as the accused man, and the remainder of the cast, the photography, lighting and all other technical credits are splendidly and effectively used.

► David Suchet, once more as Hercule Poirot, in *The Cornish Mystery.*

## ≡ 1990 ≡

## The Disappearance of Mr Davenheim (TV)

Made in England. Directed by Andrew Grieve.

### CAST
▼

| | |
|---|---|
| David Suchet | Hercule Poirot |
| Hugh Fraser | Captain Hastings |
| Philip Jackson | Chief Inspector Japp |
| Pauline Moran | Miss Lemon |
| Kenneth Colley | Matthew Davenheim |
| Mel Martin | Charlotte Davenheim |
| Tony Matthews | Gerald Lowen |
| Fiona MacArthur | Maid |
| Richard Beale | Merritt |
| Bob Mason | Sergeant |
| Peter Doran | Policeman |
| Stewart Harwood | Delivery Man |
| Jonty Miller | Mechanic |
| Malcolm Mudie | Chief Engineer |
| Patrick Page | Illusionist |

Based on the short story *The Disappearance of Mr Davenheim* (1924). 51 minutes.

*The Disappearance of Mr Davenheim*, written by Christie in 1924, opens with banker Matthew Davenheim expectantly waiting in his home for a visitor. This is Gerald Lowen, a man seeking to obtain a seat at Davenheim's bank. Davenheim asks his wife to show the visitor in when he arrives, as he is quickly walking to the local village in order to post some letters. Davenheim disappears into the fog, never to return home.

Inspector Japp, Hastings and Poirot are in a music hall watching an illusionist, and Poirot tells his companions that it is not possible to make a human being disappear, as was done in front of their eyes. It is then that Japp relates the strange story of Matthew Davenheim. When he is finished, Poirot replies, 'It is most obscure, my dear Inspector; that is why I am certain of solving it.'

Japp offers Poirot an unusual wager: £5 that the little Belgian cannot solve the case in one week without leaving his flat. Poirot, confident, accepts.

Since Poirot cannot venture out, Hastings is employed to perform the legwork in the case, interviewing the principals involved, visiting the scene of the disappearance, and reporting his findings to Poirot, who will use only the little grey cells of his brain to solve the problem.

Dragging the river, the police find Davenheim's coat but no body. Gerald Lowen is questioned by both Hastings and Japp; he seems the most likely to benefit from the disappearance and may have a revenge motive from past dealings with Davenheim. Poirot wonders if there has been murder, why no body has been found, and if it is a kidnap case, where the ransom note is.

Valuable jewels from the Davenheim safe are discovered to have been stolen, and Poirot has Hastings conduct a certain experiment that answers his questions on this point.

When Davenheim's ring is found on a pickpocket, Poirot understands that there is much more to this case than first appeared. After he is able to ascertain the answers to two seemingly trivial questions, he knows all.

*The Disappearance of Mr Davenheim* is first-class entertainment. David Suchet has fun as Poirot, performing a number of magic tricks, and there is a marvellous bit with a parrot, delivered by Stewart Harwood in an amusing cameo.

Subtle comedy is employed, as when Hugh Fraser and Philip Jackson keep running into each other in separate but parallel investigations.

The dialogue is extremely clever and witty, as in the exchanges between Suchet and Fraser: Suchet, 'And please do not fraternize with that creature. I am still training him.' Fraser, 'It's only a parrot.' Suchet, 'I was talking to the parrot.'

The technical credits, especially the photography by Ivan Strasburg, are quite good.

▲ Chief Inspector Japp (Philip Jackson, right) chases the pickpocket (Kenneth Colley) who stole his wallet in *The Disappearance of Mr Davenheim*.

# ≡ 1990 ≡

## Double Sin (TV)

Made in England. Directed by Richard Spence.

### CAST
▼

| | |
|---|---|
| David Suchet | Hercule Poirot |
| Hugh Fraser | Captain Hastings |
| Philip Jackson | Chief Inspector Japp |
| Pauline Moran | Miss Lemon |
| Elspeth Gray | Miss Penn |
| Adam Kotz | Norton Kane |
| Caroline Milmoe | Mary Durrant |
| David Hargreaves | Sergeant Vinney |
| Gerard Moran | Police Constable Flagg |
| Michael J. Shannon | Mr Baker Wood |
| Amanda Garwood | Lady Amanda Manderley |
| Paul Gabriel | Speedy Tours Rep |
| Harry Goodier | Billy Arkwright |
| Jeffrey Perry | Hotel Receptionist |
| Anna Small | Pianist |
| Miranda Forbes | Landlady |
| George Little | Dicker |
| Ned Williams | First Urchin |
| Jack Williams | Second Urchin |

Based on the short story *Double Sin* (1961). 51 minutes.

The television film of *Double Sin*, which was also the title short story in the 1961 Christie collection, begins with Poirot and Hastings out for a stroll on the common on a drizzly, chilly day. The weather reflects Hercule Poirot's own feelings; 'I am finished Hastings. I think I shall retire,' says a depressed Poirot.

Telling Poirot that he is at the height of his powers, Hastings tries his best to cheer up his little friend, so off they go to the seaside for a brief holiday.

The change of locale seems to revitalize Poirot, at least to some degree, although he still reminds Hastings that he is 'retired'. The pair are surprised by a poster announcing an upcoming lecture by Chief Inspector James Japp of Scotland Yard.

Boarding a tour bus, Poirot and Hastings encounter Mary Durrant, a young woman selling antique miniatures to a visiting American collector on behalf of her aunt. Arriving at one of several stops, Miss Durrant notices the case where she carried the antiques has been tampered with and the contents stolen.

She appeals to Hastings for help; he in turn approaches Poirot, who rebuffs him, again reminding him of his retirement. Hastings decides to help the lady in distress, and goes it alone, aided by the local police. 'I am retired – such puzzles no longer interest me,' Poirot tells him, although he does offer his friend advice.

Using Poirot as a sounding board, Hastings reports his progress; the collector has apparently already bought the antiques in question, from someone clearly not Miss Durrant.

Hastings thinks he has caught the thieves, but it turns out he has merely caught a young couple who are eloping. By now Poirot is openly interested in the affair; he visits the young woman and her crippled aunt, assuring them that he will solve the case.

Surreptitiously attending Inspector Japp's lecture, Poirot is touched to hear the Scotland Yard man praising him, referring to him as 'intelligent, brave, sensitive, devastatingly quick', and also possessing one of the most original minds of the twentieth century. Most flattering.

This serves to buoy Poirot's spirits further, and he masterfully draws the case to a surprising conclusion by bringing off a confrontation between the principals that crystalizes the case.

One could certainly run out of adjectives to describe David Suchet's performance as Poirot; like the good Inspector remarked he is intelligent, brave, sensitive and devastatingly quick; the definitive Poirot.

Philip Jackson makes a perfect Inspector Japp; he has obviously researched his role carefully, putting just the right touches of feeling and emotion into the character without falling into the trap of becoming stereotypical. Hugh Fraser also employs the proper amount of virtue and sensitivity in his portrayal of Hastings.

Pauline Moran enlivens Miss Lemon, using her grey cells a la Poirot to solve her own mystery, that of a missing latchkey.

The technical credits, as well as direction by Richard Spence and the music by Christopher

Gunning (who appeared as the bandmaster in *The Dream* in 1989) make *Double Sin* another very praiseworthy entry in the series of Poirot films made by London Weekend Television.

▲ Elspeth Grey (front) as Miss Penn and Caroline Milmoe as Mary Durrant in *Double Sin*.

# ≡1990≡

## The Adventure of the Cheap Flat (TV)

Made in England. Directed by Richard Spence.

### CAST

| | |
|---|---|
| David Suchet | Hercule Poirot |
| Hugh Fraser | Captain Hastings |
| Philip Jackson | Chief Inspector Japp |
| Pauline Moran | Miss Lemon |
| William Hootkins | FBI Agent Burt |
| John Michie | James Robinson |
| Samantha Bond | Stella Robinson |
| Ian Price | Teddy Parker |
| Anthony Pedley | Assassin |
| Jemma Churchill | Elsie |
| Peter Howell | Mr Paul |
| Jennifer Landor | Carla Romero |
| Gordon Wharmby | Records Agent |
| Nick Maloney | Bernie Cole |
| Nigel Whitmey | Luigi Valdarno |
| Luke Hayden | Carla's Husband |

Based on the short story *The Adventure of the Cheap Flat* (1924). 50 minutes.

▲ Hercule Poirot (David Suchet, left) and Captain Hastings (Hugh Fraser) in *The Adventure of the Cheap Flat.*

*The Adventure of the Cheap Flat* was written in 1924 and contained in the short story collection *Poirot Investigates*. The film opens with Poirot, Japp, and Hastings attending the cinema. Poirot does not like the excessive use of violence in the American gangster film. When Japp tells Poirot an American FBI agent is coming to London to work with him, Hercule says he hopes the agent is different from his celluloid counterpart.

A young couple, James and Stella Robinson, answer a newspaper advert for a flat. What they cannot understand is the ridiculously low rent, but nevertheless take possession immediately. Encountering their acquaintance Hastings and his friend Poirot at a cocktail party, they relate the tale of the flat. Poirot is interested in the mystery of the inexpensive rent, although Hastings believes such a trivial matter is a waste of time.

At Scotland Yard, Inspector Japp introduces Poirot and Hastings to Burt, the American FBI agent who has little respect for private detectives. It seems he is in London because a minor clerk stole some blueprints for a new submarine. A woman who now has the plans is supposedly in London to sell them.

Poirot and Hastings rent a flat in the same building as the Robinsons, and they notice a suspicious stranger who is keeping watch on the building. Hastings' imagination concocts everything from drug running to white slavery, and Poirot quips, 'You have a very fertile imagination.'

Aside from the mysterious stranger, Japp and his men are also watching the flats. It is then that Poirot realizes the cheap flat has something to do with the FBI agent's business.

Poirot tells Hastings, 'This is a plot of sinister dimensions,' and warns that the Robinsons are being used as a deadly decoy for an assassin.

Posing as a journalist, Miss Lemon is able to track down the woman with the plans at the Black Cat Club. Poirot is then able to arrange the facts of the case, which began six months before in New York, prevent a tragedy to the innocent young couple, apprehend the criminals, and recover the stolen plans.

Dramatized by Russell Murray and directed by Richard Spence, *The Adventure of the Cheap Flat* is brought to a dramatic climax. David Suchet captures the essence of Poirot's passion for order and method; Pauline Moran offers a fine performance as Miss Lemon, and the rest of the cast perform with the professionalism and finesse we have come to expect in these wonderful films from London Weekend Television.

# ≡1990≡

## The Kidnapped Prime Minister (TV)

Made in England. Directed by Andrew Grieve.

CAST

| | |
|---|---|
| David Suchet | Hercule Poirot |
| Hugh Fraser | Captain Hastings |
| Philip Jackson | Chief Inspector Japp |
| Pauline Moran | Miss Lemon |
| Lisa Harrow | Mrs Daniels |
| David Horovitch | Commander Daniels |
| Ronald Hines | Sir Bernard Dodge |
| Patrick Godfrey | Lord Estair |
| Timothy Block | Major Norman |
| Jack Elliott | Egan |
| Kate Binchy | Landlady |
| Milo Sperber | Finger |
| Henry Moxon | Prime Minister |
| Oliver Beamish | Sergeant Hopper |
| Anthony Chinn | Shi Mong |
| Roy Heather | Transport Superintendent |
| Daniel John | Urchin |
| Sam Clifton | Urchin |
| Nick Gillard | Stunts |

Based on the short story *The Kidnapped Prime Minister* (1924). 51 minutes.

Another short story from the collection *Poirot Investigates*, *The Kidnapped Prime Minister* opens with the kidnapping of the British Prime Minister while in France on his way to the League of Nations conference. He had already been shot at after a meeting with the king, and the government calls in Poirot to solve the kidnapping.

Poirot has 32 hours before the conference to find the Prime Minister and his secretary, Commander Daniels, who is also missing. Cabinet Secretary Sir Bernard Dodge is annoyed with Poirot, who conducts his investigation in England, refusing to take advantage of a destroyer specially laid on.

Checking on the scene of the shooting, Poirot also discovers that Egan, the Prime Minister's chauffer, is missing. Poirot may not have the man, but the fellow's address book stimulates the little grey cells of the Belgian.

After Daniels is found tied up in France, he is brought back to England where, to the amazement of both Hastings and Inspector Japp, Poirot gives him a very cursory examination. However, Hercule is quite pleased with the results.

Visiting the former Mrs Daniels, who had divorced her husband the previous year in a most distasteful public fashion, Poirot warns Hastings

▲ Hercule Poirot (David Suchet, left) assures Lord Estair (Patrick Godfrey) and Sir Bernard Dodge (Ronald Hines) that he will find *The Kidnapped Prime Minister*.

that 'she's a tough customer', and tells him to follow her.

It is not long before Poirot is able to solve the case, explaining to an amazed Japp that the kidnapping in France was merely a decoy; the Prime Minister had in fact never left the country.

The action comes to a head when Mrs Daniels leads Poirot and the police to a house in the country, where a conspiracy of a very high nature is uncovered.

The acting in this television drama is first rate by one and all; aside from the regulars in the series, Lisa Harrow and David Horovitch (who was seen as Inspector Slack in several of the Miss Marple films) are notable.

Ivan Strasburg's photography, and the production design by Bob Harris are excellent, and Andrew Grieve's direction is fast-paced and suspenseful. Another fine entry in the Brian Eastman-produced London Weekend Television series.

# ≡ 1990 ≡

## The Adventure of the Western Star (TV)

Made in England. Directed by Richard Spence.

### CAST

| | |
|---|---|
| David Suchet | Hercule Poirot |
| Hugh Fraser | Captain Hastings |
| Philip Jackson | Chief Inspector Japp |
| Pauline Moran | Miss Lemon |
| Barry Woolgar | Inspector Dougall |
| Bruce Montague | Hoffberg |
| Struan Rodger | Henrik Van Braks |
| Rosalind Bennett | Marie Marvelle |
| Julian Gartside | Hotel Receptionist |
| Oliver Cotton | Gregorie Rolf |
| Caroline Goodall | Lady Yardly |
| Alister Cameron | Lord Yardly |
| Stephen Hancock | Mullings |
| Ian Collier | Sergeant |
| Bill Thomas | Steward |

Based on the short story *The Adventure of the Western Star* (1924). 50 minutes.

*The Adventure of the Western Star*, written in 1924, concerns Poirot, excited at the arrival of Marie Marvelle, the famous Belgian film star. Meanwhile at Hatton Garden, Chief Inspector Japp is on surveillance duty outside Hoffberg's. After arresting jewel thief Henrik Van Braks, Japp is told by his superiors to release him (Van Braks is also an influential armaments manufacturer).

Poirot meanwhile meets Marie, who tells him that she has received three letters demanding the return of her diamond, the Western Star. Marie's husband Gregorie had purchased it under rather mysterious circumstances; Poirot suggests that he safeguard the gem, but Marie insists on keeping it in her possession. She wants to show the diamond to Lord and Lady Yardly who own the Eastern Star, a companion jewel to her own diamond. She and Gregorie also want the Yardly estate to be used in their next film.

Accompanying Poirot to the barber, Japp tells him of Van Brak and a visit Lady Yardly paid to Hoffberg's. Meanwhile Lady Yardly has called on Poirot, and Hastings believes she has also been receiving threatening letters − a false assumption of which she does not disabuse him.

Travelling down to Yardly Chase, Poirot and Hastings are told by Lord Yardly that he has never heard of a companion piece to the diamond he owns. Since his finances are rocky, he

▲ Caroline Goodall as Lady Yardly in *The Adventure of the Western Star.*

is planning to sell his gem. Lady Yardly is persuaded by Poirot to wear her diamond at dinner.

Before dinner is served, the lights go out and in the confusion, Lady Yardly's diamond is torn off of her. Hastings gives chase, recovering the necklace but the central gem is missing.

Returning to London, Poirot is informed by Marie that her gem too has been stolen. A man masquerading as her husband appropriated it from the hotel safe. Poirot discovers that the pseudo-husband was in fact the real thing, and he cleverly makes a switch with a paste imitation, recovering the real diamond while Japp and his men arrest the criminals at Croydon Airport.

*The Adventure of the Western Star* is faithful to Christie's original short story; David Suchet and Philip Jackson's usual excellent acting enliven the tale, as does Hugh Fraser, who never quite seems to grasp that there is only one diamond!

The fine direction by Richard Spence, and dramatization by Clive Exton, are up to the usual high standards set by the previous Hercule Poirot films made by London Weekend Television.

▶ Hercule Poirot (David Suchet) and Captain Hastings (Hugh Fraser) examine a vital clue in *The Adventure of the Western Star.*

# How Does Your Garden Grow? (TV)

### Made in England. Directed by Brian Farnham.

## CAST

| | |
|---|---|
| David Suchet | Hercule Poirot |
| Hugh Fraser | Captain Hastings |
| Philip Jackson | Chief Inspector Japp |
| Pauline Moran | Miss Lemon |
| Ann Stallybrass | Mary Delafontaine |
| Tim Wylton | Henry Delafontaine |
| Margery Mason | Amelia Barrowby |
| Catherine Russell | Katrina Reiger |
| Peter Birch | Nicholai |
| Ralph Nossek | Dr Sims |
| John Burgess | Mr Harrison |
| Dorcas Morgan | Lucy |
| Trevor Danby | Mr Trumper |
| John Rogan | Pathologist |
| Stephen Petcher | Photographer |
| Philip Praeger | Police Constable |

Based on the short story *How Does Your Garden Grow* (1939). 51 minutes.

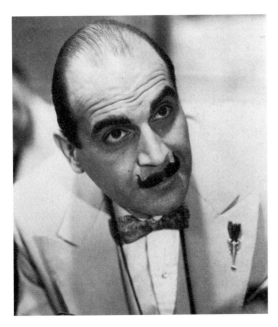

▲ David Suchet giving another fine performance as Hercule Poirot in *How Does Your Garden Grow.*

*How Does Your Garden Grow?*, written in 1939 and contained in the short story collection *The Regatta Mystery*, starts off with Katrina, a young Russian emigre, visiting a Soviet official at the Russian embassy. There is obviously something between them; they later for reasons of privacy agree to meet at London's Chelsea Flower Show.

Back at Whitehaven Mansions, Hastings is hurriedly trying to get Poirot ready, as they too are going to the flower show – it seems there has been a rose named after the great Belgian sleuth.

Katrina is a companion to wheelchair-bound Amelia Barrowby, who lives with her impecunious niece Mary and her drunken husband Henry. Dr Sims, the family physician, prescribes some powders for Amelia, arranging for Katrina to pick up the drugs.

Going to get a glass of water for Amelia, Katrina runs into Poirot, who she gives a packet of seeds. Hastings suffers an attack of hay fever throughout the show.

Back at home, Poirot finds a letter from Amelia Barrowby asking for his help as she 'fears something is wrong' with her household. Poirot makes arrangements to travel to her Surrey home the next day, accompanied by Miss Lemon (Hastings is still suffering miserably from hay fever). 'I hope we will not be too late to avert disaster,' Poirot remarks.

That same evening down in Surrey, Mary Delafontaine fixes the dinner as it is the maid Lucy's night off. Upstairs in her room, Katrina removes a powder sachet from its hidden cache. While Mary returns to her garden at the meal's conclusion, husband Henry retires to the summerhouse, disguising his drink in a weedkiller bottle. When Amelia tries to summon help, no one is there to respond; she dies, clutching her stomach. Subsequent pathology reports determine she was poisoned by strychnine.

Poirot arrives with Miss Lemon the following morning, mistaken by everyone as a lawyer; Japp is there too in the guise of a taxi driver.

It seems that Dr Sims has had certain suspicions, and Poirot must decide how, since everyone ate the same food at dinner, no one but Amelia died (or noticed the bitter taste of the strychnine). Katrina seems the likely suspect (by now Japp has announced officially it is murder) as she stands to inherit a great deal – a suspicion compounded when she flees and a bottle of poison is found in her room.

Japp is convinced of Katrina's guilt, but Poirot thinks otherwise; when comparing letters the murdered woman wrote with the one he received, there is a dissimilarity in the handwriting.

Poirot uses the famous little grey cells to solve the case – one involving oysters and oyster shells:

The acting, especially by Suchet and Pauline Moran, is particularly effective in this story. Brian Farnham's direction is subtle, complemented by Christopher Gunning's hummable series music.

▲ Margery Mason (seated) as Amelia Barrowby, Catherine Russell (left, standing) as Katrina Reiger, and Anne Stallybrass as Mary Delafontaine in *How Does Your Garden Grow*.

# The Million Dollar Bond Robbery (TV)

Made in England. Directed by Andrew Grieve.

## CAST

| | |
|---|---|
| David Suchet | Hercule Poirot |
| Hugh Fraser | Captain Hastings |
| Pauline Moran | Miss Lemon |
| David Quilter | Mr Shaw |
| Ewan Hooper | Mr Vavasour |
| Paul Young | Mr McNeil |
| Lizzy McInnerny | Miranda Brooks/Nurse Long |
| Oliver Parker | Philip Ridgeway |
| Natalie Ogle | Esmee Dalgleish |
| Christopher Owen | Chief Purser |
| Jonathan Stratt | Spivvy Passenger |
| Dallas Adams | Hood |
| Kieron Jecchinis | Tom Franklin |
| Edward Phillips | Flower Seller |
| Robin Hunter | Police Officer |
| Richard Bebb | News Reader |
| Andrew Bradford, Colin Skeaping | Stunts |

Based on the short story *The Million Dollar Bond Robbery* (1924). 51 minutes.

▲ Hercule Poirot (David Suchet) strolls the deck of the *Queen Mary* in *The Million Dollar Bond Robbery*.

*The Million Dollar Bond Robbery*, from the 1924 *Poirot Investigates* short story collection, begins when Mr Shaw is nearly killed by a hit-and-run car, and the directors of the London and Scottish Bank where he works call in Hercule Poirot. Mr Vavasour, the General Manager, believes that it was a murder attempt. It seems that Shaw is about to board the *Queen Mary* with a trunkload of Liberty Bonds worth one million dollars.

McNeil, the bank's head of security, is annoyed by the arrival of the Belgian, nevertheless showing him the case that will hold the bonds. Three keys to the case exist – Shaw, McNeil and Vavasour each have one.

Further investigation by Poirot uncovers that Assistant General Manager Ridgeway has owned a red Singer – an identical car to that which nearly killed Shaw.

Ridgeway's fiancée Esmee Dalgleish, who also happens to be Vavasour's secretary, implores Poirot and Hastings to see that no harm comes to Ridgeway.

Later that day, Ridgeway meets with a crook to whom he owes a great deal of money; mean-

▲ David Quilter (right) as Mr Shaw and Ewan Hooper as Mr Vavasour in *The Million Dollar Bond Robbery*.

while at the bank Shaw collapses after having drunk a poisoned cup of coffee.

Shaw, a bachelor, is taken home where Poirot and Hastings interview him; Vavasour and McNeil are also on hand and tell Poirot that Ridgeway was the last person in the office, therefore the one who would most likely have poisoned the coffee.

Since Shaw will be unable to make the trip, Ridgeway is selected to go in his place. Poirot and Hastings, at the request of Esmee, travel aboard the *Queen Mary* to 'keep an eye' on Ridgeway and the bonds.

While Hastings is suffering from seasickness, Poirot makes the acquaintance of the lovely Miranda Brooks. Hastings is taken with her, later emerging on deck to meet her. Believing he heard a splash, he is told by Miranda that nothing went overboard. Returning to his cabin, he sees Ridgeway's door ajar, and upon investigation discovers the bonds are missing.

McNeil is agitated at the news in London, ordering by radio a person to person search aboard the ship. All the keys are accounted for except Vavasour's, apparently stolen from his desk at the office.

Poirot and Hastings are convinced Ridgeway is innocent. Nevertheless the little Belgian tells the police to have him arrested on his return, explaining that this is for his own protection.

The action climaxes when Poirot reveals the true hiding place of the bonds and brings the criminals to justice.

Andrew Grieve directs the wonderful cast splendidly, carefully blending comedy and mystery; Suchet and Fraser are wonderful, and all other technical credits are up to the usual high standards.

## The Plymouth Express (TV)

Made in England. Directed by Andrew Piddington.

CAST

| | |
|---|---|
| David Suchet | Hercule Poirot |
| Hugh Fraser | Captain Hastings |
| Philip Jackson | Chief Inspector Japp |
| Pauline Moran | Miss Lemon |
| John Stone | Halliday |
| Kenneth Haigh | McKenzie |
| Julian Wadham | Rupert Carrington |
| Alfredo Michelson | Comte de la Rochefour |
| Marion Bailey | Jane Mason |
| Shelagh McLeod | Florence Carrington |
| Steven Mackintosh | Newsboy |
| Leon Eagles | Bank Manager |
| John Abbott | Detective |
| Steven Riddle | Barman |
| Adrian McLoughlin | Station Official |
| Nigel Makin | Reception Clerk |
| Richard Vanstone | Sergeant |
| Robert Locke | Naval Officer |
| Duncan Faber | Porter |
| Roy Alon | Stunts |

Based on the short story *The Plymouth Express* (1951). 50 minutes.

▲ David Suchet as Hercule Poirot and Pauline Moran as his secretary, Miss Lemon, in *The Plymouth Express*.

London Weekend Television's film, based on the short story in the 1951 *The Under Dog* collection, concerns Australian magnate Gordon Halliday. Halliday is worried about false rumours emanating from Paris regarding a geological survey.

Although separated from Halliday's daughter Florence, reprobate Rupert Carrington nevertheless seeks financial help from his father-in-law. While Rupert is being kicked out the door, Florence is receiving bouquets of roses from an ardent suitor – not her husband.

Hastings remarks to Poirot that certain shares he holds in Halliday's Yellow Creek Group are falling, just as Halliday appears to consult Poirot. It seems he does not like the French 'gold-digger' now pursuing his daughter.

Poirot accepts the mission, observing Florence and her suitor having tea at the Savoy Hotel. Poirot is disturbed by what he overhears, and also notes the uncanny resemblance between the suitor and Florence's husband, Rupert Carrington.

Florence and her maid Jane later board the express for Plymouth; Jane discovers that Florence has disappeared and a search for her discloses her murdered body at the end of the line.

Poirot and Hastings retrace her train journey; from the police pathologist's reports Poirot deduces that Florence must have been murdered when the train arrived in Bristol. Poirot comes upon what he believes is a vital clue in the case: a newsboy tells Poirot he saw Florence at Weston Station, the train's eventual destination. In his usual brilliant manner (and thanks in part to Miss Lemon's filing system) Poirot is able to solve this case of fraud, jewel theft, and murder.

Once more, David Suchet, born to play the part, excels as Poirot; Hugh Fraser makes a reliable Hastings and Pauline Moran an efficient Miss Lemon. Philip Jackson as Inspector Japp is a solid presence, and the remaining cast, especially Kenneth Haigh and John Stone, act their parts with distinction.

Fans of Christie will be pleased yet again – this episode, which first aired on television January 20, 1991, was not only well written, directed and acted, but remains faithful to Christie's original.

# ≡ 1991 ≡

## Wasps' Nest (TV)

Made in England. Directed by Brian Farnham.

### CAST
▼

| | |
|---|---|
| David Suchet | Hercule Poirot |
| Hugh Fraser | Captain Hastings |
| Philip Jackson | Chief Inspector Japp |
| Pauline Moran | Miss Lemon |
| Martin Turner | John Harrison |
| Melanie Jessop | Molly Deane |
| Peter Capaldi | Claude Langton |
| John Boswall | Dr Belvedere |
| Kate Lynn-Evans | Mrs Henderson |
| Serena Scott Thomas | Model Girl |
| Hilary Tindall | Commére at Fashion Show |
| Julian Forsyth | Waiter |

Based on the short story *Wasps' Nest* (1961). 51 minutes.

The short story *Wasps' Nest* can be found in the *Double Sin* story collection, which appeared in 1961. In the film, we find Poirot, Hastings and Japp at a garden fête.

While Hastings is trying out his new camera, he focuses on model Molly Deane, who we see being dragged behind a tent by a clown. Poirot meets Harrison, the son of an old friend, who tells him Molly is his girlfriend.

▶ Molly Deane (Melanie Jessop, left), Hercule Poirot (David Suchet) and Mrs Henderson (Kate Lynn-Evans) in *Wasps' Nest.*

It turns out the clown was none other than sculptor Claude Langton, who is in love with Miss Deane; apparently she does not feel the same, acting indifferent and even frosty towards him.

Harrison travels to London to Whitehaven Mansions in order to see Poirot as a sinister man may have been responsible for tampering with the brakes on Molly's car.

The same man is later seen at a fashion show, where Poirot observes him force Molly into a taxi. Hastings, ever on the alert, has taken a photo of the man. He takes the photo to Inspector Japp, who is in hospital after an appendicitis attack, but he does not recognize the chap.

By this time Poirot has discovered a great deal, and puts an end to the mystery, answering a number of riddles and foiling a suicide attempt along the way.

David Suchet has certainly captured the intricacies of the Hercule Poirot character, while Hugh Fraser is comfortable as the reliable Hastings, and Philip Jackson makes Inspector Japp a real, human character.

Brian Farnham, who also directed *How Does Your Garden Grow?*, once again does a fine job behind the camera, making *Wasps' Nest* another very enjoyable episode of this series.

# ≡ 1991 ≡

## The Tragedy at Marsdon Manor (TV)

### Made in England. Directed by Renny Rye.

### CAST
▼

| | |
|---|---|
| David Suchet | Hercule Poirot |
| Hugh Fraser | Captain Hastings |
| Philip Jackson | Chief Inspector Japp |
| Ian McCulloch | Jonathan Maltravers |
| Geraldine Alexander | Susan Maltravers |
| Neil Duncan | Captain Black |
| Anita Carey | Miss Rawlinson |
| Desmond Barrit | Samuel Naughton |
| Ralph Watson | Danvers |
| Edward Jewesbury | Dr Bernard |
| Geoffrey Swann | Police Sergeant |
| Hilary Sesta | Doctor's Receptionist |
| David Lloyd | Museum Attendant |
| Pat Keen | Civil Defence Organiser |
| Richard Bebb | Newsreader |

Based on the short story *The Tragedy at Marsdon Manor* (1924). 52 minutes.

Originally broadcast on February 3, 1991, *The Tragedy at Marsdon Manor* concerns Jonathan Maltravers and his young wife Susan.

Poirot and Hastings are in the local village at the invitation of crime novelist Samuel Naughton, a hotel landlord. Poirot is irritated that Naughton has summoned him on a literary rather than a factual problem.

Captain Andrew Black arrives from Kenya with a present for Mrs Maltravers – a woodcarving believed to have black magic powers. This interests Susan, who tells a story at dinner of a local ghost that haunts an oak tree in the garden.

The next morning Mrs Maltravers is painting when the gardener informs her that the body of her husband has been discovered under the tree

haunted by the ghost. Poirot is soon on the scene, determining that Maltravers was murdered, his body having been dragged underneath the tree from elsewhere.

Inspector Japp informs the great sleuth that Maltravers carried a large life insurance policy, and also that he was on the verge of bankruptcy.

An attempt is made later on Mrs Maltravers' life at a Civil Defence meeting, and Poirot now believes he is on to something.

Examining the picture she was painting when her husband died, Poirot finds a vital clue in helping him solve the puzzle: the broken birds eggs by the stone seat.

Poirot uses Naughton and a trick to unnerve the murderer into confessing. Later, he solves the problem of the literary killing for Naughton.

The acting in *The Tragedy of Marsdon Manor* is first rate: David Suchet captures all the eccentricities of Poirot, as well as the Belgian's ego – he is miffed when visitors to the local waxworks admire a dummy of Charlie Chaplin more than one of himself! Hugh Fraser and Philip Jackson are now practically living in their roles, and there is good work from Geraldine Alexander and Neil Duncan.

Renny Rye, who has directed a number of the Poirot films over the last two years, shows his ability for a true feeling of character, bringing out the essence of Christie's writing. The other credits are formidable as usual.

▲ Poirot (David Suchet) and policeman (Geoffrey Swann) examine a clue in *The Tragedy at Marsdon Manor.*

▲ Geraldine Alexander as Susan Maltravers in *The Tragedy at Marsdon Manor.*

# The Double Clue (TV)

Made in England. Directed by Andrew Piddington.

### CAST

| | |
|---|---|
| David Suchet | Hercule Poirot |
| Hugh Fraser | Captain Hastings |
| Philip Jackson | Chief Inspector Japp |
| Pauline Moran | Miss Lemon |
| Kika Markham | Countess Vera Rossakoff |
| David Lyon | Marcus Hardman |
| David Bamber | Bernard Parker |
| Charmian May | Lady Runcorn |
| Nicholas Selby | Mr Johnstone |
| Michael Packer | Redfern |
| William Chubb | Blake |
| Mark Fletcher | Constable |
| William Osborne | Receptionist |
| Meriel Dickinson | Katherine Bird |
| Yitkin Seow | Nacora |
| Richard Ryan | Porter |
| Martin Grace | Stunts |

Based on the short story *The Double Clue* (1961). 50 minutes.

*The Double Clue* comes from *The Double Sin* short story collection (1961). The film starts with Chief Inspector Japp, frustrated by pressure being exerted by the commissioner, consulting Poirot on four recent robberies that have taken place in high society. 'The next robbery will be the last one,' Poirot assures him.

Marcus Hardman, a jewellery collector, is having a garden party in his home. Lady Runcorn is there, along with Hardman's unsavoury sidekick, Bernard Parker, the beautiful Countess Vera Rossakoff, and South African Mr Johnstone.

Poirot is informed the next day that an emerald necklace was stolen during the house party. While Japp is interested in a constable's report of a passing tramp, Poirot takes an interest in the ivy climbing up a balcony.

Hastings and Japp are amazed at Poirot's attentions to the Countess; while he spends a day with her in the country, Hastings and Miss Lemon decide to pursue the other suspects in the case.

Spotting the tramp in the grounds of Hardman's estate, Hastings is startled when the fellow fires a shot at him and races off in an automobile. Meanwhile Poirot seems to be enjoying himself with the Countess, eventually returning to Hardman's house to explain the circumstances behind the robbery.

David Suchet, a fascinating actor, shows us another side of the many-faceted Hercule Poirot in this episode – the romantic. Although one realizes his pursuit of the Countess assists his investigation, he nevertheless shows a sensitive side we infrequently see. Director Andrew Piddington, who also did *The Plymouth Express*, displays his skill and style here. Hugh Fraser, Philip Jackson and Pauline Moran are their usual intrepid selves, and the supporting cast, comprised entirely of British television performers, all offer very fine and capable performances.

▶ Hercule Poirot (David Suchet) and Countess Vera Rossakoff (Kika Markham) in *The Double Clue*.

# The Mystery of the Spanish Chest (TV)

### Made in England. Directed by Andrew Grieve.

CAST

| | |
|---|---|
| David Suchet | Hercule Poirot |
| Hugh Fraser | Captain Hastings |
| Philip Jackson | Chief Inspector Japp |
| John McEnery | Colonel Curtiss |
| Caroline Langrishe | Marguerite Clayton |
| Pip Torrens | Major Rich |
| Malcolm Sinclair | Edward Clayton |
| Antonia Pemberton | Lady Chatterton |
| Peter Copley | Burgoyne |
| Sam Smart | Smithy |
| Edward Clayton | Rouse |
| Metin Yenal | Umpire |
| Richard Cawte | Young Officer |
| Victoria Scarborough | Party Dancer |
| Christopher Lamb | Party Dancer |
| Melissa Wilson | Maid |
| Andy Mulligan | Reporter |
| Clem Davis | Reporter |
| Roger Kemp | Doctor |
| John Noble | Rigoletto |
| Catherine Bott | Gilda |
| Arthur Howell | Stunts |

Based on the short story *The Mystery of the Spanish Chest* (1960). 51 minutes.

A slightly expanded version of *The Mystery of the Baghdad Chest*, this story is found in the 1960 short story collection *The Adventure of the Christmas Pudding*.

At the opera, Poirot is approached by Lady Chatterton, who believes that her friend Marguerite Clayton is going to be murdered by her husband Edward Clayton; ten years before, Lady Chatterton had witnessed him fight a duel.

Purchasing a knife, Clayton confides his suspicions of his wife's infidelity to his friend, Colonel Curtiss. At their club, Curtiss later warns handsome Major Rich, who Clayton had named, to stay away from Mrs Clayton.

Poirot has been invited to a party at the home of Major Rich. Clayton had shown up there to await the arrival of Rich, but disappeared before he arrived home. During the festivities, Poirot observes the interaction between Rich, Curtiss,

and Mrs Clayton, while behind a screen blood drips from a large Spanish chest.

The next day Japp drops in on Poirot to discuss the murder; he has arrested Major Rich, believing him to have committed the crime. Poirot visits Rich in jail, realizing there was no impropriety between Rich and Marguerite Clayton.

Examining the chest where the body was found, Poirot discovers a small hole in the front. After preventing an apparent suicide, Poirot uses a ruse in order to capture the wily murderer; film concludes the way it opened – with an exciting duel.

Poirot is pleased with himself, although he assumes a modest composure when being congratulated on his success.

The entire cast shines, especially John McEnery and, in a smaller part, the excellent Peter Copley. The production standards are high as usual –

another winner from London Weekend Television.

Strangly enough, the actor who plays Rouse bears the same name as that of the victim: Edward Clayton!

▲ Hercule Poirot (David Suchet, left), Lady Chatterton (Antonia Pemberton), Marguerite Clayton (Caroline Langrishe) and Major Rich (Pip Torrens) in *The Mystery of the Spanish Chest.*

# ≡ 1991 ≡

## The Theft of the Royal Ruby (TV)

Made in England. Directed by Andrew Grieve.

### CAST
▼

| | |
|---|---|
| David Suchet | Hercule Poirot |
| Frederick Treves | Colonel Lacey |
| Stephanie Cole | Mrs Lacey |
| David Howey | Desmond |
| Tariq Alibai | Prince Farouk |
| Helena Michell | Sarah Lacey |
| John Vernon | David Welwyn |
| Nigel Le Vaillant | Desmond Lee-Wortley |
| Robyn Moore | Gloria |
| John Dunbar | Peverill |
| Alessia Gwyther | Bridget |
| Jonathan S. Bancroft | Colin |
| Edward Holmes | Michael |
| Siobhan Garahy | Annie Bates |
| Susan Field | Mrs Ross |
| Gordon Reid | Chocolate Shop Owner |
| Christopher Leaver | Parsloe |
| Peter Aldwyn | Durbridge |
| Iain Rattray | Head Waiter |
| James Taylor | Waiter |
| Andrew Bradford, Colin Skeaping, Jim Dowdall, Ellie Bertram | Stunts |

Based on the short story *The Theft of the Royal Ruby* (1961). 47 minutes.

▲ Poirot displays his culinary skills in *The Theft of the Royal Ruby*. L-R: Gloria (Robyn Moore), Hercule Poirot (David Suchet), Mrs Ross (Susan Field), Sarah Lacey (Helena Mitchell), Desmond (David Howey) and Annie Bates (Siobhan Garahy).

A slightly altered version of *The Adventure of the Christmas Pudding*, the film of *The Theft of the Royal Ruby* was first shown on February 24, 1991.

Set at Christmas, Egyptologist Colonel Lacey invites antiquities dealer David Welwyn to view his collection with the intention of selling him something.

Meanwhile in a London restaurant, a drunken prince who is heir to the throne of Egypt, staggers after a female companion who has stolen his ruby. Accosted outside a chocolate shop, Poirot is taken to the foreign office and briefed on the theft. The officials persuade Poirot to accept the case, as it is imperative to British interests. The only people who knew about the gem are to be found at Kings Lacey, so Poirot spends Christmas there.

Upon arrival, Poirot is greeted by two children – his cover story is that he succeeds in seeing to it that unsuitable matches do not take place. In the kitchen he meets Sarah and Desmond, who are preparing puddings.

Poirot receives a warning later on not to eat any of the pudding. The next day Poirot overhears Desmond discussing something on the phone that arouses his interest, and at dinner Colonel Lacey finds the stolen ruby in his portion of pudding. Poirot quickly confiscates it, saying that it is merely glass.

He presents it to the ungrateful prince at a local hotel, but the Foreign Office insists that he uncovers the thief. After a game of charades, his room is burgled, but the intruder fails to discover the whereabouts of the ruby.

Poirot uses a faked murder in order to trap the jewel thief, who attempts to abscond in an aeroplane.

Once again, London Weekend Television has come up with another fine, entertaining film from an Agatha Christie short story. David Suchet, the consummate Poirot, is ably assisted by Andrew Grieve's direction and a fine cast, especially Frederick Treves, who was also notable in 1987's *Sleeping Murder*, in which he played Dr James Kennedy.

# ≡ 1991 ≡

## The Affair at the Victory Ball (TV)

Made in England. Directed by Renny Rye.

### CAST

▼

| | |
|---|---|
| David Suchet | Hercule Poirot |
| Hugh Fraser | Captain Hastings |
| Philip Jackson | Chief Inspector Japp |
| Pauline Moran | Miss Lemon |
| Mark Crowdy | Viscount Cronshaw |
| David Henry | Eustace Beltaine |
| Haydn Gwynne | Coco Courtney |
| Nathaniel Parker | Chris Davidson |
| Natalie Slater | Mrs Davidson |
| Kate Harper | Mrs Mallaby |
| Andrew Burt | James Ackerley |
| Charles Collingwood | BBC Announcer |
| Brian Mitchell | Second Actor |
| Sarah Crowden | Receptionist |
| Bryan Matheson | Butler |
| Steve Whyment | Stunts |

Based on the short story *The Affair at the Victory Ball* (1951). 50 minutes.

Readers will be able to find *The Affair at the Victory Ball*, on which this film was based, in the 1951 *Under Dog and Other Stories* collection.

The plot concerns Lord Beltaine and Viscount Cronshaw, on their way to the Victory Ball, respectively dressed like Punchinello and Harlequin, two characters from the Italian comic opera.

On their way, they stop at Broadcasting House to pick up several other attendees of the ball, while back at Whitehaven Mansions Hastings is cajoling Poirot to make an appearance; he finally agrees but insists he will not wear a costume.

At the ball Poirot observes the Cronshaw party, all of whom are dressed as Italian comedy characters. Around midnight, Hastings gallantly stands in for Cronshaw in a dance with Mrs Mallaby. While they are dancing, Cronshaw is spotted on the balcony scribbling in a small notebook. When Mrs Mallaby later goes to look for him, she finds him stabbed to death in the supper room.

Inspector Japp is summoned and immediately compares notes with Poirot. They discover the name 'Lowestoft' in the victim's tiny notebook, as well as a silver case containing cocaine. Poirot recommends to Inspector Japp that he question actress Coco Courtney, who was a member of Cronshaw's party.

She has apparently left; when the trio arrives at her flat they discover that she has died from a drug overdose.

A green pompom is found in the clenched fist of the victim, which leads Poirot to investigate the costumes worn by the various people who attended the Victory Ball. Mrs Davidson's costume is missing a pompom, but Poirot is quick to notice hers was cut off, while the one in the dead man's hand was torn off.

Reconstructing the crime to try and reveal the murderer, Poirot does just that on live radio at the BBC studios in the presence of all the suspects.

The denouement of *The Affair at the Victory Ball* is reminiscent of the style and tradition of the American writer Rex Stout in his Nero Wolfe stories, nearly all of which end with the immense detective confronting a group of suspects while reconstructing the crime.

The technical credits are outstanding, and more kudos to the casting directors for London Week-

▲ Chris Davidson (Nathaniel Parker, left), Viscount Cronshaw (Mark Crowdy), Coco Courtney (Haydn Gwynne), and Eustace Beltaine (David Henry) in *The Affair at the Victory Ball*.

end Television, who, aside from the regulars (Suchet, Fraser, Jackson and Moran) have employed a cast of theatre and television actors who are not star names. However, the actors are right for the roles, which is a lesson many would be well to learn when attempting to film Christie's (and other original) works.

# ≡ 1991 ≡

## The Mystery of Hunter's Lodge (TV)

Made in England. Directed by Renny Rye.

### CAST
▼

| | |
|---|---|
| David Suchet | Hercule Poirot |
| Hugh Fraser | Captain Hastings |
| Philip Jackson | Chief Inspector Japp |
| Diana Kent | Zoe Havering |
| Jim Norton | Roger Havering |
| Shaughan Seymour | Archie Havering |
| Roy Boyd | Jack Stoddard |
| Bernard Horsfall | Harrington Pace |
| Victoria Alcock | Ellie |
| Claire Travers-Deacon | Joan |
| Christopher Scoular | Sergeant Foran |
| Raymond Trickitt | Constable Cook |
| Arthur Whybrow | Mr Anstruther |
| Denyse Alexander | Mrs Middleton |

Based on the short story *The Mystery of Hunter's Lodge* (1924). 50 minutes.

*The Mystery of Hunter's Lodge* is contained in the 1924 *Poirot Investigates* short story collection. The film starts with Hastings, who has been invited by Roger Havering to participate in a grouse shoot on his uncle's estate. On hand are Roger, his uncle Harrington Pace, cousin Archie Havering and estate manager Jack Stoddard. The shoot ends abruptly when Archie shoots Pace in the hand; fortunately it is not a serious wound.

Maladies seem to have struck many of the guests, including Poirot, who is on hand as a spectator; he has caught a cold. Archie and Pace are not on the best of terms, the former bemoaning the fact that the lodge is so seldom used.

While Poirot returns to his hotel and takes to his bed with a fever, Roger Havering catches a train to return to London. We then see a strange, bearded figure alight from the train, stealing the railwayman's bicycle.

After Harrington Pace is murdered that same evening by a bearded stranger, local police are urged by Inspector Japp, who is now on the scene, to find Mrs Middleton, Pace's missing housekeeper.

Poirot, on the other hand, believes the missing bicycle is more important than the missing woman, and urges Japp and Hastings to look for it. It also seems that Archie Havering, an accomplished cyclist, has a great deal to gain from the death of his uncle.

▲ Poirot (David Suchet, right) gives Hastings (Hugh Fraser) a tip in *The Mystery of Hunter's Lodge*.

Both the items are eventually discovered, but the woman turns out to have been bogus; the real Mrs Middleton had been discharged before the murder.

Poirot, who has appropriated the pseudo-Mrs Middleton's apron, enlists the aid of a foxhound to come up with the necessary evidence to prove the identity of the murderer, which he does at Hunter's Lodge via flashbacks in his usual urbane style.

*The Mystery of Hunter's Lodge*, aired on March 10, 1991, was the eighth in the series directed by Renny Rye, which he does with his usual skill and flair.

David Suchet, Hugh Fraser, and Philip Jackson are all splendid, and the supporting cast is first rate, especially veteran character actor Bernard Horsfall as the murdered man.

# ≡ 1992 ≡

## The ABC Murders (TV)

Made in England. Directed by Andrew Grieve.

### CAST

▼

| | |
|---|---|
| David Suchet | Hercule Poirot |
| Hugh Fraser | Captain Hastings |
| Philip Jackson | Chief Inspector Japp |
| Nicholas Farrell | Donald Fraser |
| Donald Douglas | Franklin Clarke |
| Pippa Guard | Megan Barnard |
| Nina Marc | Thora Grey |
| Donald Sumpter | Cust |
| Cathryn Bradshaw | Mary Drower |
| Jeremy Hawk | Deveril |
| Michael Mellinger | Franz Ascher |
| Miranda Forbes | Mrs Turton |
| Lucinda Curtis | Mrs Marbury |
| Ann Windsor | Miss Merrion |
| Peter Penry-Jones | Superintendent Carter |
| David McAlister | Inspector Glen |
| Vivienne Burgess | Lady Clarke |
| John Breslin | Mr Barnard |
| Norman McDonald | Mr Strange |
| Campbell Graham | Mr Downes |
| Allan Mitchell | Dr Kerr |
| Philip Anthony | Doctor |
| Alex Knight | Andover Police Sergeant |
| Claude Close | Doncaster Sergeant |
| David Richard-Fox | Scotland Yard Sergeant |
| Clifford Milner | Constable |
| Gordon Salkilld | Commissionaire |
| Andrew Williamson | Man in Library |
| Jane Birdsall | Nurse |
| Bill Weston, Paul Weston, Eddie Powell, David Cronnelly | Stunts |

Based on the novel *The ABC Murders* (1936). 99 minutes.

▲ Members of the cast of *The ABC Murders* (L-R) Pippa Guard, Miranda Forbes, Philip Jackson, David Suchet, Donald Douglas, Nina Marc, Nicholas Farrell and Hugh Fraser.

*The ABC Murders*, one of Agatha Christie's best stories, had been filmed in 1966 with light actor Tony Randall cast in the role of Hercule Poirot, under the title *The Alphabet Murders*.

The 1992 television film, first broadcast on January 5, returned the story's title to its original, as well as adhering strictly to period setting.

The story opens as Hastings returns from a visit to South America where he has, among other things, been hunting. Poirot is pleased with his gift of a cayman, but perplexed by a letter he has recieved from someone signed 'ABC' and warning him to look out for Andover on the 21st of the month. Later, Inspector Japp discovers that a woman with the initials A.A. has been found battered to death in Andover.

Poirot's next letter points to Bexhill-on-Sea; Poirot hurries down but the victim, Betty Barnard, is discovered strangled on the beach. Just as in the first crime, a copy of an ABC railway guide is left at the scene of the murder.

The newspapers generally assume the crimes to be the work of a lunatic, but Poirot believes the criminal has a particular hatred of him, making a personal challenge (much in the same way Jack the Ripper taunted press and police in 1888).

The next letter, apparently through a delay in the post, arrives on the day the crime is to take place, in Churston. Japp, Poirot and Hastings take the sleeper train, but millionaire Sir Carmichael Clarke has already been killed. Poirot then gathers relatives and employees of all three victims together in order to prompt any recollections that may link the three crimes.

At this point we are introduced to a shabby fellow, one Alexander Bonaparte Cust, who becomes confused and upset when reading an account of the crimes in a public library. Meanwhile, Poirot receives another letter, informing him the next murder will take place in Doncaster. Despite elaborate police surveillance at the local racecourse, where the crime is expected, the murderer strikes once more – this time in the local cinema.

Mr Cust has also been to the cinema and, back at his hotel, appears shocked to discover blood on his cuff and a knife in his pocket. While the police are searching for him, Cust stumbles into the local station. A highly suggestible and neurotic man (apart from being an epileptic), Cust thinks he may have committed the murders, but denies having written the letters to Poirot.

Although authorities are convinced they have the right man, Poirot disagrees, returning to the scene of the Bexhill killing with all the interested parties. There on the beach, he explains his theory of an extremely complex case; not surprisingly he is quite correct.

*The ABC Murders*, adapted by Clive Exton and produced by Nick Elliott, is yet another fine example of the exemplary care that has gone into all the productions made by London Weekend Television.

David Suchet, Hugh Fraser and Philip Jackson can by now all play their parts in their sleep; however, they give finely-tuned, wide-awake performances, full of detail and substance.

One can only continue to applaud these dramatizations, as they are all well cast and straightforward in their adherence to period and the substance of Christie's original works.

▲ Hercule Poirot (David Suchet, standing), flanked by Captain Hastings (Hugh Fraser, left) and Chief Inspector Japp (Philip Jackson), explains his views in *The ABC Murders*.

## Death in the Clouds (TV)

Made in England. Directed by Stephen Whittaker.

### CAST
▼

| | |
|---|---|
| David Suchet | Hercule Poirot |
| Philip Jackson | Chief Inspector Japp |
| Sarah Woodward | Jane Grey |
| Shaun Scott | Norman Gale |
| Richard Ireson | Inspector Fournier |
| David Firth | Lord Horbury |
| Cathryn Harrison | Lady Horbury |
| Amanda Royle | Venetia Kerr |
| Eve Pearce | Madame Giselle |
| Gabrielle Lloyd | Elsie |
| Jenny Downham | Anne Giselle/Madeleine |
| Roger Heathcott | Daniel Clancy |
| Guy Manning | Jean Dupont |
| Harry Audley | Raymond Barraclough |
| John Bleasdale | Mitchell |
| George Rossi | Zeropoulos |
| Nick Mercer | Policeman |
| Hilary Waters | Paris Hotel Receptionist |
| Russell Richardson | French Registrar |
| Yves Aubert | Smart Man |
| Hanna Maria Pravda | Concierge |
| Artro Morris | French Proprietor |
| Raymond Sawyer | French Desk Clerk |

Based on the novel *Death in the Clouds* (1935). 103 minutes.

*Death in the Clouds*, which had its title changed to *Death in the Air* when released in the United State, finds Hercule Poirot staying in Paris at the Ritz Hotel. His fellow guests include Lord and Lady Horbury and their companion, the Hon. Venetia Kerr. At the French Open Tennis Championship, stewardess Jane Grey meets dentist Norman Gale. In the bar, they later observe Lady Horbury's startled reaction to the presence of a woman in black, one Madame Giselle.

Lady Horbury is later seen visiting Madame Giselle and afterwards losing at the casino table. Lord Horbury, upset as his wife has behaved badly (she was accompanied to the casino by a handsome young actor), vows to return to England. Meanwhile Venetia takes Poirot to the men's final of the tennis match in return for his having shown her round at an art gallery.

The next day, Norman Gale, Lady Horbury, Venetia, archaeologist Jean Dupont, detective writer Daniel Clancy, and Madame Giselle are on Poirot's flight back to England. Jane Grey is the stewardess on duty, accompanied by steward Mitchell.

As Poirot falls asleep, a meal is served, disturbed only slightly by the presence of a wasp, which is slain by Dupont. Poirot is awakened when it is discovered that Madame Giselle is dead; initially it is thought that she was stung by the wasp, but it is later revealed that she was killed with a poisoned dart.

As the police have been alerted on the ground, Inspector Japp is waiting at Croydon Airport when the plane lands. A search of everyone's luggage reveals nothing pertinent, but a blowpipe is found next to Lady Horbury's seat.

▲ ▶ Hercule Poirot (David Suchet) displays his multi-purpose walking stick in *Death in the Clouds*.

Inquiries reveal that Madame Giselle had been a known blackmailer and moneylender, but police are unable to gain any clues from her papers, as Madame Giselle's maid has burned them all.

Poirot attacks the case from another angle, and finds that a good many of the passengers on the fatal flight had some connection or knowledge of blowpipes. Lord Horbury volunteers the information that his marriage is on the rocks and that his wife knew the murdered woman.

After being married in a Paris registry office, a woman goes to the police, claiming to be the daughter of the dead Madame Giselle. The latter's maid confirms the existence of an illegitimate daughter, who was sent away as a baby.

On a flight over to Paris with Inspector Japp, Poirot makes experiments with a blowpipe, proving the impossibility of Lady Horbury having fired the dart. Steward Mitchell tells them that Madame Giselle, a frequent flyer on the London–Paris run, usually took the early flight; an office clerk admits that he took a bribe from a man to tell the victim the early flight was filled.

After Poirot discovers that Madame Giselle's maid and daughter are one and the same (the 'maid' was also on the flight), he is unfortunately unable to prevent her death on board a train. But is this suicide, or murder?

Assembling everyone in his hotel suite, Poirot explains the solution of the crime. Two vital clues, he tells them, were an empty matchbox and two coffee spoons on Madame Giselle's saucer.

*Death in the Clouds*, shown for the first time on January 12, 1992, is a first-rate television production.

Dramatized by William Humble and directed by Stephen Whittaker, it is an ingenious story, certainly well made by a group of talented professionals. David Suchet, as Poirot, goes this one without Hastings, but Philip Jackson (in his twenty-eighth appearance in the role) is on hand here, wonder-fully portraying the Scotland Yard man.

Sarah Woodward, Shaun Scott, David Firth, Cathryn Harrison and Amanda Royle offer fine work among a cast of television actors who were obviously chosen for their suitability to their characters than for 'name' appeal. This is just one of many reasons to praise the makers of Christie television films in England during the last decade.

Another reason, particularly evident in *Death in the Clouds*, is the wonderful photography. Combine this with good acting, directing, writing and the fine costumes (which truly deserve compliments) and music, and you have the recipe for excellence and success.

## One, Two, Buckle My Shoe (TV)

Made in England. Directed by Ross Devenish.

CAST

| | |
|---|---|
| David Suchet | Hercule Poirot |
| Philip Jackson | Chief Inspector Japp |
| Carolyn Colquhoun | Mabelle Sainsbury Seale |
| Joanna Phillips-Lane | Gerda Grant |
| Peter Blythe | Blunt |
| Chris Spicer | Claudio |
| Michael Tudor Barnes | Don Pedro |
| Alan Penn | Leonato |
| Guy Oliver Watts | Benedick |
| Joe Greco | Alfred |
| Laurence Harrington | Henry Morley |
| Karen Gledhill | Gladys Neville |
| Sara Stewart | Jane Olivera |
| Kevork Malikyan | Amberiotis |
| Oliver Bradshaw | Mr Hendry |
| Cassandra Holliday | Receptionist, Russell Hotel |
| Stephen Bird | Pageboy |
| Rosalind Knight | Georgina Morley |
| Trilby James | Agnes |
| Nicholas Brook | Waiter, Astoria |
| Tom Durham | Lionel Arnholt |
| Christopher Eccleston | Frank Carter |
| Dawn Keeler | Mrs Pinner |
| Helen Horton | Julia Olivera |
| Keith Woodhams | Desk Clerk, Astoria |
| Jean Ainslie | Mrs Hendry |
| John Carlin | Dr Bennett |
| George Waring | First Coroner |
| Eileen Maciejewska | Manageress, Carlyle Hotel |
| Ben Bazell | Sergeant Beddoes |
| Mark Heal | Police Constable |
| John Warner | Second Coroner |
| Nigel Bellairs | Leatherman |
| John Peters | Sergeant |

Based on the novel *One, Two, Buckle My Shoe* (1940). 103 minutes.

*One, Two, Buckle My Shoe*, written at the time of Dunkirk in 1940, was known in the United States firstly as *The Patriotic Murders* and later as *An Overdose of Death*. The *New York Times*, reviewing the book on March 2, 1940, stated: 'It's a real Agatha Christie thriller: exceedingly complicated plot, briskly simple in narrative, with a swift course of unflagging suspense that leads to complete surprise. After closing the book one may murmur "farfetched" or even "impossible". But any such complaint will be voiced only after the story has been finished; there won't be a moment to think of such things before.'

The film begins in India in 1924, with an

▲ David Suchet played the dapper Poirot for the thirty-third time in *One, Two, Buckle My Shoe*.

English touring company. Gerda Grant confides the news of her engagement to the dashing Alistair Blunt to her fellow actress, Mabelle Sainsbury Seale.

Many years later, as Poirot is visiting the dentist, Mabelle, who works there, is just leaving, and runs into Alistair Blunt and his niece. Later at her hotel, she meets Mr Amberiotis, an acquaintance from her India days, who reacts oddly when she tells him of the chance encounter with Blunt. The last we see of Mabelle is as she enters the flat where Gerda is supposed to live.

Morley, the dentist, complains that his secretary's absence is likely due to an assignation rather than a sick aunt, but her boyfriend arrives in a state of agitation, and soon after, Blunt. Outside the office, Poirot retrieves a broken shoe buckle for a woman calling herself 'Miss Sainsbury Seale', but who is in fact not Mabelle. After the arrival and departure of Amberiotis, pageboy Alfred discovers Morley dead on the surgery floor; he appears to have shot himself.

Subsequent police inquiries lead Inspector Japp to the conclusion of suicide, which is further strenghthened when Amberiotis is discovered dead in his hotel room, from an overdose of novacaine. The inquest brings in a verdict of death by suicide on Morley, concluding the dentist had shot himself after realizing his fatal mistake of injecting Amberiotis with a dose much too high.

Miss Sainsbury Seale has now disappeared, and Blunt's niece Jane relates how they met her outside the dentist's office, and the connection with the old days in India. The flat where Mabelle was visiting Gerda turns out to be rented by a Mrs Chapman, who has also disappeared. A search of the flat uncovers a large fur chest, containing a body with a battered face and a distinctive pair of buckled shoes.

Japp bursts in on the wrong Chapmans, a honeymoon couple, which leads Poirot to visit Somerset House in search of a certain certificate. The dentist that has taken over for Morley says the dental records of the corpse prove her to be one of Morley's patients – a Mrs Chapman.

After a visit to Blunt at Exsham Manor, Poirot employs his famous little grey cells to solve this difficult case involving blackmail, dual identity, and murder.

*One, Two, Buckle My Shoe* showed that Christie indeed was a person who was in touch with current affairs. Although the war itself was not directly mentioned in the story, Hitler and

▲ Inspector Japp (Philip Jackson, left) collars a suspect in *One, Two, Buckle My Shoe*.

Mussolini are, and the tone of Fascism is felt with the Blackshirt Organization (which Christie doubtless derived from the real life British Union of Fascists).

It is impossible not to be impressed with this film, another fine production from London Weekend Television. One runs out of worthy adjectives; the technical credits are all exemplary, as we have come now to expect, and there is a fine sense of period atmosphere.

Aside from the two stars, David Suchet and Philip Jackson (Suchet in his thirty-third rendering of Poirot and Jackson playing Japp for the twenty-ninth time), who shine as usual, the acting is first rate down to the tiniest part, with Peter Blythe and Carolyn Colquhoun especially fine in two of the larger roles.

## ≡ 1992 ≡

## They Do It With Mirrors (TV)
Made in England. Directed by Norman Stone.

### CAST
▼

| | |
|---|---|
| Joan Hickson | Miss Marple |
| Jean Simmons | Carrie Louise Serrocold |
| Joss Ackland | Lewis Serrocold |
| Faith Brook | Ruth Van Rydock |
| David Horovitch | Detective Chief Inspector Slack |
| Ian Brimble | Detective Sergeant Lake |
| Neal Swettenham | Edgar Lawson |
| Gillian Barge | Mildred Strete |
| Christopher Villiers | Alex Restarick |
| Jay Villiers | Stephen Restarick |
| Holly Aird | Gina Hudd |
| Todd Boyce | Walter Hudd |
| Saul Reichlin | Dr Maseryk |
| John Bott | Christian Gulbrandsen |
| Matthew Cottle | Ernie |
| David Doyle | Neville |
| Jake Wood | Bert |
| Tom Kerridge | Keithie |
| Brenda Cowling | Mrs Rodgers |
| Anne Atkins | Woman Police Constable |
| Stee Billingsley, Rachel Bond, Bryn Walters | Dancers |

Based on the novel *Murder With Mirrors* (1952). 96 minutes.

The eleventh television film starring Joan Hickson as Miss Marple, *They Do It With Mirrors* had been filmed in 1985 with Helen Hayes in the role of the clever spinster.

The film opens with Ruth Van Rydock (Faith Brook), a friend of Miss Marple's, convinced that something is wrong at Stonygates, a reformatory for young criminals. Ruth's sister, Carrie Louise Serrocold, and her husband Lewis live at the large estate; the latter being an ardent social reformer and founder of the institute.

Miss Marple arrives and renews her acquaintanceship with Carrie Louise, whom she has not seen for some time. Miss Marple suspects, or rather intuitively feels, that something is amiss. She also discovers that the authorities are putting pressure on the Serrocolds to close the institute.

We are soon introduced to other characters: Mildred Strete, Carrie's widowed daughter, who fusses and frets over her mother, and Carrie's granddaughter Gina and her American husband Walter Hudd, who suspects that Gina has too strong an interest in Carrie's stepsons Alex and Stephen Restarick.

After Edgar Lawson, a disturbed young man whom Lewis has taken under his wing, disturbs an afternoon tea party, a telegram arrives from Christian Gulbrandsen announcing his arrival the following day.

After Gulbrandsen's arrival, Miss Marple overhears him discussing how 'Carrie Louise must not learn the truth' with husband Lewis.

Later that evening, Ruth has a surprise for everyone: an old film of herself and Carrie Louise as young girls on a European tour.

Before the film begins, Gulbrandsen retires to his room in order to write an important letter. Meanwhile, downstairs, the film is interrupted when Edgar bursts in and begins an argument with Lewis, who he accuses of being his enemy. Calming the lad down, Lewis persuades him into the adjoining study, locking the door behind him.

As the others watch the film, they can hear Edgar's shouts and Lewis's calm responses coming from the next room. As the lights fuse, stopping the film and plunging the room into darkness, two shots are heard apparently coming from the room next door. As some of the men are about to break in the door, Lewis himself steps out. Edgar is lying sobbing on the floor, and there are two bullet holes in the wall behind Lewis's desk. In the ensuing confusion, Mildred tells everyone that Christian Gulbrandson has been murdered.

The police are summoned and duly arrive; Lewis shows Chief Inspector Slack the letter Gulbrandsen was apparently typing, while Miss Marple expresses her regret to Ruth concerning the unforeseen tragedy; even she is baffled.

It appears that all along someone has been trying to poison Carrie Louise, as her medicine contains arsenic. Slack decides to interrogate Edgar (who has told Miss Marple he is the son of Winston Churchill!), and as matters reach a climax, Miss Marple finally deduces who must be the killer. The clue was given to her by Inspector Slack's secret hobby.

As usual, another wonderful film has been made by the BBC. T.R. Bowen, who has become the essential element in the continuing success of these films, once again adapted the novel. The stunning atmospheric pictures were created by cameraman John Walker, and Alan Spalding's production design provides a late-1950s setting.

Brian Willis designed the costumes, Christine Walmesley-Cotham did the make-up, Sheila O'Neill the choreography and Ken Howard the music. All are first rate and professional, and make *They Do It With Mirrors* most enjoyable.

George Gallaccio, the producer, and director Norman Stone also continue the high standards they established with the Hickson–Marple productions.

Joan Hickson's Miss Marple is welcomed after an absence of some three years, and there is good work from Jean Simmons, Faith Brook, David Horovitch and Ian Brimble, the latter two repeating roles they essayed previously. Joss Ackland, a marvellous actor, also gives polish to the role of Lewis Serrocold.

The rest of the cast are uniformly good, and the highly talented team of production personnel, many of whom have contributed to the success of the previous Miss Marple films, make this another piece of fine entertainment.

▲ Joan Hickson (seated) as Miss Marple, Jean Simmons as Carrie Louise Serrocold and Joss Ackland as Lewis Serrocold in *They Do It With Mirrors.*

# The Mirror Crack'd From Side to Side (TV)

### Made in England. Directed by Norman Stone.

CAST

| | |
|---|---|
| Joan Hickson | Miss Jane Marple |
| Claire Bloom | Marina Gregg |
| John Castle | Inspector Craddock |
| David Horovitch | Superintendent Slack |
| Gwen Watford | Dolly Bantry |
| Barbara Hicks | Miss Hartnell |
| Ian Brimble | Sergeant Lake |
| Barry Newman | Jason Rudd |
| Norman Rodway | Dr Gilchrist |
| Glynis Barber | Lola Brewster |
| Constantine Gregory | Ardwyck Fenn |
| Margaret Courtenay | Miss Knight |
| Amanda Elwes | Margot Bence |
| Trevor Bowen | Raymond West |
| Elizabeth Garvie | Ella Zeilinsky |
| Christopher Good | Reverend Hawes |
| Rhoda Lewis | Mrs Brogan |
| John Cassady | Guisseppe |
| Judy Cornwell | Heather Badcock |
| Christopher Hancock | Arthur Badcock |
| Anna Niland | Cherry Baker |
| Rose Keegan | Gladys Dixon |
| Michael Stroud | Delancey |
| Reggie Oliver | Chris |
| Celia Ryder | Mrs Hopkins |
| John Croft | Inch |
| Vince Rayner | Station Master |
| Stuart Harrison | Equerry |

Based on the novel *The Mirror Crack'd From Side to Side* (1962). 115 minutes.

Christie's 1962 novel had been previously filmed in 1980 as *The Mirror Crack'd*, with Angela Lansbury as Miss Marple and an international all-star cast featuring Elizabeth Taylor, Rock Hudson, Kim Novak, Edward Fox, and Tony Curtis.

*The Mirror Crack'd From Side to Side*, dramatized by T.R. Bowen, is set in the village of St Mary Mead, home of Miss Jane Marple. The story concerns an American film crew shooting a picture at Gossington Hall, home of Miss Marple's friend Dolly Bantry.

The film will feature Marina Gregg, who is making a return to the screen after an absence of several years; her husband, Jason Rudd, will direct it. Also in the cast is Lola Brewster, a rival of Marina. Her husband, Ardwyck Fenn, is the producer.

After local Heather Badcock drinks a poisoned cocktail at a party, Miss Marple becomes interested. It is without doubt a case of murder, although the Badcock woman seems to have taken the drink when it was intended for someone else. Who then is the intended victim? Further inquiries seem to point to Marina; the victim took the actress' drink when her own was spilled.

Miss Marple's nephew, Chief Inspector Dermot

▲ Stars of *The Mirror Crack'd From Side to Side* include Joan Hickson (Miss Marple), Claire Bloom (Marina Gregg, seated) and Barry Newman (Jason Rudd).

Inspector Craddock in the 1986 film *A Murder is Announced*, repeats the role here and is quite good. David Horovitch and Ian Brimble, who portray Superintendent Slack and Detective Sergeant Lake respectively, do so for the fifth time.

Gwen Watford previously played Dolly Bantry in the 1985 *The Body in the Library*, while Barbara Hicks, who is seen here as Mrs Hartnell (the same role she played in *Murder at the Vicarage* in 1988) had also appeared in *Murder She Said* (1962) and *Evil Under the Sun* (1982). Margaret Courtenay, seen here as Miss Knight, was also in the 1980 version, *The Mirror Crack'd*. That time she appeared as Mrs Bantry.

The dramatization is first rate, as are the costumes and sets. Producer George Gallaccio, and director Norman Stone (who helmed *They Do It With Mirrors*) also do quality work, which helps to make another memorable feature.

▲ Joan Hickson (left foreground) plays Miss Marple for the twelfth time in *The Mirror Crack'd From Side to Side*. In the background are Barry Newman and Claire Bloom.

Craddock, along with local Superintendent Slack, does most of the leg work in the case while Miss Marple relies on her intellect. Only after a following murder and several accidents is Miss Marple able to solve this baffling case.

Christie's publishers had established a tradition in later years of 'A Christie For Christmas', bringing out her books for release at the Christmas holidays. The BBC has carried on the tradition, showing *The Mirror Crack'd From Side to Side* at Christmas 1992.

Joan Hickson, now 86, who has developed quite a following, plays the intelligent amateur sleuth Miss Jane Marple with aplomb for the twelfth time. Sadly, this may well be the last time, as the BBC apparently has no plans to produce any more Miss Marple films in the immediate future.

The entire cast does a fine job, including Claire Bloom, Glynis Barber, and Norman Rodway. There are a number of alumni on hand from other Christie films. John Castle, who played

## The Adventure of the Egyptian Tomb (TV)

### Made in England. Directed by Peter Barber-Fleming.

### CAST

| | |
|---|---|
| David Suchet | Hercule Poirot |
| Hugh Fraser | Captain Hastings |
| Pauline Moran | Miss Lemon |
| Rolf Saxon | Dr Ames |
| Oliver Pierre | Henry Schneider |
| Anna Cropper | Lady Willard |
| Peter Reeves | Sir John Willard |
| Grant Thatcher | Sir Guy Willard |
| Bill Bailey | Felix Bleibner |
| Paul Birchard | Rupert Bleibner |
| Jon Strickland | Dr Leonard Fosswell |
| Simon Cowell-Parker | Nigel Harper |
| Mozaffar Shafeie | Hassan |
| Bob Wisdom | Waiter |

Based on the short story *The Adventure of the Egyptian Tomb* (1924). 51 minutes.

Taken from the short story of the same title in 1924's *Poirot Investigates*, *The Adventure of the Egyptian Tomb* concerns archaeologist Sir John Willard, who dies of a heart attack shortly after opening a pharoah's tomb. The press immediately capitalizes on the death, dredging up stories of 'cursed' tombs.

When fellow excavator Bleibner dies of blood poisoning two weeks later, followed by the suicide of Bleibner's nephew, Lady Willard consults Poirot to deal with the curse of Men-her-Ra.

It seems that Lady Willard now fears for the life of her son, Sir Guy Willard, who is in Egypt carrying on with the excavation. Poirot assures her that he will do what he can.

Poirot and Hastings set sail for Egypt, a voyage that turns out to be agony for the poorly-travelled Poirot. A week later they land in Alexandria; Hastings extolls the virtues of the Sphynx and the Pyramids while Poirot complains about the sand, among other things. A camel ride to the excavation provokes further groans and lamentations from the detective.

▶ Hastings (Hugh Fraser, left) and Poirot (David Suchet) arrive in Alexandria, Egypt in *The Adventure of the Egyptian Tomb*.

▲ Hercule Poirot (David Suchet) selects his camel to ride in *The Adventure of the Egyptian Tomb*.

Upon arriving at the camp they are met by Dr Fosswell, who informs them that party member Henry Schneider has died of tetanus. Poirot notes that this is the fourth recent death connected with the expedition. Dr Ames assures Poirot that tetanus was definitely responsible for Schneider's death.

The Egyptian servant Hassan warns Poirot that 'there is evil in the air around us', and later that evening after dinner a strange figure is seen prowling around the camp. The figure has the head of a dog (Anubis, the jackal-headed god of departing souls, according to legend) and mysteriously vanishes before it can be tracked.

While Poirot has been all the while dwelling on the more superstitious aspects of the situation, the case is finally solved when Poirot is ostensibly poisoned. The story concludes as Poirot explains all to the befuddled Hastings.

With only minimal changes to the story, such as the changing of the character Tosswill's name to Fosswell, *The Adventure of the Egyptian Tomb* is yet another excellent television film from London Weekend Television.

The photography is first rate, as well as all other technical credits, and the acting by Suchet and Fraser is up to their usual high standards. Very good performances are also turned in by Rolf Saxon, Oliver Pierre, and Anna Cropper (who played Anthea Bradbury-Scott in the 1987 Christie film *Nemesis*).

## The Adventure of the Italian Nobleman (TV)

Made in England. Directed by Brian Farnham.

### CAST

| | |
|---|---|
| David Suchet | Hercule Poirot |
| Hugh Fraser | Captain Hastings |
| Philip Jackson | Chief Inspector Japp |
| Pauline Moran | Miss Lemon |
| Arthur Cox | Dr Hawker |
| Sidney Kean | Count Foscatini |
| Leonard Preston | Mr Graves |
| Vincenzo Ricotta | Mario Asciano |
| David Neal | Bruno Vizzini |
| Anna Mazzotti | Margherita Fabbri |
| Janet Lees Price | Miss Rider |
| David Verrey | Chef |
| Alberto G. Janelli | Darida |
| Vittorio Amandola | Secretary |
| Ben Bazell | Sergeant Beddoes |
| Barrie Wilmore | Regents Court Manager |
| David Willoughby | Lad in Showroom |
| Michael Tudor | Man in Peabody Buildings |

Based on the short story *The Adventure of the Italian Nobleman* (1924).
51 minutes.

Contained in the *Poirot Investigaes* short story collection, *The Adventure of the Italian Nobleman* begins with a friend and neighbour, Dr Hawker, visiting Poirot and Hastings at home one evening. Miss Rider, the doctor's housekeeper, suddenly arrives with the news of a desperate phone call to the doctor from a Count Foscatini, a patient who was apparently being attacked at the time of his call for help.

Poirot and Hastings accompany the good doctor to the Count's Regents Park flat. After obtaining a passkey to the flat from the court manager, they discover the body of the Italian, his head bashed in by a marble statuette.

After ascertaining that no one else is in the flat, they notice the remains of a dinner that was apparently eaten by the Count and two others. Inquiries of the kitchen staff corroborates this.

Graves, the Count's valet-butler, tells Poirot of a visit by two other men: middle-aged Mario Asciano and another Italian of about 25. Inspec-

tor Japp arrives and soon starts setting the official wheels in motion.

Asciano is traced and subsequently arrested and charged with the Count's murder. Only when the Italian Ambassador asserts that the prisoner was with him at the embassy on the evening in question is the latter released.

Asciano visits Poirot at the latter's invitation, admitting that he visited the murdered man on the morning before his death. He also tells the Belgian that the Count was a bogus Count but a genuine blackmailer. After his departure, Poirot knows all he needs to know. He calls Hastings' attention to the clues of the drapes that were not drawn and the black coffee, which enable him to catch a most brilliant criminal.

*The Adventure of the Italian Nobleman* is quite good entertainment. The story has been somewhat expanded in that several characters are presented that are not in the short story.

The cast are exceptionally fine, with David

Suchet, Hugh Fraser, Philip Jackson and Pauline Moran all in their usual good form. The supporting players are also well cast, especially veteran character actor Arthur Cox, who had previously portrayed Inspector Marriott in several of the episodes in the 1984 *Partners in Crime* series.

◀ The intrepid Poirot (David Suchet, left) and faithful Hastings (Hugh Fraser) in *The Adventure of the Italian Nobleman.*

# ≡ 1993 ≡

## The Case of the Missing Will (TV)

Made in England. Directed by John Bruce.

### CAST

| | |
|---|---|
| David Suchet | Hercule Poirot |
| Hugh Fraser | Captain Hastings |
| Philip Jackson | Chief Inspector Japp |
| Pauline Moran | Miss Lemon |
| Mark Kingston | Andrew Marsh |
| Jon Laurimore | Walter Baker |
| Terrence Hardiman | John Siddaway |
| Rowena Cooper | Sarah Siddaway |
| Beth Goddard | Violet Wilson |
| Edward Atterton | Robert Siddaway |
| Gillian Hanna | Margaret Baker |
| Susan Tracy | Phyllida Campion |
| Neil Stuke | Peter Baker |
| Richard Durden | Dr Pritchard |
| Scott Cleverdon | President |
| George Beech | First Undergraduate |
| Alistair Petrie | Second Undergraduate |
| Stephen Oxley | Doctor |

Based on the short story *The Case of the Missing Will* (1924). 51 minutes.

▲ David Suchet as the Belgian sleuth, Hercule Poirot, in *The Case of the Missing Will*.

*The Case of the Missing Will* is yet another short story taken from the marvellous 1924 collection, *Poirot Investigates*. The tale involves Violet Wilson (her name was Violet Marsh in the short story) seeking the assistance of Poirot.

Her uncle, the late Andrew Marsh, had been Violet's guardian since the death of her mother some years ago. Marsh had accumulated a large estate and left a peculiar will that challenged Violet to match her wits with the dead man. She is given a year's time, after which the estate would pass to charity.

Poirot believes that her uncle hid either a large sum of money or a second will somewhere about the house. Along with Hastings, Poirot sets off for the estate. He learns from the Bakers, a couple who had cared for the old man, that a second will definitely did exist (they had signed two wills) and also that some seemingly unnecessary repair work had been done on the house a while back.

Tracking down the firm that did the repair work, Poirot learns that a secret cavity was built in one of the chimneys. But when he investigates, all he finds in it is a charred bit of paper.

Although Poirot believes that the case is now over, his little grey cells get to work and he is able to see what he had overlooked. When Hastings points out to Poirot that it was in fact the uncle that had the greater wit, Poirot disagrees. He reasons that the young woman's wit was superior because she had the sense to employ the brilliant Hercule Poirot!

*The Case of the Missing Will* is very well made technically and artistically. The lighting and costumes are especially good.

On the acting side, Suchet, Fraser, and Jackson are up to their usual high standards. Nonregulars that give notable performances include the superlative, versatile Jon Laurimore, and Mark Kingston as Andrew Marsh. Terrence Hardiman, as John Siddaway (he had been seen in 1987 in *Sleeping Murder*) and Rowena Cooper (likewise seen before, in 1984's *The Case of the Missing Lady*) as Sarah Siddaway are both quite good.

Those who have read the short story will note that several changes have been made in this film, most noticeably the addition of characters. Aside from the usual name changes, be they major or minor, there were no characters with the surname Siddaway in the short story, or for that matter, Japp.

# ≡ 1993 ≡

## The Chocolate Box (TV)

Made in England. Directed by Ken Grieve.

### CAST

| | |
|---|---|
| David Suchet | Hercule Poirot |
| Philip Jackson | Chief Inspector Japp |
| Rosalie Crutchley | Mme Deroulard |
| Geoffrey Whitehead | Xavier St Alard |
| David De Keyser | Gaston Beaujeu |
| Mark Eden | Superintendent Boucher |
| Anna Chancellor | Virginie Desmesne |
| James Coombes | Paul Deroulard |
| Jonathan Hackett | Claude Chantalier |
| Preston Lockwood | Francois |
| Jonathan Barlow | Jean-Louis Ferraud |
| Lucy Cohu | Marianne Deroulard |
| Michael Beint | Coroner |
| Kirsten Clark | Jeanette |
| Linda Broughton | Denise |
| Richard Derrington | Henri |

Based on the short story *The Chocolate Box* (1924). 51 minutes.

The short story *The Chocolate Box* (in the *Poirot Investigates* collection) begins one evening with Poirot recounting to Hastings that not all of his cases have been successful ones. Poirot then begins to narrate one of his rare failures, which occurred many years previously when he was on the police force in Brussels.

For the television film, Hastings is absent and Chief Inspector Japp (who did not appear in the written work) is on hand.

The case involves one Paul Deroulard, an anti-Catholic French deputy who is awaiting the portfolio of a minister. When the deputy suddenly dies of an apparent heart attack, Poirot comes into the case.

A young lady, Virginie Desmense, believes that Deroulard has been murdered. Arriving at Deroulard's home, Poirot encounters the elderly mother of the deceased, and several others, none of whom believe there has been any crime. Xavier St Alard had been a guest at the time of the deputy's death.

◄ Poirot in uniform: David Suchet in *The Chocolate Box*.

Further investigations lead Poirot to the conclusion that Mademoiselle Desmense has been suffering a delusion. Everything appears normal. Everything, that is, except a box of chocolates. For although the box is blue, the lid of the box is pink. Although he as yet cannot see the significance of this, Poirot nevertheless notes that here at least is something out of the ordinary.

When Poirot questions Francois, servant to Deroulard, he reveals that the deceased was very fond of sweets, especially chocolates. A discreet search produces an empty box; this time the box is blue and the lid pink.

A chemist informs Poirot that although not strictly speaking a poison, a certain prescription taken in large doses can prove fatal. Poirot next discovers an empty bottle of just such a prescription, and feels certain that he knows the murderer, but upon returning to Deroulard's house discovers that he was wrong.

Ken Grieve, who also directed *The Jewel Robbery at the Grand Metropolitan*, shows a steady hand at the helm of this film. Technical credits are up to their normal standards, which are quite excellent, and the acting is classy, especially by Rosalie Crutchley, Geoffrey Whitehead, David De Keyser and Mark Eden.

One does tend to wonder, however, why so many changes have been made in this film from the original work. Although period setting is quite excellent, there seems to be little reason for the omission of Hastings, the removal of the character John Wilson, the adding other characters, and the name changes.

# ≡ 1993 ≡

## Dead Man's Mirror (TV)

### Made in England. Directed by Brian Farnham.

CAST

| | |
|---|---|
| David Suchet | Hercule Poirot |
| Hugh Fraser | Captain Hastings |
| Philip Jackson | Chief Inspector Japp |
| Zena Walker | Vanda Chevenix |
| Iain Cuthbertson | Gervase Chevenix |
| Fiona Walker | Miss Lingard |
| Richard Lintern | John Lake |
| Emma Fielding | Ruth Chevenix |
| Tushka Bergen | Susan Cardwell |
| Jeremy Northam | Hugo Trent |
| James Greene | Snell |
| Derek Smee | Auctioneer |
| John Rolfe | Registrar |
| John Croft | Lawrence |

### Based on the short story *Dead Man's Mirror* (1937). 51 minutes.

*Dead Man's Mirror*, taken from the *Murder in the Mews* short story collection, is actually a short novel (87 pages) that expands somewhat Christie's earlier short story entitled *The Second Gong*. Although the basic plots of the two stories are similar, the character names, locales, and dialogue have been changed.

The story concerns eccentric Gervase Chevenix, who writes to Poirot, asking the detective to come to his home to investigate a matter of fraud.

On Poirot's arrival, Sir Gervase is found in his locked study, apparently having committed suicide. The most perplexing clue is a mirror in the room seemingly shattered by a bullet, but not directly in the line of fire. Aside from investigating members of the family and houseguests, Poirot must use his little grey cells in regards to a quirk in the eccentric victim's will.

Chief Inspector Japp of Scotland Yard is also present, but Poirot proves to him that despite the seemingly impregnable room, the case is one of murder and not suicide. And, with his usual aplomb, Poirot also proves who is responsible.

Those who have read *Dead Man's Mirror* will not fail to notice a number of changes and omissions in this film. In the majority of these London Weekend Television productions, the films were based upon short stories approximately twelve to twenty pages in length, resulting in films about 50 minutes long. *Dead Man's Mirror* was 87 pages long, resulting in a necessary tightening of the action and dialogue when trans-ferred to the small screen.

Director Brian Farnham, who had previously directed the Poirot films *How Does Your Garden Grow?* (1991), *Wasps' Nest* (1991), and *The Adventure of the Italian Nobleman* (1993) again does a reputable job here.

Mr Satterthwaite, a Christie character often associated with the mysterious Harley Quin, is completely cut, although he appears in the first chapter of the story. Also, local policeman Major Riddle has been replaced by Chief Inspector Japp of Scotland Yard.

David Suchet displays his precise and methodical talents with the usual élan; Hugh Fraser is earnest and Philip Jackson dogged. The talented Iain Cuthbertson is especially well cast as the murdered knight, while Fiona Walker and Zena Walker also do justice to their roles.

▲ The dapper Poirot (David Suchet) in *Dead Man's Mirror*.

# 1993

## The Underdog (TV)

Made in England. Directed by John Bruce.

### CAST

David Suchet · · · · · · · · · · · · · · · · · · · · · Hercule Poirot
Hugh Fraser · · · · · · · · · · · · · · · · · · · Captain Hastings
Pauline Moran · · · · · · · · · · · · · · · · · · · · Miss Lemon
Denis Lill · · · · · · · · · · · · · · · · · · · · · · · Sir Reuben
Ann Bell · · · · · · · · · · · · · · · · · · · · · · Lady Astwell
Bill Wallis · · · · · · · · · · · · · · · · · · · · Horace Trefusis
Andrew Seear · · · · · · · · · · · · · · · · · Humphrey Naylor
Ian Gelder · · · · · · · · · · · · · · · · · · · · Victor Astwell
Jonathan Phillips · · · · · · · · · · · · · · · · · · · · Charles
Adie Allen · · · · · · · · · · · · · · · · · · · · · · · · · Lily
John Evitts · · · · · · · · · · · · · · · · · · · · · · · Parsons
Michael Vaughan · · · · · · · · · · · · · · · Police Sergeant
Lucy Davidson · · · · · · · · · · · · · · · · · · · · · Gladys
Charles Armstrong · · · · · · · · · · · · · Golf Club Receptionist

Based on the short story *The Under Dog* (1951). 51 minutes.

*The Underdog* was taken from the short story collection of the same name. The original work was 65 pages long. All the stories in this collection had previously been published in British magazines between 1923 and 1926.

The *New York Times*, reviewing the collection on October 14, 1951 said: 'The stories' interest is, it must be admitted, more historical than intrinsic. All feature Hercule Poirot (on his own in the novelette, Boswelled by the faithful Captain Hastings in the eight short stories), and all are routine puzzles strongly influenced by the form, if not the spirit, of the Sherlock Holmes stories and evincing nothing of the novelistic skill or technical mystery brilliance with Christie was later to display.'

The *New Yorker* wrote on September 8, 1951: 'The title novelette is fully up to the author's present standard (it would take a remarkably alert reader to single out the murderer before the last page in each story), the style is brisk and lady-like, and nearly all the people involved, with the exception of M. Poirot, and a few servants, and two or three persons connected with the police, are prominent members of a vanished society. Reading Miss Christie is likely to remind you of the hammocks of long-ago summers, but that may not be so bad, all things considered.'

In *The Underdog*, Lily Margrave, paid companion to Lady Astwell, visits Poirot to seek his assistance in the gruesome murder case of Lady Astwell's husband, Sir Reuben Astwell. He had

▲ Pauline Moran appears as Miss Lemon is *The Underdog*.

been bludgeoned to death in the tower retreat of his large estate.

The most likely suspect appears to be surly Charles Leverson, a nephew of the Astwell's who was heard arguing with his late uncle. Lady Astwell, however, is of the opinion that someone else murdered her husband, and it is up to Poirot to find the killer.

John Bruce, who skillfully directed *The Case of the Missing Will*, again does fine work in *The Underdog*. David Suchet excels as Poirot, assisted by the faithful Hastings (Poirot went solo in the novelette) faultlessly played by Hugh Fraser. Ann Bell, as Lady Astwell, and Denis Lill as the titled victim, also offer fine performances. All technical credits here are exemplary.

# ☰ 1993 ☰

## Yellow Iris (TV)

Made in England. Directed by Peter Barber-Fleming.

### CAST

▼

| | |
|---|---|
| David Suchet | Hercule Poirot |
| Hugh Fraser | Captain Hastings |
| Pauline Moran | Miss Lemon |
| David Troughton | Barton Russell |
| Geraldine Somerville | Pauline Weatherby |
| Hugh Ross | Stephen Carter |
| Stefan Gryff | General Pereira |
| Yolanda Vasquez | Lola |
| Arturo Venegas | Hotel Receptionist |
| Joseph Long | Luigi |
| Leonard Maguire | Mr Grove |
| Robin McCaffrey | Iris Russel |
| Dorian Healy | Anthony Chapell |
| Neil Todd | Reporter |
| Kit Jackson | Stage Manager |
| Carol Kenyon | Singer, Buenos Ares |
| Tracy Miller | Singer |
| Domini Winter | Choreographer |
| Maurice Lane | Choreographer |
| Di Cook, Leigh Miles, Mola Haynes, Di Holmes, Lindsay Ashton, Mick Davion, Carl Newman, John Willet, Gerry Zuccarello, Vince Williams. | Dancers |

Based on the short story *Yellow Iris* (1939). 51 minutes.

*Yellow Iris*, taken from the 1939 *Regatta Mystery* collection, opens with Poirot receiving a mysterious telephone call telling him of a life or death situation about to take place at a restaurant. The unidentified female caller tells him a clue is a yellow iris.

Arriving at the restaurant, Poirot notices pink tulips at all tables except one – that table has a vase of yellow irises. Poirot learns that the table in question has been reserved for wealthy American Barton Russell, former Poirot acquaintance Anthony Chapell, Pauline Weatherby, diplomat Stephen Carter, and dancer Lola Valdez.

Poirot believes one of the two ladies is the person who telephoned him, and while he is endeavouring to ascertain which it might be, Russell proposes a toast to his late wife. Her Christian name had been Iris; hence the flowers.

Russell goes on to tell Poirot that Iris had died four years ago that very evening at a dinner party attended by himself and the other four. The late Mrs Russell had been poisoned, and although the verdict at the time was suicide, Russell believes she was murdered – by one of the people now present at the table.

Russell apparently is trying to recreate the same atmosphere and set of circumstances that occurred four years earlier – the same type restaurant, same music, etc.

The lights are dimmed and when they return to normal, Pauline takes a drink of champagne and drops dead, in the same manner as Iris four years before. However, this turns out to be merely a faked death, contrived by Poirot to prevent a genuine one.

*Yellow Iris* is a first-class dramatization of the 21-page short story. Peter Barber-Fleming, who ably directed *The Adventure of the Egyptain Tomb*, also does well here, getting the most of a talented cast. David Suchet, as usual, is excellent as the Belgian sleuth.

Purists will be happy to note that names have not been changed and the original work remains unaltered in its transformation to the small screen except for the characters played by Hugh Fraser and Pauline Moran.

▲ Yolanda Vasquez as Lola in *Yellow Iris*.

▲ David Suchet as Poirot strikes a dignified pose in *Yellow Iris*.

# ≡ 1993 ≡

## The Jewel Robbery at the Grand Metropolitan (TV)

Made in England. Directed by Ken Grieve.

CAST

| | |
|---|---|
| David Suchet | Hercule Poirot |
| Hugh Fraser | Captain Hastings |
| Philip Jackson | Chief Inspector Japp |
| Pauline Moran | Miss Lemon |
| Trevor Cooper | Ed Opalsen |
| Sorcha Cusack | Margaret Opalsen |
| Arthur Cox | Dr Hawker |
| Karl Johnson | Saunders-Worthington |
| Elizabeth Rider | Grace |
| Hermione Norris | Celestine |
| Simon Shepherd | Andrew Hall |
| Tim Stern | Bellboy |
| James McCusker | Journalist |
| Andrew Carr | Hubert Devine |
| Graham Rowe | Hotel Manager |
| Colin Stepney | Guest |
| Simon Malloy | Excited Man |
| Eileen Dunwoodie | Jolly Lady |
| Doreen Taylor | Stall Lady |
| Peter Kelly | Lucky Len |
| Jo Powell | Lucky Len Woman |

Based on the short story *The Jewel Robbery at the Grand Metropolitan* (1924).
51 minutes.

This story, found once more in the *Poirot Investigates* short story collection, concerns Hastings and Poirot taking a short holiday in Brighton, staying at the Grand Metropolitan Hotel.

At dinner, while Poirot remarks on the abundance of all the fabulous jewellery seen on various women, Hastings meets some friends of his, the Opalsens. Mrs Opalsen insists on going to her room to fetch her pearl necklace to show Poirot. After an absence of some time, Mr Opalsen goes off in search of his wife. Hastings wonders when they will come back. 'They will not come back,' states Poirot, 'because my friend, something has happened.'

And of course he is right; the valuable necklace has been stolen. A search of the Opalsen's maid and the hotel chambermaid reveals nothing; however the necklace is found in the maid's room under a mattress. Poirot however does not be-

lieve that Celestine has stolen the necklace, and tells Hastings that the pearls that have just been found are imitations.

Further inquiries of the chambermaid and valet convince Poirot that he knows who the perpitrator of the theft is; all he needs now is corroboration.

*The Jewel Robbery at the Grand Metropolitan*, directed by Ken Grieve (who was also responsible for *The Chocolate Box*), is a first-rate entry in this series produced by London Weekend television by Brian Eastman, and marks the forty-first time that David Suchet has played Poirot. He has become regarded by a growing legion of fans as the master interpreter of this role.

Hugh Fraser, Philip Jackson, and Pauline Moran also excel as usual, and certainly have been definite assets to the success of these wonderful television films. (Fans of Christie and the series will be happy to learn that plans to produce further episodes are being discussed at the time of this writing.)

Arthur Cox repeats his role as Dr Hawker, first seen in *The Adventure of the Italian Nobleman*, and the remainder of the cast are first rate, down to the tiniest part. Fans of Christie as well as people who merely enjoy television of the highest quality will rejoice in the meticulous care taken by London Weekend Television to even the smallest of details. Music, costumes, lighting, and period atmosphere are once again to be commended.

▲ Chief Inspector Japp (Philip Jackson, left), Hastings (Hugh Fraser) and Miss Lemon (Pauline Moran) in *The Jewel Robbery at the Grand Metropolitan*.

# INDEX

# INDEX